The swing of a highly materialistic culture toward spiritual values and goals is, of course, not a usual event. More often, a culture that has lost its hope and enthusiasm simply dies. But I do not think this will be the case with America, for not only is America inherently great, America also has been greatly blessed. If a seed of spirituality has been planted in the heart of a nation, then times of inner erosion can act as awakeners of that seed; it will surely stir and sprout. Such a seed was planted in the heart of America some eighty years ago by the towering prophet of this age — Swami Vivekananda. That is the wonderful hope.

— MARIE LOUISE BURKE
in her book, *Swami Vivekananda Prophet of the Modern Age.*

When considering the Indian influence in America, a special place must be reserved to the Vedanta Societies throughout the country. Historically, the Vedanta Society was the first Eastern religious tradition that took roots on our soil, having been brought here late in the nineteenth century by Swami Vivekananda, the chief disciple of the great Indian Master, Sri Ramakrishna. Intellectually, the influence of this form of Vedanta has been enormous.

— JACOB NEEDLEMAN
in his book, *The New Religions*

Under the leadership of men trained in the spirit of Vivekananda and Ramakrishna, the Ramakrishna Centers are living examples of how timeless truths of the past have value when they are continuously relived and reinterpreted in the present. The Ramakrishna Centers in the West are playing their own part quietly in helping to prepare the way for the united pilgrimage of mankind toward self-understanding and peace.

— DR. FLOYD H. ROSS
Professor of World Religions,
University of Southern California,
in *Vedanta and the West*

MEDITATION
ON
SWAMI VIVEKANANDA

Published
in commemoration of
the Centenary of the
The Vedanta Society of New York,
New York, N.Y.

SWAMI VIVEKANANDA (1863–1902)

"My ideal indeed can be put into a few words, and that is: to preach unto mankind their divinity, and how to make it manifest in every movement of life."

MEDITATION ON SWAMI VIVEKANANDA

Swami Tathagatananda

Foreword by
Swami Bhuteshananda

THE VEDANTA SOCIETY OF NEW YORK
CENTENARY CELEBRATION (1894-1994)

Published by
Miss Jeanne Genêt
Secretary
The Vedanta Society of New York
34 West 71st Street
New York, N.Y. 10023.

First Edition: August 1994.
In commemoration of
the Centenary Celebration (1994) of
The Vedanta Society of New York,
New York, N.Y.,
founded by
Swami Vivekananda
in 1894.

Library of Congress Catalog Card Number: 94-60790
International Standard Book Number 0-9603104-0-1

Set in 11-point Times Roman by Vignesh Laser Printers, Madras-600 005.
Cover design by Sri G. B. Anand, Madras-600 078. Processed at Print Systems &
Products, Madras-600 008. Printed in India by Sharada Press, Mangalore-575001.

Dedicated

to

the loving memory

of

Swami Bodhananda,

Spiritual Leader

from 1912-1950

of

The Vedanta Society of New York,

New York, N.Y.

Ramakrishna Math
P.O. Belur Math
Dist. Howrah
West Bengal-711202
March 4, 1994

FOREWORD

Great personages like Swami Vivekananda are born rarely; their lives and words are simple, but so profound and powerful that deep thought and meditation on even a small incident or idea will suffice to transform a person totally. To understand the spirit of Swamiji's life and words, we need proper attention and deep thinking. The present work, *Meditation on Swami Vivekananda*, is an attempt by Swami Tathagatananda to inspire its readers to understand Swamiji and his universal ideas. The book, containing articles written on different occasions, is sure to bring home some of Swamiji's basic thoughts.

I hope *Meditation on Swami Vivekananda* will be well received by readers, enabling them to go deep into Swamiji's ideas and ideals.

SWAMI BHUTESHANANDA
President
Ramakrishna Math &
Ramakrishna Mission

PREFACE

Since the advent of Shri Ramakrishna on the spiritual horizon of mankind, a new epoch of spiritual fraternity has been steadily unfolding. The West has been evincing its keen interest in the ancient truth of Indian heritage. Shri Ramakrishna proclaimed the fundamental unity of all religions to a world plagued by hostility, disharmony and persecution, all in the name of religion. Various dogmatic theologies and their anti-rational and anti-humanistic attitudes denigrated the image of religion. Religious truths and categories like God, Soul and immortality lost their reality and made religion a mockery. Religion itself was finally abandoned in the modern period.

Into that bleak, hostile world, Swami Vivekananda preached the sublime truth of Vedanta, the philosophic system of the Upanishads. Vedantic idealism brings a new perspective in making the motive of spiritual harmony a fundamental and supreme fact of life. Truth is one — it can be approached by different methods. Swami Vivekananda, with his vast spiritual experience and universal outlook, proclaimed in the West that the infinite can be realized in diverse ways, and thereby became an epoch maker of religious fraternity. Vedanta has permeated the modern mind with its catholicity, universality and spiritual unity.

A new spirit of universality has dawned upon the world. Our present age is pressing this truth home. This great intellectual system of the world as enshrined in Vedanta has cast its charming spell on the modern mind. Vedanta aims at the development of individual life in all its phases, culminating in one's crowning spiritual achievement. It does not advocate mere adherence; it encourages discrimination, intellectual comprehension and meditation. It is the improvement of inner life which constitutes the goal of religious life. A great spiritual luminary like Swamiji — with his illuminating message born of intuitive personal experience — is surcharged with spirituality, capable of transforming others' lives. His message gives us a glimpse of deep spiritual insight and perennial inspiration for improving our life and environment.

The year 1994 is a very important year for us as it happens to be the centenary year of The Vedanta Society of New York, founded by Swami Vivekananda in 1894. On this auspicious occasion, it is our great joy and satisfaction to offer to the devotees and admirers of Swami Vivekananda this humble work, *Meditation on Swami Vivekananda.* We hope this book will help the reader, at least partly, to understand Swamiji's comprehensive philosophy of life.

The first two chapters give a general insight into Hinduism. These and the remaining chapters contain the universal teachings of Swamiji.

The incident narrated in one of the chapters (about Madame Calvé and her first meeting with Swami Vivekananda) reveals how the strength of Swamiji's character, the purity and integrity of his purpose, carried conviction with all those who came into contact with him and how he was a lighthouse of inspiration to drooping souls.

A living gospel of Practical Vedanta, Swamiji has left a rich legacy of his exemplary devotion to his mother for the benefit of the entire humanity. Chapter 20 depicts Swamiji's extraordinary devotion to his mother.

The spirit of Hindu scriptures — practice of being good and doing good — was fulfilled by Buddhism which was nothing but Practical Vedanta. Swami Vivekananda was one of the few great thinkers of India to acknowledge the greatness of Buddha's flaming message. The chapter on Buddha contains Swamiji's heartfelt tributes to him.

The last chapter on Josiah John Goodwin is included here in view of his singular contribution in recording Swamiji's speeches. We want to remember him on this occasion.

Some of these chapters were published as articles in *Prabuddha Bharata* and *The Vedanta Kesari* between 1966 and 1994. I am grateful to the authorities of these journals for their kind permission to reproduce my articles in the present volume. I extend my thanks to all those publishers and authors from whose works I was authorized to take excerpts.

While preparing the manuscript, I received the voluntary assistance of typing and editing from many friends in India and the United States. I also wish to express my sincere gratitude to each and every one of them.

I am beholden to Srimat Swami Bhuteshanandaji, the Revered President of Ramakrishna Math and Ramakrishna Mission, who very kindly wrote a much valued foreword for this book. My respectful salutations to him.

My special gratitude is to Swami Jyotirmayananda, author of the monumental book *Vivekananda — A Comprehensive Study*, who has taken the entire responsibility of the publication of this book. But for his spontaneous and wholehearted cooperation, it would not have been possible to bring out the book within a very short time. I am also grateful to Prof. Hariharan, the Librarian of the Ramakrishna Math Library, Madras, and Prof. C. S. Ramakrishnan, the former Joint Editor of *The Vedanta Kesari,* for their singular and active cooperation at various stages of the publication. I would also like to express my sincere thanks to Dr. Jayanta Sarkar of The University of Maryland, and to Dora, Helen, Nitai and Bhavani for their kind help in various ways. I am also thankful to Shri Manohar Kamath, Director, Sharada Press, Mangalore (south India), for the elegant printing and binding of the book.

I shall consider these efforts fruitful if this book, small though it is, enables anyone to gain an insight into the themes discussed or provides inspiration to read more about them.

Om Shri Ramakrishnarpanam astu!

SWAMI TATHAGATANANDA

The Vedanta Society of New York
34 West 71st Street
New York, N.Y., 10023
Shri Ramakrishna's Birthday,
Monday, March 14, 1994.

CONTENTS

ILLUSTRATIONS

SWAMI VIVEKANANDA
A Brief Introduction

Narendranath Dutta, who became a legendary figure in history as Swami Vivekananda, was born in Calcutta on Monday, the 12th of January, 1863. He was one of the greatest prophets the world has produced. He lived barely 40 years and died on July 4, 1902. Within this short span of life, he left a rich legacy of spectacular achievements in the religious and cultural history of the world. He was a man of versatile genius — a multi-faceted personality. In him we find the great heart of Lord Buddha, the penetrating intellect of Shri Shankara, the love of Shri Chaitanya, the burning renunciation of Lord Jesus Christ, and the dynamism of St. Paul — all harmoniously blended in his magnificent personality. He was fearless in disseminating his message to mankind, regardless of caste, creed, colour, and nationality. A distinctive characteristic of Swami Vivekananda was the comprehensiveness of his vision. He was remarkably universal to the very core of his luminous being. Behind his universal outlook was his great spiritual realization — apprehension of the Reality in and beyond appearances. This Reality, the Atman, is ever pure, immortal, and blissful. Atman is distinct from, yet immanent in the world of change and process. He realized the epochal truth that the pure Atman, the real Self behind our tiny and fleeting ego, is the real source of strength and other human excellences. "Each soul is potentially divine. The goal is to manifest this divinity within by controlling nature, external and internal," said Swami Vivekananda. Elaborating this point he said: "That is your own nature. Assert it, manifest it . . . Nature is like that screen which is hiding the reality beyond. Every good thought you think or act upon is simply tearing the veil, as it were, and the purity, infinity, the God behind manifests itself more and more." As a spark of blazing fire — if fanned properly — has all the capacity of generating a huge conflagration, so the tiny human being by manifesting the divinity within, may become fully divine. The real well-being of man depends entirely upon the recognition of this vital point in human life. This faith in our innate divine nature is the essential prerequisite of any healthy scheme of life. Said Swamiji: "This infinite power of the spirit, brought to bear upon matter, evolves material development; made to act upon thought, evolves intellectuality, and made to act upon itself makes man a God . . . Be and make. Let this be our motto. Say not man is a sinner. Tell him that he is God." His great mission was "to rouse in all people the awareness of the ever-present focus of human dignity, namely the Atman, the Divine Spark, and to help them manifest that Glory in every movement of their life." He was the Prophet of the "Gospel of Man-making." He saw the divine Self in every person and looked upon the human form as the temple of God. This transcendental experience of the spiritual unity of life made him really universal. It is absolutely different in character from the so-called universalism based on humanism, as these idealists never recognized the spiritual dimension of life.

In his integral vision of truth there was no cleavage between science and religion, the East and the West, secular and spiritual, work and worship. Therefore, he exhorted all categories of people to develop their natural potentialities without ever forgetting the true goal of life — manifesting the divinity within. He laid equal emphasis on all aspects of life, bringing harmony in the culture of head, heart and hand. In him we find a happy synthesis of secular aspirations and spiritual development. He was looked upon as a great champion of nationalism, awakening the national consciousness, restoring the real glory of India and giving a spiritual foundation to the national movement; we thus feel justified in addressing him as, "Patriot Saint." The impact of his message is stated by C. Rajagopalachari thus: "Vivekananda saved Hinduism and saved India. But for him, we would have lost our religion and would not have gained our freedom. We therefore owe everything to Swami Vivekananda." This great ambassador of a spiritual mission was never a parochial nationalist; spiritual regeneration of the entire mankind was the real goal of his message. Truly speaking, he was a global citizen accepting everyone and rejecting none. His life and message provide necessary momentum to bring forth the spiritual vision of a cosmic civilization.

The aims and aspirations of life are to experience the spiritual excellences of the divine through self-culture. This demands growth, maturity and a higher evolution — certainly not the stagnation produced by impulsively seeking only material satisfaction. Swamiji gave stern warnings about the evil consequences of rampant materialism seeking power without spiritual maturity. Unregenerate men, confining themselves to the study of nature, oblivious of the role of the spirit that enlivens and animates it, get only a partial view of truth and consequently lose sight of the whole. A new portal of life never opens before them. "The excess of knowledge and power without holiness," says Swamiji, "makes human beings devils." Marie Louise Burke writes: "The West, horrified by the destructive powers of the nuclear forces is really corroborating the teachings of Vivekananda in that 'a man with excess of knowledge and power without holiness is a devil'." He was essentially and primarily a great spiritual teacher of mankind. He was an eternally perfect Sage commissioned by Shri Ramakrishna to teach and serve humanity. The stupendous spiritual power stemming from his illumined life made immediate impact on his vast audience. Romain Rolland wrote in his biography in 1928: "I cannot touch these sayings of his, scattered as they are through the pages of this book at thirty years' distance, without receiving a thrill through my body like an electric shock. And what shock, what transport, must have been produced when, in burning words, they issued from the lips of the hero!" He was a monk par excellence. Sister Nivedita said: "Vivekananda will ever remain the archetype of the *sannyasin* . . . Burning renunciation was chief of all the inspirations that spoke to us through him. 'Let me die like a true *sannyasin* as my Master did,' he exclaimed once passionately, 'heedless of money, of woman, and fame! And of these the most insidious is the love of fame'." He remained ever a pure child of God, absolutely untouched by the glamour of materialism, always radiating an uplifting, transforming, and ennobling influence on others. He was the true interpreter of Hinduism and projected its bright image to India and abroad. His signal contribution in discovering the real import of Vedanta, the glory of our ancient culture, and the greatness of Shri Ramakrishna are of momentous importance to the entire humanity. "In his *guru,* Ramakrishna Paramahamsa, Vivekananda found the key of life . . ." Nivedita further writes, "the *shastras,* the *guru,* and the Motherland, are the three notes that mingle themselves to form the music of the works of Vivekananda." Shri Ramakrishna was the synthetic genius of philosophy and religion in modern times. There is but one substance, one life, one reality in, as and through the world. The Unitary Consciousness of pure Advaita, exemplified in the life and teachings of Shri Ramakrishna, was expounded by Swamiji in language which is simple, persuasive, practical, and profound. The fundamental spiritual truth of Indian culture is elucidated in *The Complete Works of Swami Vivekananda* in the most helpful manner to the rational, scientific mind. Swamiji's works contain the bread of life for the starving souls. This Great Gospel of the future, containing the life-giving universal wisdom of India, will be accepted by an enlightened mankind as a great gift to posterity.

1

THE INDIVIDUAL AND THE SUPREME

Each of us has two kinds of consciousness: individual and universal. Individual consciousness, or ego, separates us from God and from other beings. This individuality is self-reinforcing; it binds us to our egocentric view of life. When the ego is completely gone, when we become soul-conscious, we realize the Supreme Truth: the unity of existence.

Even before this complete awakening, a vague sense of a shared consciousness moves us to seek peace, harmony, and fraternity with others. Something within moves us to think of God and to develop a larger awareness. We cannot rest, feeling we are completely separate from others; part of us wants to break the barriers and be free. In our best moments we see that life is essentially divine; we also feel that we are bound by ego, unable to express our full divine potential.

We feel helpless because we are not aware of our own divinity. Vedanta boldly proclaims that every living being is essentially divine. The soul of everyone is pure, good, beautiful, and blissful. It is infinite and eternal. It is free from all bondage, limitation, and sorrow. It is one with God, the Supreme Spirit.

The individual seems finite, but this is only the outer expression of the inner source, God, who is free from bondage and beyond all relations. This idea takes deep root in our minds and drives us to seek the experience of oneness. Even partial self-realization makes us aware of our universal nature. We hear the call of our own greater self — the higher or real self. We try to respond to this divine call through spiritual growth.

The higher self of the individual is called the Atman. Body and mind cover the Atman, like a coat, but are not part of it. The body is made of parts; it must fall apart in time. The Atman is single, simple, and divine. It is the source of life, the organizing and sustaining power. Without the Atman nothing lives.

The *Katha Upanishad* illustrates the relationship between body, mind, and self with this analogy: "The body is a chariot. Know the Atman as the master of the chariot, *buddhi* (intelligence) as the charioteer, and *manas* (sensing, feeling mind) as the reins."[1] In the next verse, we are told that the five senses are the horses and the objects of sense are the roads on which we travel. The senses are higher, or more subtle than the objects of sense; mind, subtler than the senses; *buddhi*, subtler than the mind; and the Atman, subtler than *buddhi*. The finer a substance, the harder it is to hold it. The Atman, like space, is subtle, vast, and free; yet it joins itself to body and mind to experience the world. The Atman wills its own embodiment.

This knowing Self, the cause of our birth in the world, is unborn, immortal, and abiding. It has no cause. It is not affected by death. For our spiritual growth and real well-being, we should know the Atman while we are living. In the Upanishad we read:

As a razor stays hidden in its sheath,
as fire lies dormant in wood,
so the soul fills the whole body,
even to the tips of the nails.
People do not see the soul directly;
what they see is an imperfect image.

When it breathes it is called *prana*,
when it sees it is called vision,
when it hears it is called hearing,
when it thinks it is called mind.
These are names for its functions (*karma nama*);
all are centered in the soul.[2]

This Atman, as pure awareness, is the eternal witness of all the mind's changes. It is the light of pure consciousness that illumines every mental action. Hence, the Atman is "known through every pulsation of knowledge and awareness."[3] Shankara's comment on this verse of the *Kena Upanishad* is illuminating:

The Atman is aware of every mental state.
He sees and knows each one as it flows by.
As he is essentially pure awareness,
we cannot, with our minds,
distinguish him from the mental states.
His reflection is seen by the mental states,

in and through the mental states –
how else could they know him?[4]

The Atman is the light of pure consciousness that illumines all mental activities. Thus, the Atman is "known through every pulsation of knowledge and awareness."[5]

"This Brahman is immediate and direct. It is the innermost Self of all."[6] The Atman that lies in the innermost part of the body (*antaratman*) is dearer than sons, dearer than wealth, dearer than anything else. "The husband is dear to one, not because he is the husband; but when one craves (*kamana*) for the husband, the husband is dear because of love for the Self (*atmapriti*)."[7] Wife, son, wealth — everything is desired for our own satisfaction (*atmapriti*). This is one of the most illuminating passages in the Upanishads about the nature of the Self. It compels us to admit that things are dear to us only to the extent that we see ourselves projected in them. Things become dear to us because the soul is the dearest object of our life.

After expounding this thought-provoking idea, the great Yajnavalkya exhorts his dear wife, "Oh Maitreyi, this Atman has to be seen. This Atman has to be heard about, this Atman has to be meditated upon and known. Only then is everything known, because the Atman fills everything — there is nothing else to know."[8] The objective world of earthly possessions and enjoyments affords the discriminating student opportunities to seek God. God, the inner self of all, attracts us through all. This is the real secret of our love for each other.

A sincere seeker who systematically follows spiritual disciplines can experience this profound truth. Our experiences and memory demand the unity and unchangeability of the experiencer, the subject. Only the immortal Atman is the real experiencer, the real subject without any object or, "objectless subject." A pure soul, seeking earnestly, can find the Atman. "Of all things, this Self alone should be realized; one knows everything through it. Just as one can get at (an animal) through its footprints, so can one get at the Self through its footprints in the sands of experience."[9]

Everything that is composed of parts must change. The Atman, simple and not compound, never changes. Incorporeal, it is not tied to anything physical. The Atman is the ever-pure, untainted, eternal witness. It is luminous intelligence, nameless, formless, and deathless. It appears to be enclosed by the body and the body's adjuncts, the senses. Vital force, mind, *buddhi,* and ego stand as a bulwark hiding the Atman. When we get rid of body-consciousness, the self-effulgent Atman stands revealed.

The absolute Brahman is "beyond the range of speech and thought" — we cannot define or limit it as an object of relative experience. Still, the Upanishads point to Brahman through its characteristic expressions in the human mind: "Brahman is truth, consciousness, infinity."[10] "Brahman is consciousness, bliss."[11] Shri Ramakrishna said of Brahman:

"What Brahman is cannot be described. All things of the world — the Vedas, the Puranas, the Tantras, the six systems of Philosophy — have been defiled, like food that has been touched by the tongue, for they have been read or uttered by the tongue. Only one thing has not been defiled in this way, and that is Brahman. No one has ever been able to say what Brahman is."[12]

While coming out of *samadhi,* Shri Ramakrishna could not utter even the most sacred word "OM." He had to come down three levels, as it were, to utter it. But *saguna* Brahman, or Cosmic Brahman, or the Personal God immanent in the cosmos, suffers no change. Brahman always remains undifferentiated and infinite. The cosmos is essentially the Absolute Brahman appearing as names and forms.

The Immanent Brahman is all-transcendent. The infinitude of God is in no way affected by His immanence. The Absolute cannot be divided. "The personal is the Absolute looked at through the haze of *maya* — ignorance."[13] Hinduism accepts pure consciousness as the ultimate reality. It is non-dual, non-relational, non-compound, unitary, universal. It is prior to every form of existence, the starting point of all experiences. It is self-existent and self-luminous. This reality, in Hindu tradition, is known as Brahman — an entity whose greatness, power, or expansion none can measure. Shankara gives an idea of Brahman in the *Brahma Sutras*:

> This universe of name and form supports many agents, their actions and experiences, and the results of actions. Its space, time, and causation are governed by laws. Human reason cannot grasp the true nature of its creation. The projection, sustenance, and dissolution of this universe can only come from Brahman, the omniscient, omnipotent source.[14]

"This universal intelligence," says Swami Vivekananda, "is what we call God."

Again defining Brahman, Shankara says in his commentary on the *Taittiriya Upanishad*: "Brahman is defined as the Reality from which beings are never separated — neither during their origin, sustenance, nor dissolution."[15] The central idea of the Upanishads is that Brahman is Atman.[16] In the *Brihadaranyaka Upanishad*, Brahman and Atman are not discussed separately; Brahman is always identical with Atman.[17]

Jivatman, the individual soul, is only an "abridged edition," as it were, of the *Paramatman*. This has been expounded in the great dictum *prajnanam Brahma*: consciousness (manifest in the individual self) is Brahman.[18] Here we get the identity of the individual self and the Supreme Self, in their essential nature as pure consciousness beyond all distinctions. Divine splendor, chained to a body-mind, appears to be finite. With illumination, its true identity is revealed.

The analogy of the wave and the ocean will help us to understand. The wave, limited by its apparent form, is small in comparison with the vast ocean. When the wave loses its individual character and merges with the ocean, it gains its true identity. As pure and simple water, the wave is always one with the ocean. The wave has no life apart from the ocean. The ocean takes the form of a wave due to *upadhis* (adjuncts).

The experience of finding identity between man and God finds utterance in the words, "I am Brahman."[19] Jesus articulates the same ancient and eternal truth when he says, "I and my Father are one." In the Upanishad, *Paramatman* and *jivatman* — Brahman and *jiva* — have been compared to two birds.[20] Swami Vivekananda narrates this picturesque parable in his own inimitable way:

Upon the same tree there are two birds, one on the top, the other below. The one on the top is calm, silent, and majestic, immersed in its own glory; the one on the lower branches, eating sweet and bitter fruits by turns, hopping from branch to branch, is becoming happy and miserable by turns. After a time the lower bird eats an exceptionally bitter fruit and gets disgusted and looks up and sees the other bird, that wondrous one of golden plumage, who eats neither sweet nor bitter fruit, who is neither happy nor miserable, but calm, self-poised, and sees nothing beyond his Self.

The lower bird longs for this condition, but soon forgets it, again begins to eat the fruit. In a little while, he eats another exceptionally bitter fruit, which makes him feel miserable, and he again looks up, and tries to get nearer to the upper bird. Once more he forgets and after a time he looks up, and so on he goes again and again and again until he comes very near to the beautiful bird and sees the reflection of light from his plumage playing around his own body, and he feels a change and seems to melt away; still nearer he comes, and everything about him melts away, and at last he understands this wonderful change. The lower bird was, as it were, only the substantial-looking shadow, the reflection of the higher; he himself was in essence the upper bird all the time. This eating of fruits, sweet and bitter, this lower, little bird, weeping and happy by turns, was a vain chimera, a dream: all along, the real bird was there above, calm and silent, glorious and majestic, beyond grief, beyond sorrow. The upper bird is God, the Lord of the universe, and the lower bird is the human soul, eating the sweet and bitter fruits of the world. Now and then comes a heavy blow to the soul.

For a time, he stops the eating and goes towards the unknown God, and a flood of light comes. He thinks that this world is a vain show. Yet again the senses drag him down, and he begins as before to eat the sweet and bitter fruits of the world. Again an exceptionally hard blow comes. His heart becomes open again to divine light; thus gradually he approaches God, and as he gets nearer, he finds his old self melting away. When he has come near enough he sees that he is no other than God, and he exclaims, "He whom I have described to you as the Life of this universe, as present in the atom, and in the suns and moons — He is the basis of our own life, the Soul of our soul. Nay, thou art That."[21]

Paramatman, like the luminous sun, seems to be eclipsed by clouds of ego. When the clouds of ignorance disperse, the ever-bright sun of God shines in the pure heart.

God, when formless, has no gender. Taking the form of a *jiva,* God is seen as male, female, or neuter, depending on the kind of body. The body is a temple of God and God resides in the heart of a *jiva.* Brahman is also called *akasha.* "The characteristics of subtlety, incorporeality, and all-pervasiveness are common to *akasha* and Brahman."[22] The sole purpose of life is to realize the Truth through spiritual transformation. The highest Truth, called *Sat,* Brahman, *Bhuman,* or Atman, is non-dual, all-pervasive, all-inclusive, subtlest, smallest of the small and greatest of the great. It is hard to think about. Yet common people can approach Brahman because it lives in our heart. We can meditate on Brahman in the small space in our heart.[23] The outer sky (*akasha,* Brahman) and the small space within (*hridayakasha, jivatman*) are of the same nature. This truth is concisely stated in another *mahavakya* (great saying): "This Atman is Brahman."[24]

During deep sleep, we are happy to have a rest from tension and fears, a break from our desires and impulses. In that period of deep sleep we are at one with Brahman, though unconsciously. Although resting on Brahman, the *jivatman* does not realize oneness with Brahman, pure existence.[25] This contact motivates a rare few to study the character of deep sleep and to find the bliss of Brahman behind the joy of sleep. The *jiva* experiences "vague ignorance, and a mood of bliss" during deep sleep.

The Upanishads also discuss how transmigration takes place. "When a man's death is imminent, the *jivatman* leaves the body and moves away, guided by the *paramatman.*"[26] The fruits of his good and bad *karma* invariably cling to him, determining his future. Of course, the prevailing thought in his mind at the moment of death sets his immediate course.[27]

Man enjoys life according to his deserts; he learns good lessons through experience. Finally, he learns the hard lesson that he is responsible for everything. The law of *karma* does not let him lay responsibility on anyone but himself. In this way, man gains a complete victory over his impulses and approaches the final phase of liberation through good *karmas*. Desire is the root cause of his painful suffering; he must wake from spiritual slumber by sheer earnestness, through meditation and other spiritual practices. He cannot avoid suffering without freeing his mind of desires. The *jivatman* reveals its pristine glory when completely free from ignorance. It is pure subject — objectless consciousness, bliss. The soul finds its eternal rest in God.[28] The absolute reality is Brahman — *Satchidananda* (Existence, Consciousness, Bliss). Brahman projects this world through its *maya-sakti* (magic power), just for its own play *(lila)*.

One primary idea possessed the seers of India since the days of the *Rig-Veda*: *jivatman* and *Paramatman* are one. With intuitive perception, they discovered one unchanging Supreme Reality, Brahman, underlying the objective universe.[29] The same Brahman, as the immortal consciousness in man, is called Atman. Brahman and Atman, identical in nature, are the first principle.[30] A superficial view of man cannot reveal his immortal divinity; but, over an immeasurably long course of evolution, the individual attains freedom through spiritual transformation. Swami Vivekananda says, "No books, no scriptures, no science can ever imagine the glory of the Self that appears as man, the most glorious God that ever was, the only God that ever existed, exists, or ever will exist."[31]

Spirituality, according to Vedanta, is a truth to be communicated and verified like science. Shri Ramakrishna vindicated that truth in our age. The eternal truth revealed itself to him. He saw with open eyes that God has become everything:

> The Divine Mother revealed to me in the Kali temple that it was She who had become everything. She showed me that everything was full of consciousness — the water vessels were consciousness, the doorsill was consciousness, the marble floor was consciousness — all was consciousness.[32]

Further, he says: "Now I see that it is God alone who is moving about in various forms; as a holy man, as a cheat or a villain."[33] The great saying of Vedanta — "Thou art That"[34] — stands vindicated.

2

THE CONCEPT OF GOD IN HINDU RELIGION

The Hindus believe that religion is realization — the truth of religion must be intuitively experienced in life. Hindus are not satisfied with an implicit faith in certain dogmas or doctrines about God, the human soul, or the final goal of life. Their rational minds demand the highest truth. Hindus do not submit to the authority of any prophet or teacher. They enjoy absolute freedom of thought, will, and emotion: they may even pursue spiritual life without believing in God. The one requirement is that they lead moral lives, earnestly disciplining body and mind, purifying themselves. Religion is a way of life which ennobles their character, enlightens their view of life, and deepens their knowledge of nature, man, and God.

The loftiest ideal of Hinduism is to see human beings as the living temples of God. God is infinite, immortal, and eternal. The universe is His body. To the Hindus, man is essentially a spiritual being; the cosmos ultimately a spiritual entity. The microcosm is identical with the macrocosm.

In Vedic literature, God is essentially a transcendent Being. *Ekam Sat*,[1] "that breathed without air, by its own power."[2] The absolute Reality is one and without a second, the Sole Reality beyond time, space, and causation. It is not related to anything else. It is pure spirit, an undifferentiated, homogeneous mass of consciousness, free from attributes. It is addressed as silence, or as *neti neti* (not this, not this).[3] It is also called *Satchidananda*.

The use of the expression *Satchidananda* does not mean that the Absolute can be determined or limited in any way. The word *Sat* means Being. "It stands for that which is existence itself, extremely subtle, indefinable, all-pervading; It is one taintless, indivisible, pure consciousness." *Sat* should not be confused with what we call the phenomenal existence of things as perceived by the senses. As a mirage cannot be seen without the desert, nor a painting without the canvas, so the reality called *Sat* is the support of the world of appearances that we see. If nonbeing were the fundamental nature of things, we could not explain the "isness" that we always perceive. To quote Swami Vivekananda, "All that we see and feel about things is pure and simple existence, 'isness'."[4] "No illusory perception is possible without a substratum," says Shankara in his commentary on the *Mandukya Karika*.[5]

Likewise, the word *chit,* consciousness, does not mean empirical consciousness. God is pure consciousness,[6] not a self-conscious personality. Life depends on sentience. Thus, consciousness is at the root of life. Consciousness, or God, is the timeless being of the cosmos, the first principle implicit in all our experience. It is self-existent, self-luminous, beginningless and endless. God as pure consciousness, is all-pervading. It illumines everything: nothing else illumines it.[7] The whole universe of animate beings and inanimate objects comes from pure consciousness. Everything is sustained, and ultimately dissolved, by consciousness. "One self-effulgent being, hidden in all beings, and all-pervading, is the inner self of all animate beings."[8] Absolute consciousness is directly and immediately present as the soul of all beings. The fundamental difference between matter and spirit is that spirit is self-aware, while matter is not. One tiny insect is aware of itself, but the sun is not aware of its own existence. Therefore, Hinduism rejects the idea (popular in secular scholarship) that the world is a product of unconscious matter, and that life and consciousness have evolved from this dull matter.

The word *ananda*, or bliss, does not mean sensual pleasure. *Ananda* is the absolute bliss found when subject and object become one — when "I" consciousness is lost. All pleasures derive from God, the Supreme Source; sensual pleasures are merely a drop in the infinite ocean of bliss. "No one can live without that bliss."[9] *Sat, Chit,* and *Ananda* — Existence, Consciousness, and Bliss Absolute — are co-dependent. Any one of them implies the other two. They are not attributes of Brahman — they are the very essence of Brahman. These epithets are more negative than positive; Brahman alone, beyond diversity, is indescribable and incomprehensible.[10] Nonetheless, as Shri Ramakrishna says, the pure mind can comprehend Him — the non-dual, impersonal God of Advaita Vedanta.

Non-dual Reality, as we have described it, cannot create the world of multiplicity. Thus we come to the concept of a Personal God — *saguna* Brahman or *Ishwara* — Brahman linked with *maya-shakti*. *Maya-shakti* is the creative power of God, also called *Devatmashakti* — God's self-conscious power.[11] This mysterious power, *maya*, is the essence of relative existence.[12]

Nirguna Brahman, transcending all natural objects, is experienced only in deep meditation when subject and object coalesce. It is known by its transcendental attributes: *satyam* (truth), *jnanam* (knowledge), *anantam* (infinity), and *advaitam* (non-duality, oneness). When we adopt a transcendent point of view, we speak of non-dual Brahman. The same non-dual Brahman, projecting the cosmos through *maya-shakti*, we call the immanent God. This manifested God appears as the Personal God, as souls, and as the world. The word "Personal" means that He has holy attributes, not that he has a body like a human being. The individual soul (*jiva*), the world of experience (*jagat*), and their Supreme Ruler (*Ishwara*) are the three main categories of the cosmos. Non-dual monism sees the soul, the world, and the Personal God as three simultaneously arising, interdependent forms of relative existence. This is a most valuable understanding.

The human mind naturally thinks of God in relation to the universe. Though immanent in the cosmos, God is all-transcendent, unaffected by diversity. Though *saguna*, God is *nirguna* as well. There is no real conflict between the two aspects, dynamic and static. Says Swami Vivekananda:

> These are various forms of that same Oneness, of which all these various ideas of the world are but various readings, and the Personal God is the highest reading that can be attained to, of that Impersonal, by the human intellect.[13]

Although the Upanishads refer to both *nirguna* Brahman and *saguna* Brahman, there is only one Brahman. *Nirguna* is Brahman as It is. *Saguna* is the same Brahman when it comes within the purview of discussion, adoration, and dedication. *Nirguna* is Brahman in Reality; *saguna,* in relativity. *Nirguna* Brahman manifests itself to us as *Ishwara*, the God we worship. As the God of transcendence, He is the subject of our contemplation and communion. As the God of immanence, He receives our love and devotion. God's transcendence and immanence are complementary. Thus, the infinite God, the God of transcendence, is the same God of immanence who reaches us through *maya-shakti,* while ever remaining beyond the cosmos. Shri Ramakrishna, a great illumined soul of modern India, throws light on this enigma:

> When I think of the Supreme Being as inactive, neither creating, nor preserving, nor destroying, I call Him Brahman or *Purusha,* the Impersonal God. When I think of Him as active, creating, preserving, destroying, I call Him *Shakti* or *Maya* or *Prakriti*, the Personal God. But the distinction between them does not mean a difference. The Personal and the Impersonal are the same Being, in the same way as milk and its whiteness, or the diamond and its lustre, or the serpent and its undulations. It is impossible to conceive of the one without the other. The Divine Mother and Brahman are one.

Further, he says:

> Brahman and *Shakti* are identical. If you accept the one, you must accept the other. It is like fire and its power to burn. If you see the fire, you must recognize its power to burn. You cannot think of fire without its power to burn, nor can you think of the power to burn without the fire. You cannot conceive of the sun's rays without the sun nor can you conceive of the sun without its rays.... You cannot think of milk without the whiteness, and again, you cannot think of the whiteness without the milk. Thus one cannot think of Brahman without *Shakti*, or *Shakti* without Brahman.
>
> One cannot think of the Absolute without the Relative, or of the Relative without the Absolute. The Primordial Power is ever at play. She is creating, preserving, and destroying in play, as it is were. This power is called Kali. Kali is verily Brahman and Brahman is verily Kali. It is one and the same Reality. When we think of It as inactive, that is to say, not engaged in the acts of creation, preservation and destruction, then we call it Brahman. But when It engages in these activities, then we call It Kali or *Shakti.*[14]

Says Swami Vivekananda:

Who is *Ishwara*? *Janmadyasya yatah* — "From whom is the birth, continuation, and dissolution of the universe." —He is *Ishwara*— "the Eternal, the Pure, the Ever-Free, the Almighty, the All-Knowing, the All-Merciful, the Teacher of all teachers"; and above all, *Sa Ishwara anirvachaniya-premasvarupah* — "He the Lord is, of His own nature, inexpressible Love." These certainly are the definitions of a personal God. Are there then two Gods — the "Not this, not this," the *Sat-chit-ananda*, the Existence-Knowledge-Bliss of the philosopher, and this God of Love of the *bhakta?* No, it is the same *Sat-chit-ananda*, who is also the God of Love, the Impersonal and the Personal in one. It has always to be understood that the Personal God worshiped by the *bhakta* is not separate or different from the Brahman. All is Brahman, the one without a second; only the Brahman, as unity or absolute, is too much of an abstraction to be loved and worshiped; so the *bhakta* chooses the relative aspect of Brahman, that is, *Ishwara,* the Supreme Ruler. To use a simile: Brahman is the clay or substance out of which an infinite variety of articles are fashioned.

As clay, they are all one; but form or manifestation differentiates them. Before everyone of them was made, they all existed potentially in the clay, and, of course, they are identical substantially; but when formed, and as long as the form remains, they are separate and different; the clay-mouse can never become a clay-elephant, because, as manifestations, form alone makes them what they are, though as unformed clay they are all one. Ishwara is the highest manifestation of the Absolute Reality, or in other words, the highest possible reading of the Absolute by the human mind. Creation is eternal, and so also is *Ishwara*."[15]

Shri Ramakrishna, to whom both aspects of God were a matter of direct knowledge and immediate experience, had seen the Divine in everything and in every being. He said, "It was revealed to me that all these are one substance, the non-dual and indivisible consciousness."[16] The entire cosmos is soaked with Divinity, but the cosmos does not cover His entire Being; He is also beyond the cosmos. The cosmos exists as a portion of His Being.[17]

In the Upanishads, the Impersonal God is generally referred to as It or That and not as He or She. The personal God is referred to as He or She or It, according to the mood of the devotee. The Hindu mind knows the futility of addressing the timeless, nameless, ineffable, Impersonal God by any name or form. Yet, the mystics enjoyed a deep sense of satisfaction in glorifying and singing the blessedness of the Supreme Spirit seen in personal form. The very name and form of God have a purifying and transforming influence. Through such worship, a true devotee seeks the inner truth and enjoys pouring out his deep feelings.

The seers report that the Supreme Being remained alone in His undifferentiated unity until He decided: "I am one, I shall become many; I shall grow forth."[18] Thus, the transcendent, indivisible, incomprehensible existence of the Impersonal God appears before us in and through the entire cosmos. Here we find the Personal God with His immanent qualities: Bliss (*ananda*), Immortality (*amrita*), Peace (*shanti*), Auspiciousness (*shaiva*), Holiness (*shuddha apapavidda*), and Beauty (*saundarya*). He is the Supreme God within and beyond the cosmos, its Master, the source of soul power whose unalterable laws the entire cosmos obeys, and whose shadow is immortality and death.[19]

The all-pervading, self-effulgent God is the only source of all virtue, happiness, peace, wisdom, power, and knowledge. He is the pure, holy, and benevolent one. He is the dearest of friends, the most affectionate parent, and the most loving saviour — "The goal, the support, the lord, the witness, the refuge, the friend, the origin, the dissolution, the firm ground, the storehouse, and the undying seed."[20] These suggestions can be found in the *Rig-Veda* as well.

Hinduism, discovering the ground of existence, addresses embodied beings as the Children of Bliss.[21] Says Swami Vivekananda, "Ye are the children of God, the sharers of immortal bliss, holy and perfect beings. Ye divinity on earth — sinners! It is a sin to call a man so; it is a standing libel on human nature."[22] The goal of Hinduism is to unfold the potential divinity within us. God lies planted deep within every life. God, in Hinduism, is not only the creator of the world, but also the immortal inner guide.[23]

A human being can evolve into an illumined soul only because the Divine Spark is within. To a Hindu, this is the real cause of evolution: the Immortal within us impels us to realize the true nature of the Self. Evolution postulates involution. Swami Vivekananda expressed it well:

> From the lowest protoplasm to the most perfect human being, there is really but one life. Just as in one life we have so many various phases of expression, the foetus developing into the baby, the child, the young man, the old man; so, from that protoplasm, up to the most perfect man, we get one continuous life, one chain. This is evolution; but each evolution presupposes an involution. The whole of this life — which slowly manifests itself, evolves itself from the protoplasm to the perfected human being, the Incarnation of God on Earth — the whole of this series is but one life, and the whole of this manifestation must have been involved in that very protoplasm. This whole life, this very God on Earth was involved in it, and slowly came out, manifesting itself slowly, slowly, slowly.[24]

In fact, says Shankara, "Truly, God is the only transmigrant."[25]

In addition, God intervenes in history as the *avatar* or Incarnation to overthrow the forces of evil and to create a center of spiritual regeneration. Such an advent generates a new creative force in the world, based on righteousness. In this way, God restores moral equilibrium and sets an inspiring example of spirituality through His exalted life and blessings. This is the Gracious God's periodic move to maintain world order.[26]

From this brief discussion on the concept of God, which even the mystics do not fully know, we recapitulate the main ideas:

- God is the Supreme Reality.
- The individual self is one with the Supreme Self.
- All existence is ultimately one.
- God fills everything.

- He is both Personal and Impersonal.
- The Personal aspect of Brahman is what we call *Shakti* or *Ishwara* or God.
- Brahman and *Shakti* are inseparable, like fire and its heat.

The universe comes out of Brahman, rests in Him, and merges in Him.[27]

This cycle continues throughout eternity. Just as the spider is said to bring forth its web from within itself and again retract it, so God projects and absorbs the universe. Just as herbs shoot up from the earth, or hair grows out of living bodies, so the cosmos emerges from God.[28]

Thus, Hinduism teaches us to see and experience oneness in the manifold. The Upanishads exhort us repeatedly in a clear, unambiguous, and triumphant voice: "You have to see this Atman!"[29] Therefore, "Arise, awake, and stop not till the goal is reached!" God is intra-cosmic, not extra-cosmic. He is the soul of life and the soul of the universe, whose subtle presence illumines our minds and lets us unravel the secrets of nature, within and without. God is the Lawgiver as well as the laws. This law — known as *rita,* the "fixed way or course" — rules the whole gamut of cosmic activity. Hinduism removes the inveterate conceptions that God is far away and unknowable, that people are weak and mortal, that dull matter runs the world, and that the cosmos is created out of nothing. Hinduism teaches that religion is not based on dogma or blind faith — the truth of religion can be realized in this life, through struggle.

God is eternal and infinite. He is the inexhaustible source of all life and of the whole universe. Outdated and anthropomorphic conceptions of God, cherished in many cultures, may find some light in Vedanta philosophy. Vedanta does not present truth in dogmatic terms; as such, religious persecution is almost nil in the history of Hinduism. To a Hindu, God is the loving, living, eternal guide. His wisdom is revealed in the cosmos; His almightiness forms the distant nebula and grows the grass under our feet. His infinite love impels Him to create, preserve, and redeem millions and millions of living beings, and to lead humanity through infinite stages of evolution. Again, His unbounded love is reflected in the sense of justice we feel, deep in our hearts — conscience, the silent voice of God.

God, ever watchful, maintains His creation through His laws — *rita* and *satya.* Hindus do not believe in a cruel, anthropomorphic God who is jealous, angry and punitive. Freedom gives man moral responsibilities. He is accountable for his actions — as he sows, so he reaps. Such is the Divine Law. The law of *karma,* to a Hindu, is not about retribution — it describes the natural consequences of our actions. "As one acts, so one becomes. The doer of good becomes good, the evildoer becomes evil."[30] Virtue leads to happiness; weakness leads to misery. Divine order is the nature of the world. The common man may see the world as a multitude of different things, but an intelligent person certainly sees the universe as one whole. An eternal law lies behind the universe, keeping all things within their limits, eliminating chaos, and maintaining harmony, rhythm, and order.[31]

The concept of the "adorable Lord of the world," the Divine who resides in the hearts of all beings, guiding and constraining our growth, plays a vital role in the spiritual life of the Hindu. The sincere feeling of deep, loving adoration, nurtured in the depth of one's heart, is called love for God. Hindus worship a living, loving and concerned God, who always hears our deepest prayers. He is nearer than our arteries; He is our Inner Self. These lovers of God find, as the mystics say, that one universal God lives within us. God is *sarva-bhuta-antar-atman,* the Inner Self of all beings. Thus there is only one religion; different faiths are different paths leading to the same goal.

The urge to seek God is the perennial urge of human life. The search is eternal; thus religion has survived the ravages of time, as well as the impulsive nature of man. God is our very own. He is the moral prop of our life. He is truth, beauty, righteousness, and immortality. Yet again, He is not separate from us, nor from the universe for all are in Him. We live, move, and have our being only in Him.

3

THE FUNDAMENTAL TEACHINGS OF VEDANTA

Down through the ages, India has been the eternal source of spiritual inspiration for humanity. "Evidently . . . India was the birthplace of the fundamental imaginings, the cradle of contemplative religion and the nobler philosophy."[1] This source has been authenticated, amplified, elucidated and rejuvenated by eminent mystics throughout the ages. The Indian mind, despite depressed situations in external life, kept this life-giving and sustaining philosophy and religion in its culture. "In all nations there are minds which incline to dwell on the conception of the fundamental Unity . . . . This tendency finds its highest expression in the religious writings of the East, and chiefly in the Indian Scriptures, in the Vedas, the *Bhagavad Gita,* and the *Vishnu Purana,*" declared Ralph Waldo Emerson.

In the Hindu view, philosophy and religion are not contradictory, but complementary. Religion is the practical side of philosophy. The Supreme Reality is at once the Absolute of philosophy and the God of religion. India's spiritual and cultural heritage dates back to time immemorial. The essential concepts of Hinduism regarding God, nature, and the soul have been traced to the days of the *Rig-Veda,* the earliest of the four Vedas, the basic Hindu scripture. "What extracts from the Vedas I have read fall on me like light of a higher and purer luminary . . . simple, universal," wrote Henry Thoreau. The timeless Reality in man and nature was discovered in the Vedic age. Absolute faith, based on verification with regard to the fundamental and an amazing flexibility in readjusting the external, have been a fact of the lifestyle through which the Hindu faith has survived and flourished throughout the ages. That is why it is said to be "ever-aging but never old." It may be remembered that Hinduism is older than any other religion of the world. Hinduism regards as its supreme authority the religious experience of the ancient Vedic sages. It has no single founder; the ancient seers acted as various channels for transmitting to humanity the spiritual truths they experienced.

Indian idealism "marched out of her, but every word has been spoken with a blessing behind it, and peace before it. We, of all nations of the world, have never been a conquering race, and that blessing is on our head, and therefore we live."[2] Again, Swami Vivekananda, the modern incarnation of the spirit of Vedanta, said, "Like the gentle dew that falls unseen and unheard, yet brings into blossom the fairest of roses, has been the contribution of India to the thought of the world."[3]

This view of Swamiji was shared by Will Durant. "Perhaps in return for conquest, arrogance and spoliation, India will teach us the tolerance and gentleness of the calm mature mind, the quiet content of the unacquisitive soul, the calm of the understanding spirit, and a unifying, pacifying love for all living beings."[4]

The dominant feature of Hinduism is her emphasis on the development of spiritual life, which finds fulfillment in seeking God within and without. Hence, Hinduism as a religion is both a way of understanding and a scheme for living. The goal of religion is the union with Divinity, which is the "soul of Truth, the delight of life, and the bliss of mind, and the fullness of peace and eternity."[5] This passion for divine life, this search for eternal life in divine excellences, in the midst of the evanescent joys of life, welling forth from the deepest recess of the Hindus, found its eloquent and sincere expression in one of their most familiar prayers: "Lead me from the unreal to the Real, from darkness to Light, from death to Immortality."[6] The great thinkers of the world speak eloquently about the glory of this message contained in Vedanta. The Spanish lover of Vedanta, J. Mascaro, described it as the "Himalayas of the Soul." Upon reading the Latin translation of the Upanishads when it first appeared in the West, the German philosopher Schopenhauer made the significant remark that the Upanishads would be a great source of inspiration and enlightenment to the generations to come. He further said, "In the whole world there is no study except that of the original (of the Upanishads) so beneficial, so elevating . . . it has been the solace of my life, it will be the solace of my death." In the preface to his book, *The World as Will and Idea*, he wrote, "I believe that the influence of the Sanskrit literature will penetrate no less deeply than did the revival of Greek literature in the fifteenth century." He also made a prophecy: "They are destined sooner or later to become the faith of the people." Max Mueller, who drank profusely the divine nectar gathered from Vedanta throughout his long life, remarked, "(Vedanta) is the light of the morning, like the pure air of the mountains, so simple and so true, if once understood." Paul Deussen wrote, "On the tree of Indian wisdom there is no fairer flower than the Upanishads, and no finer fruit than the Vedanta philosophy . . . ."

This philosophy of the Upanishads, as a whole, has made its impact on great minds. Its attraction to the Western mind is very deep and pervasive. It has exerted a permanent influence on Schopenhauer, Hartmann, Nietzche, Paul Deussen, Max Mueller, W. B. Yeats, G. W. Russel, Romain Rolland, Horace Wilson, Sir Monier Williams, Louis Renou, Keyserling, Somerset Maugham, T. S. Elliot, and a host of others in Europe.

In the United States, we find its tremendous influence on the works of Emerson, Thoreau and Walt Whitman, Aldous Huxley, Gerald Heard, Christopher Isherwood, Marie Louise Burke, Huston Smith, and many others. The influence of Vedanta can be attested to by their writings, coloured by Vedantic thought. Vedanta or the Upanishads occupy a unique place in the history of Indian philosophy. They constitute the concluding portion of Vedic literature and are therefore called Vedanta. In a deeper sense, they contain the very essence of the Vedas. They primarily refer to knowledge, and only secondarily to a book. Vedanta upholds the view that truth is not the monopoly of any race. It is a world literature, it is a universal phenomenon. It reveals the immanence of God in nature and the divinity of man. These may be regarded as the fundamentals of Vedanta which for this reason is also addressed as Eternal Religion (*Sanatana Dharma*).

The scientists, through their painstaking and dedicated research, "discover" certain laws of nature; this knowledge is verifiable by others. In the same way Indian sages, *rishis*, through their elevated minds discovered the spiritual truths extant in the Vedas. Only after attaining high spiritual eminence can the mystery of the inner world be discovered through intuitive knowledge. These laws or the facts of their discovery are not "created" by the sages. Vedanta in this sense is *apaurusheya,* impersonal, and thus universal and eternal. Vedanta philosophy exhorts us to verify these eternal truths of spiritual life through our personal endeavor geared to achieve final liberation from bondage.

Swami Vivekananda threw light on this point: "By the Vedas no books are meant. They mean the accumulated treasury of spiritual laws discovered by different persons in different times. Just as the law of gravitation existed before its discovery and would exist if all humanity forgot it, so is it with the laws that govern the spiritual world. The moral, ethical, and spiritual relations between soul and Soul and between individual spirits and the Father of all spirits, were there before their discovery, and would remain even if we forgot them.

"The discoverers of these laws are called *rishis*, and we honour them as perfected beings. I am glad to tell this audience that some of the very greatest of them were women."[7]

Unlike other world religions, Hinduism — rather, *Sanatana Dharma* — has no founder. It is not on the authority of a single individual, but on the intuitive knowledge of the host of mystics. These highly illumined souls do not give us a set of finished and final dogmas or conventional creeds which are to be accepted. Rather, Vedanta tells us repeatedly that experience is very vital to spiritual development: "Religion is realization," as Swamiji said, and not a matter of blind faith in following certain socio-religious practices or external forms of religion. One of the most remarkable features of Vedanta is the intensity of emotion that it inculcates in the seeker of Truth. Therefore, it puts strenuous emphasis on practice to establish a definite relationship with God. "Religion is a question of being and becoming, not of believing."[8]

Truth of Vedanta being the fruits of discovery in the laboratories of our Soul, Vedanta keeps its mind open to accept the revelation of truth from other lands, genuine expressions of man's highest spiritual experience. Vedanta claims to be as much a revelation as the other religions of the world. It goes even a step further and contends that it is a continuous revelation. It does not believe in truth which has been revealed once and for all. Vedanta always encouraged freedom of thought. Infinite Truth has to express itself in infinite ways and in infinite time. It cannot be a sealed book. This catholic outlook and the scientific temper coupled with its sincere passion for various facets of truth have kept it a living philosophy of life. It accepts different types of mind and, therefore, does not prove itself oppressive and monotonous, static and insipid, by keeping everybody in the pigeonhole of a single creed. It recommends different disciplines for different persons which are helpful for their growth. Hence, wide latitude is granted to the people to have their personal religion. That is why, within Hinduism we find the bewildering variety of its expression in its sects and rituals, in its beliefs and worship. This attitude of spiritual struggle to experience truth, as opposed to adopting some external format of religion, has saved Hinduism from the vice of elitism. "The emphasis on the goal of spiritual life bound together worshippers of many different types and saved the Hindus from spiritual snobbery."[9]

Another important feature of Vedanta which it has practised throughout its long career is its wide toleration. It is not a policy but an article of faith. Hence, harmony and positive fellowship based on understanding, sympathy, and reverence for the views of others is prevalent among Hindus. Vedanta is accommodative. Hinduism does not advocate the theory that acceptance of one faith is indispensable for salvation, and that the rejection thereof is an unpardonable sin. It teaches not only toleration but universal acceptance.

"Mark, the same earnest man who is kneeling before the idol tells you, 'Him, the sun cannot express, nor the moon, nor the star; the lightning cannot express Him, nor what we speak of as fire; through Him they shine.' But he does not abuse anyone's idol or call its worship sin. He recognizes in it a necessary stage of life. 'The child is father of the man.' Would it be right for an old man to say that childhood is a sin or youth a sin?

"If a man can realize his divine nature with the help of an image, would it be right to call that a sin? Nor even when he has passed that stage, should he call it an error? To the Hindu, man is not traveling from error to truth, but from truth to truth, from lower to higher truth. To him, all the religions, from the lowest fetishism to the highest absolutism, mean so many attempts of the human soul to grasp and realize the Infinite, each determined by the conditions of its birth and association, and each of these marks a stage of progress; and every soul is a young eagle soaring higher and higher, gathering more and more strength, till it reaches the Glorious Sun."[10]

Thus, rational in its outlook, accommodative in spirit, scientific in temperament, putting emphasis on intuitive experience, practising peaceful coexistence down through the ages, Vedanta has attracted the loving attention of the thinking mind of the world. It does not expect people to submit themselves to the authority of anybody — prophet or teacher.

One Supreme Reality is the sole support and substance of the manifold. This Reality is called the Brahman, out of which the world has originated. The universe is sustained by Brahman and ultimately it is dissolved in Brahman; therefore, Vedanta does not accept the theory that the objective universe has emerged from dull, insentient matter, and that life and consciousness have originated out of matter devoid of consciousness. Brahman is the very essence of *Existence, Consciousness* and *Bliss.* It is by the light of Brahman's consciousness that we become aware of everything. The phenomenal existence is an appearance; it disappears when the knowledge of Reality is gained. But Vedanta does not essentially denounce the world. We are to see God in everything. This is deification of the world: "The whole world is full of the Lord." In this way, we can make spiritual progress.

Brahman is all-pervading and nothing can exist independent of it. While Brahman is immanent, it is also transcendent at the same time. When seen through time, space and causality, Brahman is immanent. Brahman is one undivided whole. Brahman is not confined to this universe, but is above and beyond it. It transcends the entire range of cause and effect. This is transcendental Brahman and it can be experienced only in deep *samadhi.*

Non-dual Brahman cannot function as a world-cause. The totality of God's power is called *maya.* The term *maya* is applicable to God's creation, as well as His creative powers. Brahman is the material as well as the efficient cause of the universe. He is not only the Creator but also the created. In the Vedantic view, there cannot be creation out of nothing, for existence cannot come out of nonexistence. There cannot be anything outside of God. According to Vedanta, an extra-cosmic God is a naive conception of God. Brahman associated with *maya* is the origin, support, and the goal of the universe. This is called *saguna* Brahman (Brahman with attributes) who is immanent in the universe as the Supreme Self and acts as God, the Almighty Lord of the universe. He controls the universe from within. God is both Personal and Impersonal. The term "Personal" is used to indicate that He has attributes; it does not mean that God has a form like a human being. Personal God, apart from *maya,* His limiting adjunct, is no other than Impersonal God.

Swami Vivekananda said, "The very idea of causation exists only in the phenomenal world, and God as the cause of the universe must naturally be thought of as limited, and yet, He is the same Impersonal God."[11]

Though the Hindu pantheon teems with millions of deities, God is One. Formless God assumes various forms by His *maya.* These forms are like different garments under which God is always the same. Since God and His glories are infinite, approaches to Him may be innumerable. "All these forms are of one God, for God is multiform. He is formless and with form and many are His forms which no one knows."[12]

Vedanta is dominated by one supreme conception, which is that there is identity between the individual and God in their essential nature as Pure Consciousness. As long as the individual is under the spell of ignorance about his divinity, he is bound in every respect. Like the ocean and its waves, there is a difference between man and God. As pure and simple water the wave is identical to the ocean. The oneness of the individual and God is the most inspiring message of Vedanta. Atman (Self) and Brahman (Universal Self) are one. Man is Divine, the Divine Spark within man is his Self, is his real Soul. He is not a sinner, it is blasphemy to call him so. Evil is real to us but not to God as He is in Himself. Shri Ramakrishna once compared God to a snake and evil to its poison: what we call poison is not poison to the serpent. Therefore, immutable God is not affected in any way by the evils of the world.

Vedanta exhorts us to accept the world as a battlefield where we are to struggle hard for our freedom from bondage. The story of evolution is the story of the manifestation of this inherent perfection through suitable change in the environment and the organism. The glorious future of this struggle culminates in our attainment of perfection. Religion at this stage becomes a spiritual adventure, and the seeker of truth enters into a world of higher life. He loses all his human weaknesses and enjoys the divine bliss. This is the acme of spiritual life. Spiritual unity, which transcends all worldly distinction, is the solid universal ground of human fraternity.

Vedanta is the religion of optimism. It constantly assures us of our final redemption through successive births. Divinity being our real nature, nobody is condemned forever. From this we get the idea that the goal of life is to attain perfection through the fullest manifestation of our innate divinity deeply imbedded within us, in character development, in the spiritual transformation of life, and in the cultivation of our divine consciousness. Vedanta accepts life as a whole. All aspects of life are given full scope for their development through its participation in socioeconomic programmes. But, Vedanta does proclaim that the highest goal of life can be fulfilled only in spiritual consummation.

Religion is realization. Religious truth has to be experienced through *inner development.* It is to be noted that the purification of the mind and the intense longing for God are very essential. Religion is never for hugging mere dogma or creed, or having a faith in tradition. The divine essence being our inherent property, we feel the compulsive urge from within to seek divine fulfillment through the development of moral and spiritual excellence. This feeling for divine life, this hunger and thirst, this compulsive urge for mystical experience is the beginning of religion. This idea of religion as a Godward impulse is necessary to gain a foothold in the realm of divinity. To such persons, fully roused from the stagnation and resignation of a novitiate, religion becomes a great source of inspiration. Such persons transform dogma- ridden, primitive religion into a practical field to achieve the highest excellences of spiritual life through lifelong struggle. Swami Vivekananda's clarion call to mankind to realize the oneness of existence — of God, man and nature — through living spiritual idealism is the "new religion of the age." It has no church, no books, no founder, no creed, and no priest. The teaching of the Eternal Religion, the whole of Vedanta, has been expressed succinctly by Swami Vivekananda. "Each soul is potentially divine. The goal is to manifest this Divinity within by controlling nature, external and internal. Do this either by work or worship or psychic control or philosophy — by one or more or all of these — and be free. This is the whole of religion. Doctrines, or dogmas, or rituals, or books, or temples, or forms, are but secondary details."[13]

God is the Supreme Self, which brings forth all existence, conscious and unconscious, animate and inanimate, with the help of His *maya,* which belongs to Him. God is the source of orderliness, as He is the greatest lawgiver. He is not an extra-cosmic God, but an intra-cosmic one. This concept of law, in Vedanta, is known as *rita,* "the fixed way or course."[14] The doctrine of *karma* is the counterpart of this law of causation, and more precisely, an extension of the physical law of causation to the moral world. The law of *karma* is the direct corollary of *rita.*

This law of *karma* is one of the most important contributions which India has made to the religious thought of the world. The doctrine of *karma* is the pivot on which the entire structure of Hindu philosophy and culture stands. It is the most original and important conception of Hinduism. It has a tremendous practical bearing on the individual and his destiny. The word *karma* means action. It also suggests the effects thereof. The doctrine of *karma* means that all actions are governed by a law. Vedanta proclaims that as we sow, so we reap. "A man becomes good by good action and bad by bad actions."[15] This is a very logical and scientific theory. Newton's third law of motion states, "To every action there is an equal and opposite reaction."

The truth of this physical law is equally applicable in religious life, too. This theory of *karma* does not espouse fatalism; it stands instead for our freedom of will. We are the architects of our fate. Morally good actions have a spiritual impact on our mind, and morally degraded thoughts and actions have a weakening effect on our mind. This is not guided by any external and irrational agent; it is the effect of *karma* that visits us. "All that we are is the result of what we have thought," said Swami Vivekananda. Hence, it is not a retributive or an inexorable law. Divine Grace does intervene and the effect of *karma* can be partially or wholly mitigated. Paul Deussen appreciated this law as it took away the bitterness from life.

Karma affords us freedom and opportunity to come out of the vicious circle. Swami Vivekananda said, "The only way to come out of bondage is to go beyond the limitations of the law, to go beyond causation."[16] *Karma* binds, but unselfish *karma* liberates us. This is *karma yoga.*

Vedanta preaches the doctrine of non-duality and non-difference. Oneness of life and all existence is the message. Its assurance of joy, strength, faith and vision of life, its call for devotion, fellow-feeling and dedication, are of momentous importance today. Discrimination between person and person originates from our "die-hard ignorance." Our spiritual maturity makes us friends of humanity. It is our very spiritual impulse, if properly nurtured, that helps us to abide by ethical principles. "Thou shalt love thy neighbor as thyself," said Jesus Christ.[17] Swami Vivekananda shone a floodlight on this point: "The rational West is earnestly bent upon seeking out rationality. It is very practical as its central focus is on man who is the epitome of the universe. Man in Vedanta is divine. Self, Atman of Vedanta, is self-luminous, eternally pure and blissful. As the Self is not a created entity, it is immutable and eternal. Some religions lay emphasis on the weaknesses of man and demand the help of God who alone can redeem him. Vedanta emphatically extols the divinity of man. Vedanta recognizes the oneness of man and God, and thereby removes the deep-seated misconception of his weakness. Again, by declaring God as the innermost Self of each person — Atman, it removes our die-hard ignorance of God, that He is extra-cosmic. Infinite God is within us and we all can feel the strength within."

Swami Vivekananda preached untiringly this gospel of Atman and wanted to rouse people from their spiritual stupor to actualize the tremendous potentiality out of such awakening. "Teach yourselves, teach everyone his real nature, call upon the sleeping soul and see how it awakes. Power will come, glory will come, goodness will come, purity will come, and everything that is excellent will come when this sleeping soul is roused to self-conscious activity."[18]

The goal of Vedanta is to attain *moksha* — spiritual freedom — the masterword in Indian philosophy. This spiritual attitude, moulded by Vedanta, has saved India from destruction. Philosophy in India has its origin, not in wonder or inquisitiveness, but in the practical need to enjoy everlasting life in divine bliss and thereby solve the problems of life. The occupation of mind with this practical question certainly provides much better incentive for such preoccupation than mere intellectual curiosity or removal of doubts. Hence, Vedanta is essentially a value-oriented "way of life and the view of life." Therefore, Vedanta gives us a blueprint of healthy values of living.

As opposed to Western thinkers, Vedanta does not treat the study of philosophy as merely an intellectual pastime. The problem of anxiety can never be forgotten by such diversions. Hence, Vedanta holds that the saving values of life — being conscious of our own divinity and constant meditation on Atman (Self) — are to be pursued seriously. Constant meditation with deep conviction will transform our whole personality. "The earnestness of the search for truth is one of the delightful and commendable features of the Upanishads."[19]

Only the direct, immediate and intuitive experience of Atman can make us perfectly happy. This experience is, necessarily, the greatest value in life. This concept of Atman, the Self of man, the immortality of Soul, is one of the greatest contributions of Vedanta to humanity. Swamiji said, "No books, no scriptures, no science, can ever imagine the glory of the Self that appears as man, the most glorious God that ever was, the only God that ever existed, exists, or ever will exist."[20] Vedanta is concerned with this value. Even for the intellectual, Vedanta is a great source of inspiration and enlightenment. Its fearless quest for Truth, its love of freedom in that pursuit, its boldness and sweep of thought, its dynamic outlook on life, are of momentous importance today. It's synthetic view of unity in variety, its harmony of religions, its cosmology and, above all, its peaceful approach toward the goal of life, are the immortal themes. In religion, Vedantic attitude is the common basis of world religions. It expounds the essential unity of all traditional faiths, recognizing that there are many paths to the temple of Truth.

In today's world, Indian wisdom is important for our very survival. Its quest for higher values of life, its emphasis on nonviolence, its love for the spiritual over the material, its affirmation and realization of the divinity inherent in man, and its comprehensive, synthetic philosophy of the harmony of religions, is universal, positive and humane. This spirit gives rise to those values of peace, tolerance and nonagressiveness which will help to usher in a new climate of friendship and unity for mankind.

The modern relevance of the Indian spirit has been appreciated by many Western thinkers. We conclude with a quotation from one of them. Highlighting the need for the accommodative spirit of Hinduism, Toynbee said, "At this supremely dangerous moment in human history, the only way of salvation for mankind is the Indian way. The Emperor Asoka's and the Mahatma Gandhi's principle of nonviolence and Shri Ramakrishna's testimony to the harmony of religions; here we have the attitude and the spirit that can make it possible for the human race to grow together into a single family — and, in the Atomic Age, this is the only alternative to destroying ourselves.

"In the Atomic Age, the whole human race has a utilitarian motive for following this Indian way. No utilitarian motive could be stronger or more respectable in itself. The survival of the human race is at stake. Yet even the strongest and most respectable utilitarian motive is only a secondary reason for taking Ramakrishna's and Gandhi's and Asoka's teaching to heart and acting on it. The primary reason is that this teaching is right — and is right because it flows from a true vision of spiritual reality."[21]

4

VEDANTA AND SWAMI VIVEKANANDA

In his lecture, *Vedanta and Indian Life*, Swami Vivekananda remarked: "The Upanishads are the great mine of strength. Therein lies strength enough to invigorate the whole world; the whole world can be vivified, made strong, energized through them. They will call with trumpet voice to the weak, the miserable and the downtrodden of all races, all creeds and all sects, to stand on their feet and be free. Freedom, physical freedom, mental freedom and spiritual freedom are the watchwords of the Upanishads."[1] And in his lecture, *The Mission of the Vedanta* he said, "Teach yourselves, teach everyone his real nature, call upon the sleeping soul and see how it awakes. Power will come, glory will come, goodness will come, purity will come, and everything that is excellent will come, when this sleeping soul is roused to self-conscious activity."[2]

Swamiji looked upon Vedanta as a great source of inspiration. The Vedantic doctrine of Atman points out that the human spirit is in reality identical with the Supreme Being. Atman is one and universal. The primary message of Vedanta, according to Swamiji, is the proclamation of man's true nature as the birthless, deathless Spirit, ever free, perfect and ever pure. The human being is not really the weak and grovelling creature that he seems to be — a creature who is at the mercy of a hundred forces of nature and a slave to irresistible passions. The consciousness of bondage, of weakness and of impurity is present in us, because we have forgotten our identity, and the moment we assert our divinity again, that inalienable nature of ours, which no amount of self-hypnosis can really change, will manifest itself. The world of matter which appears so vast and so overpowering is only a misreading of the nature of the Supreme Atman. The next important teachings of Vedanta that caught the imagination of Swamiji were those about *abhaya* (fearlessness), *shraddha* (faith and reverence) and *tyaga* (renunciation).

Vedanta does not preach a static view of life. It is a perennial source of strength and creativity. Its theme is the freedom of the human spirit. It underlines the infinite dimensions of the human personality. It explains every great movement, social, political or religious — nay, the entire gamut of life itself as an expression of the urge for freedom that is inherent in man. The Atman is the basis of our consciousness, our happiness, nay, even of our very existence. One man differs from another in body, color, race, or mental attitudes, but not in this essential truth of his being, his self. This is the real point behind universal religion and the brotherhood of man. The discovery of this truth is indeed of momentous importance. Sister Nivedita has aptly described Swamiji as "the worker at foundations." He is the only man who has utilized the life-giving message of Vedanta for the regeneration of India and for the establishment of Universal Religion. The base of his mission is a spiritual non-dualism and not any eclectic, exotic, superficial, pseudo-universal religious propaganda indulged in by modern intellectuals having no insight into the spiritual unity of man. Vivekananda saw to it that Vedanta no longer remained confined to the forest and given over to scholastic speculation, but was made the property of the masses for lifting them up in the spiritual scale, as well as for sustaining them in the struggle of life. The concept of Atman has not been applied previously for the elevation of the collective life of the people and for providing a solid basis for all-round prosperity. In the light of the gospel of Neo-Vedanta there is "no distinction henceforth between sacred and secular. To labour is to pray. To conquer is to renounce. Life is itself religion. To have and to hold is as stern a trust as to quit and avoid."[3] Taking his stand on this set principle, the great Swami deduced a series of consequences bearing vitally on the entirety of life, thought and activity. The situation that faced Swamiji in his time was a very complex and baffling one. India was groaning under the heels of the foreign conqueror. It was no longer isolated and was exposed to the influence of Christian missions, English education, Western culture, and materialism augmented by science and technology. Hence the Indian Renaissance that began with the advent of Rammohan Roy was not confined to religion. People were interested in many things — politics, social reform, science and materialism. Religion itself was caste-ridden; rituals and superstition were choking it. Atheism was rampant; poverty, stagnation and exploitation were the order of the day. What was needed was all-round reconstruction at a rapid pace. The modern age was different from the age of religious revolution of the Upanishadic era and the times of expansion and consolidation of the *Gita* message. In Swamiji's view, man had too long been obsessed with the idea of sin and weakness. It was high time for man to wake up to the consciousness of his own divine nature which was his birthright. This alone was rightly considered to be a panacea for all maladies of stagnant and moribund life. Self-knowledge alone could foster love and mutual understanding between man and man. It alone would summon men and women everywhere to the mighty adventure of freedom and fearlessness, sympathy and service, and to the spiritual realization of inner unity, and thus help the solving of the formidable problems of life. An overemphasis on the *jnana* attitude was a historical necessity — for counteracting the pernicious and debasing effects of the feeling of unworthiness of man, which feeling was engendered by slavery. The Swami said, "Strength is the medicine for the world's disease."[4] To him, spirituality was strength and strength was the test of true realization. Vedanta in his hands became a gospel of intense activity and connoted the widest expansion of the spirit. It became a great force for the moral regeneration of an India that was haunted by the spectre of fatalism, defeat and decay. Again and again the Swami reminded his countrymen of their glorious spiritual heritage and stressed the special role his generation had to play in the evolution of modern renascent India. The reconstruction of India had to be based, he said, on the bedrock of her spiritual resources, on the Upanishads, which were an inexhaustible mine of infinite strength. He taught that without faith in the Atman — ever free, pure, immortal, self-luminous, as the Upanishads describe it, men could not be strong and invincible. That period in India's history in which Swamiji lived and worked was characterized in part, by the search for ideologies. Swamiji presented Vedanta as a fearless philosophy of life which helped man to frame ideas for himself "with the intensity of the fanatic and the extensity of the materialist". In Swamiji, Hinduism got a fresh lease on life and vigour. He impregnated Hinduism with the ideal of complete self-dedication to the service of humanity. He encouraged the study of new knowledge for the improvement of the secular life of the people. He also made Hinduism dynamic by enkindling in it the zeal for dissemination of the gospel of universal truths for the welfare of humanity at large. He emphasized a twofold application of Vedanta in practical life: (1) arousing man's faith in himself, and (2) serving brother-men in the spirit of serving God. A distinctive character of the Swamiji's message was its comprehensiveness. His message was meant for all grades of life. In conformity with the Vedic teachings, he recognized a twofold way — the *pravritti marga* and the *nivritti marga.* He declared, "Our duty is to encourage everyone in his struggle to live up to his own highest ideal, and strive at the same time to make the ideal as near as possible to the truth." An outstanding discovery of the Swami has to be mentioned here. His historical knowledge and insight unveiled to him the supreme fact that spirituality was the very lifeblood of India and that her regeneration had to be worked up on a spiritual basis. Underlying all diversities of sects, castes, doctrines, rites, customs etc., there was a spiritual unity in Indian life which his extraordinary genius clearly saw. No extraneous forces could, he knew, help the growth of a nation as much as the slow-moving yet formative forces of its own national life could. The life force of India, he saw, was religion and religion alone. He said, "In India, religious life forms the centre, the keynote of the whole music of national life, and if any nation attempts to throw off its national vitality, the direction which has become its own through the transmission of centuries — that nation dies, if it succeeds in the attempt." Swamiji not only preached this ideal, but he went a step further and warned the country that India's special gift to the world throughout the ages had been the profound truths of spiritual life and that on her regeneration depended the regeneration of the world.

The spirit of Vedanta, asserted Swamiji, was through and through permeated by the idea of renunciation. The alpha and omega in India was renunciation. Give up, says the Veda, give up. *Na karmana, na prajaya dhanena, tyagenaike amritattvam anasuh* ('Neither through *karma,* nor through progeny, nor through wealth, but only through renunciation have some attained immortality'). So he emphasized the twin ideals of our culture — renunciation and service. It was Swamiji's philosophy of mobility and vitality based on the message of the *Aitareya Brahmana* — *charaiveti* — "move on" — which gave a tremendous inspiration to the new forces operating in modern India. Said he, "My hope is to see again the strong points of India, reinforced by the strong points of this age, only in a natural way. The new state of things must be a growth from within." Swamiji's all-encompassing vision took into its ken those who aspired after temporal values as well as those who sought spiritual bliss. He said, "With us the prominent idea is *mukti* — there was a time in India when *dharma* was compatible with *mukti.* There were worshippers of *dharma* such as Yudhishthira, Arjuna, Bhishma and Karna, side by side with the aspirants for *mukti* such as Vyasa, Suka, Janaka. On the advent of Buddhism, *dharma* was entirely neglected and the path of *moksha* alone became predominant. The central fact is that the fall of our country, of which we hear so much spoken, is due to the utter want of this *dharma.* Without enjoyment, renunciation can never come." Hence, Swamiji deviated from the traditional way, by not imparting the cardinal Vedic teaching of the divinity of the soul exclusively to the seekers of spiritual knowledge. He democratized it and proclaimed its message to one and all, to the spiritual seekers as well as to the materialists. He recommended its application not only for spiritual development but also for material and intellectual development. He said, "This infinite power of the spirit brought to bear upon matter evolves material development; made to act upon thought, evolves intellectuality and made to act upon Itself, makes man a God. Manifest the divinity within and everything will be harmoniously arranged around it." He also enjoined on the monks of his Order a twofold duty: While striving for his own liberation the seeker should work for the good of the world as well. And here lay the originality of the Swamiji. He, with his *guru,* Shri Ramakrishna, for the first time in the history of Indian philosophy, combined the Monistic Vedantic theory of the oneness of Brahman with the Monotheistic Vedantic practice of universal love and service. Vedic seers, Jains, Buddhists, Monotheistic Vedantists and many others preached and practised the ideal of service to humanity. But none before had preached the ideal of service to man as God Himself. In fact, in the whole history of mankind, as has been well stated, none has proclaimed the glory and grandeur of man — his absolute divinity, infinite greatness, immeasurable dignity in such a vehement manner as Swamiji.

He elevated and sublimated the empirical to the transcendental, instead of denying the former. "The Vedanta does not in reality denounce the world — it really means deification of the world — giving up the world as we think of it, as we know it, as it appears to us and to know what it really is. . . . You can have your wife but you are to see God in the wife. In life and in death, in happiness and in misery, the Lord is equally present. The whole world is full of the Lord. Open your eyes and see Him. This is what Vedanta teaches." And, this may be taken as one of the best commentaries on the Vedanta. He emphasized equally the twin aspects of Supreme Godhead — the transcendental and the immanent. Swamiji pointed out that the Vedanta, in all its forms, is intensely practical. Two celebrated *mantras* — *sarvam khalvidam Brahma* (The world is Brahman),[6] and *ayamatma Brahma* (The soul is Brahman)[7], give the most comprehensive view of the state of things in the universe. Swamiji had to deal with the active, busy, complex life of intellectual triumph and material achievement — a life which demanded the spiritualizing principle of *karma.* Idleness in the garb of contemplation was no longer to be tolerated. He had to rouse all to action. In fact, he presented *karma yoga* to people, with a broad and elevated outlook, without denying the bliss and glory of the real meditative life.

In his view, all domestic, social, and humanitarian deeds could be performed in the spirit of service to God. His message was the logical conclusion of the teachings of the Vedanta, the *Gita* and the *Bhagavatam.* Truly speaking, it was not at all a new message. But its practical application in every department of life had not been tried before. Such a course had been recommended by Shri Ramakrishna himself. "No, not kindness to living beings, but service to God dwelling in them," said he. He further said, "If God can be worshiped through a clay image, then why not through a man?" It was to the singular credit and eternal glory of Swamiji that he exhorted us to practise this teaching in the modern age for the welfare of the suffering humanity. He blended the ethical and the spiritual ideals beautifully. His message was for men of realization, too. Serving man even after attaining the Supreme Bliss had to be regarded as a very high state — a state of super-knowledge and super-devotion. Shri Ramakrishna and his disciples have emphasized the ideal of living in the world as a free soul for the well-being of humanity. This is the *vijnani* stage of evolution. Swamiji linked Vedanta and Buddhism. His view was that one was incomplete without the other. Swamiji felt the need of all the three systems of philosophy. He brought out their inner glory, inherent beauty, and infinite wealth, through his message and synthesized in a simple, straightforward and charming manner all the three systems. In his view the oneness of Advaita had to be reached through Dvaita and Vishishtadvaita, as the three were not contradictory, but complementary.

This synthesis of Dualism, Qualified Monism and Monism was the work of the mastermind of Swamiji. It was indeed a marvellous "discovery." The Advaita, as propounded and practised by Swamiji, was therefore marked by a wonderful spirit of acceptance of diversity. Thus the originality of the Swami lies in that, though a staunch Advaitin, he recognizes the supreme importance and absolute necessity of feeling in one's spiritual life. "It is feeling that is life, the strength, the vitality, without which no amount of intellectual activity can reach God." This feeling or love is the logical and living outcome of his realization of the basic and infinite unity of creation. Love and knowledge are by no means opposed, but are rather complementary — like the hard stem and the soft petal of a flower. The hiatus between the ideal and the practical has been beautifully bridged by his emphasis on the practice of Vedanta in life. Swamiji has thus carved a place for himself as the modern apostle of Advaita, of cosmic unity. His words have become the modern hymn of Advaita: "I see God in all that exists. I see him as completely in the least fragment as in the whole cosmos. . . ."

Swamiji indeed had "the head of Shankara and the heart of Chaitanya, the eyes of a Monist and the hands of a Monotheist, the tenacity of a scholar and the tenderness of a lover, the devotion of a Theist and the spirit of service of a Humanist." We may call his interpretation of the Vedanta doctrine by a new name, *manava advaitavada* or "Humanistic Monism." For who ever sang *manavamahatmya*, or the glory of man, in sweeter tunes than he? "No books, no scriptures, no science can ever imagine the glory of the Self that appears as man, the most glorious God that ever was, the only God that ever existed, exists or ever will exist. Bold, brave beyond the conception of the present day stand the giant minds of the sages of the Upanishads, declaring the noblest truths, that have ever been preached to humanity, without any compromise, without any fear. This, my countrymen, I want to lay before you. . . . go back to your Upanishads, the shining, the strengthening, the bright philosophy, and part from all these mysterious things, all these weakening things. Take up this philosophy; the greatest truths are the simplest things in the world, simple as your existence. The truths of the Upanishads are before you. Take them up, live up to them, and the salvation of India will be at hand."[8]

Such were the ringing words of Swamiji.

5

SWAMIJI'S PRACTICAL VEDANTA – I

Summing up the lessons of India's political history, Will Durant in *Our Oriental Heritage* says, "Weakened by division, it succumbed to invaders; impoverished by invaders, it lost all power of resistance, and took refuge in supernatural consolations; it argued that both mastery and slavery were superficial delusions, and concluded that freedom of the body or the nation was hardly worth defending in so brief a life."[1]

Time and again did Swami Vivekananda turn the searchlight inward and declare that our internal dissensions, selfishness, and mutual jealousy and hatred were among the principal causes of our degeneration; that these sordid vices ate into the very vitals of the nation and promoted slavery. The Swami's penetrating observations in this context may be profitably read by everyone wishing the well-being of the country: "What we in India have are only deep-rooted envy and strong antipathy against one another, morbid desire to ruin by hook or by crook the weak, and lick the feet of the strong. . ." Unfortunately, even today these defects of our national character continue to be present in menacing proportions.

The wailings of the nation's soul, incarcerated like Prometheus, had already begun to be heard in the last century. The first faint murmurings of a new life were already audible to the pioneers of awakened India. But it fell to the lot of Swamiji to give the nation the lead that would truly rehabilitate it. "India was hauled up out of the shifting sands of barren speculation wherein she had been engulfed for centuries by the hand of her own *sannyasin*."[2]

It is indeed a fascinating exercise to read the story of the life of Swamiji in the context of the national awakening. Swamiji had the unique advantage of coming into intimate contact with a super-personality like that of Shri Ramakrishna. He saw the living image of wisdom and love in his master. He had not been inspired very much by his study of the dry pages of philosophy, although he was a voracious reader, but the living truth, embodied in the personality of Shri Ramakrishna, went deep into his mighty soul. In Shri Ramakrishna was the reality which the books only brokenly described. Swamiji gave his impressions of his master to Nivedita in such a way that she says, "In his *guru* (Ramakrishna), Vivekananda found the key to life." Shri Ramakrishna's realization of the presence of Divinity in the phenomenal world and his understanding of the fundamental unity of all faiths and beliefs opened the eyes of Swamiji to the fact that all is Brahman, that *jiva* is no other than *Shiva*, that every creature is God Himself in a particular garb of name and form. Therefore, to him, service to man was divine worship. In respect of this attitude, he was in a sense different from the traditional monists for whom the world is unreal and who naturally feel that compassion for agonized humanity and sympathy for sufferers would be tantamount to an affirmation of the reality of illusory appearance. Shri Ramakrishna, by means of his unique *sadhana*, imparted to the monistic Vedanta a practical mould by emphasizing a positive aspect. The trans-empirical awareness of identity upon which the doctrine of pure Advaita is ultimately based was of course Shri Ramakrishna's fundamental philosophy. And he stood with the traditional Advaitins to acclaim identity as the fundamental stuff of reality. Yet he refused to remain forever absorbed in *samadhi.* His spiritual life was a perpetual transition from unity to plurality and vice versa. Swamiji's *nirvikalpa samadhi* gave him the incontrovertible certitude of the teachings of his *guru.*

Following the pathway treaded by his master, Swamiji seized the essential truth of religion, viz, the oneness of *jiva-Brahma.* His own supreme realization of the unity of existence and of the divinity of the soul dissolved the breach between the spiritual and the secular, between the self-repose of the soul and the action — service of deified man, between perfect detachment and disinterested service guided by an integrated vision. The spiritual ideal is for life, and life must be lived truly and well in all its spheres — private, social and international. Swamiji wished that the eternal faith should become dynamic and living and be a force for waging a relentless struggle for the all-round development of the human personality. Swamiji yearned to raise mankind to higher and still higher levels of existence by the gradual spiritualization on the vital plane, by the sanctification of the empirical, and the deification of the material. He made a very bold attempt to convert the metaphysical abstraction of Vedanta into a vibrant, living force. He worked for bringing the Vedanta from the forest to the battlefield of life. He did not want us to make use of the Vedanta force exclusively for the super-mundane quest. His mission was to transfer the emphasis from involvement in metaphysics to living a life of practical righteousness, and from striving for individual salvation to laboring for the salvation of all beings. "The abstract Advaita," he urged, "must become living, poetic, in everyday life." Thus *Brahmanubhuti,* the Universal Consciousness, the highest spiritual realization visualized by the monistic school of philosophy, was brought in letter and spirit by Swamiji into his advocacy of dynamic religion and Practical Vedanta. His grand message is a call of awakening to the totality of our manhood, to the all-ness of our personality. The modern apostle of monism that Swamiji was, he breathed a new life into the moribund Hinduism. To quote a writer, "This new Shankaracharya may well be claimed to be the unifier of Hindu ideology. Travelling all over India he not only aroused a sense of Hindu feeling, but taught the doctrine of Universal Vedanta as the background of the new Hindu reformation."[3]

Swamiji, though a staunch monist, never preached a world-denying, pessimistic and negative philosophy of life. In his interpretation of Vedanta, the world does not get totally negated and annihilated, but is sublimated, transformed and deified. The world thus transformed and deified is the real world; and Swamiji was the first to proclaim this truth in clear, unequivocal and emphatic terms. It is not possible to come across a finer statement of the quintessence of the Advaita Philosophy than in his brilliant lecture, *God in Everything,* in London on October 27, 1896.

Thus theoretically Swamiji's message is one of *sarvatma-vada,* and practically, it is one of *sarva-seva-vada.* There are monists who vehemently support the first, but do not pay any heed to the second. It was Swamiji, who for the first time, combined gloriously, the Advaita doctrine of the oneness of the soul with the Vaishnava doctrine of service to all. His crystal-clear and trenchant exposition of *maya*, of *karma*, of Vedanta, and privilege — of Practical Vedanta, is a new light shed on philosophy. His brilliant and exhilarating message of spiritualistic humanism is voiced thunderingly all through his fiery speeches and writings. He was an eternal pilgrim to the city of God and still a valiant warrior in the cause of suffering humanity. His magnificent and colorful personality had immense lustre added to it because of this twofold characteristic.

Truth is not a closed book. The newness of Swamiji's message lay in the turn given by him to life's motif. It was one of his greatest services to the welfare of mankind that he showed how pure religion can face all the challenges and help man in his evolutionary process. No higher stroke of his genius can be looked for than in his thesis of Practical Vedanta. It has no parallel in history. As Romain Rolland says, "He (Swamiji) surrounded service with a divine aureole and raised it to the dignity of a religion." For nearly ten centuries, Advaita philosophy had been a series of footnotes to Shankara. All religious movements that shook the community had aimed either at strengthening orthodoxy or expanding the fold of social workers, and were narrowly spiritual in appeal or much too mundane. In Swamiji, the urges of the total life in all its aspects found a voice that struck the consciousness of the people. For the first time in the history of the world, the harmony of religions took deep root in the human soil. For the first time in Indian history, philosophy and religion were examined from a modern historical background and spiritual treasures were successfully pressed into the service of enriching the secular life. Swamiji re-oriented the whole outlook of religion and life by his emphasis on *atmano mokshartham jagaddhitaya cha* — for the liberation of the self and for doing good to mankind. India had known orders of *sannyasins* for ages upon ages, but never before were they consecrated to the service of that God whom we mistakenly call man. Never before was Vedanta interpreted as a mine of strength; never before had

Vedantic catholicity as Swamiji conceived and realized it, made such an impact on human life. Never before had the conception of the all-round development of the human personality been based on the four *yogas.* Never before had this lucid exposition of Vedanta been made: "If the many and the One be indeed the same Reality, then it is not all modes of worship alone, but equally all modes of work, all modes of struggle, all modes of creation, which are paths of realization. No distinction henceforth between sacred and secular. . . . Life is itself religion." Addressing a London audience with, *The Absolute and Manifestation* in 1896, Swamiji said: "Buddha laid stress upon the moral side of the philosophy, and Shankaracharya, upon the intellectual. Shankara worked out, rationalized, and placed before men the wonderful, coherent system of Advaita." And the great Swami applied the truths of Vedanta to the solution of all social and national and international problems so that man's life on earth might become saner, richer, and fuller.

6

SWAMIJI'S PRACTICAL VEDANTA - II

Vedanta is a living philosophy which is interested in the study of a whole Reality — the timeless Reality in man and in nature. It discovered the Oneness of God, the divinity of mankind, the identity of the individual with Godhead, and the harmony of faiths. Religion is realization. The truth of Vedanta is living and poetic. The practice of this truth will enrich our total life. Religion means a way of life that enables us to know the Divine within as well as without — in other words, Self-realization. It caters to the vital need of nourishing man and giving him real fulfillment in life. Vedanta views life in all its aspects. Its main aim is man — man in the perennial quest of Truth, Beauty and Goodness in their absolute sense. Vedanta also investigates the external world, but its main passion is the study of the inner life of man. The study of external nature culminates in material prosperity; the study of inner nature gives a clue to the spiritual treasure which ultimately brings spiritual fulfillment, as well as all-round growth.

The teaching of Vedanta is addressed to all humanity — to all people struggling to have freedom from bondage. Therefore, universality and humanism are two of the essential characteristics of this fruitful study. Vedanta seeks the real welfare, peace and spiritual fulfillment of man as such, and not man chained by sect or race. It is concerned with man in his depth, beyond the frontiers of narrow and parochial dissension. This original incentive to seek the genuine welfare of man in himself, unlike philosophies elsewhere and unlike other philosophies of India, has saved Vedanta from becoming a mere academic quest. It is a living philosophy, and its universalism, freshness, intensity, courage, and broadness of outlook have captivated the mind of the scholars of all nations.

Vedanta has twice saved India from materialism. According to Swami Vivekananda, Buddha first brought the essence of Vedanta to light, gave it to the people, and saved India. Again Shankara revived it. Buddha preached the moral excellences of life and the spirit of unselfish service. Shankara gave the intellectual support. He gave a complete philosophy based on reason. He rationalized it and placed before us the wonderful, coherent system of Advaita. This time we see Swami Vivekananda extolling this message of Vedanta for the regeneration of all humanity. The passion for purity, knowledge and freedom were preserved and amplified by every subsequent age of Indian thought. But in the modern period, Swami Vivekananda infused life into it and gave it dynamism. Through his great life, he made Vedanta a living and practical philosophy.

Religion, by which we mean a spiritual view of life, nourishes a culture which, in turn, supports people by guiding them to find the excellences of life. Without this nourishment people stagnate and, consequently, religion is lost. Therefore, a great culture is the product of a deep spiritual quest which sets the tone of that culture. Indian culture, inspired by messengers of spiritual truth, has acquired a spiritual direction. That India is mainly based on this spiritual outlook can be seen both from its spiritual earnestness and from its variety of religious expression. Saints and illumined souls always did receive far greater honor than any celebrity. The nature and character of spontaneous ovation accorded to Swamiji after his triumphal return to India, speaks highly of her spiritual culture.

The Indian Renaissance owes its birth and growth to spiritual leaders from Rammohan Roy to Swami Vivekananda. Romain Rolland, in his *Life of Ramakrishna*, presents this great spiritual luminary and his chief disciple, Swami Vivekananda, as "the splendid symphony of the Universal Soul," and reports, "Ramakrishna is the consummation of the two thousand years' spiritual life of three hundred million people."[1] In the same vein, Swami Vivekananda asserts that Ramakrishna "in fifty-one years lived the five thousand years of national spiritual life, and so raised himself to be an object-lesson for future generations."[2] Swami Vivekananda dived deep into the ocean of Spirit in all its magnificent beauty. His entire message to humanity was based on his firsthand spiritual realization. This unique capacity gave a halo to his personality and a solid foundation to his mission. His ability to teach from experience commands respect from the world. His fresh, invigorating, practical and rational message has found a loving place in our minds. What we urgently need today is a scheme of life which is spiritually inspiring, morally ennobling and physically strength-giving. We need a new gospel of life. Swami Vivekananda gave humanity the lofty message of Vedanta, which addresses human beings as divine. Only this divinity of man can inspire us to find dignity in life and the assurance of bright future possibilities. This noble philosophy of life, based on the solid spiritual experiences of the mystics, when accepted with earnestness and understood in real perspective, will be the new ethos of the people.

Swami Vivekananda, whose singular passion in life was man — the whole man in all his aspects — gave articulation to his deep feeling in this worshipful attitude:

> May I be born again and again, and suffer thousands of miseries, so that I may worship the only God that exists, the only God I believe in, the sum total of all souls — and above all, my God the wicked, my God the miserable, my God the poor of all races, of all species, is the special object of my worship.[3]

He also stated:

> All the ideas that I preach are only an attempt to echo his (Ramakrishna's) ideas.[4]

It may be remembered that Swami Vivekananda was moulded by the life and teachings of Shri Ramakrishna, who poured out his pent-up emotion to Mother Kali with the same pathos: "Mother, I do not want *moksha*. Let me live in the midst of your created beings and lift them up, try for their liberation."[5] And again he said: "We heard the Master say sometimes at Dakshineswar that he was not afraid to be born lakhs of times to do good to living beings."[6]

However, Swami Vivekananda gave a new direction to philosophy and religion, and made Vedanta a practical system to be espoused by the common people. God-centered philosophy was made man-centered. The system which was confined to a few seekers of Truth began giving the eternal bread of life to the millions. The traditional Vedanta has now become, through new interpretation, a source of inspiration for everyday life, and has been labelled the Neo-Vedantic Movement. Dr. S. C. Chatterjee said, "The main outline of this new Vedanta was given by Shri Ramakrishna and it was Swami Vivekananda who filled it with elaborate reasoning so as to work up a philosophy proper. It has been very aptly said that Swami Vivekananda is a commentary on Shri Ramakrishna. But the Commentator with his giant intellect and profound understanding made such a distinctive contribution, that his commentary becomes itself a philosophy, just as Shankara's commentary on the *Vedanta Sutras* is by itself a philosophy."[7]

This Neo-Vedantic Movement of Swami Vivekananda not only opened a new and vital chapter of our spiritual life, but also enhanced the prestige of this life-giving system. The very call of Swami Vivekananda — "Back to the Upanishads!" — ushered in an era of new vitality and dynamism in Hinduism. The constructive genius of Swami Vivekananda made this new gospel of living a universal, catholic and nonsectarian voice unlike previous movements that are negative, destructive, condemning and abusive. One of the brilliant landmarks of this progressive and creative message is that it is geared to the all-round happiness of the people, and thus paves the way for modernism. It bridges the gulf between science, religion and philosophy. Besides all the achievements, it freed Vedanta from lifeless scholastic arguments and the narrow groove of academic discussion in which it lay buried for many centuries. The new Vedanta eschews the abstract reasoning and discussion of mere intellectual faith. It has become a new gospel of work and creative progress, fertilizing every aspect of human life. The life-giving ideas of Vedanta have to be practised in life. Once Swami Vivekananda expressed his deep feeling of sorrow and hope in this way:

> Knowledge of the Advaita Vedanta has been hidden too long in caves and forests. It has been given to me to rescue it from its seclusion and to carry it into the midst of family and social life.

> The drum of the Advaita Vedanta shall be sounded in all places, in the bazaars, from the hilltops and on the plains.[8]

Swamiji wanted us first to bring transformation in our own mind, which will then lead to an awakening of the Soul. As a true reformer, he believed in the enduring benefit of moral and spiritual awakening of people, which alone can bring forth new humane developments among mankind. He found the real source of that true reformation in the philosophy of Advaita. Let human ships float on the bosom of the divine waters of life. The strong conviction of Soul-consciousness alone will motivate people to go forward. We know that even in India this blueprint for a new culture based on spiritual life was never presented on a massive scale. The old ideas of philosophy, leading to lifeless academic discussion, never showed any concern for the well-being of the people. Swamiji wanted to place before mankind the powerful idealism of Advaita, to make it a powerful vehicle of social transformation through spiritual transformation. In his famous letter to Alasinga Perumal, dated February 17, 1896, he gave an outline of his plans:

> The dry, abstract Advaita must become living — poetic — in everyday life; out of hopelessly intricate mythology must come concrete moral forms; and out of bewildering *yogi-ism* must come the most scientific and practical psychology — and all this must be put in a form so that a child can grasp it. This is my life's work.[9]

Again, he said, "My ideal, indeed may be put into a few words, and that is to preach unto makind their divinity and how to make it manifest in every movement of life."[10] Swamiji's four lectures on *Practical Vedanta* given in London, in November, 1896, together with other lectures, especially his lecture on November 12, 1897, at Lahore, give us a new, hitherto unknown and most comprehensive philosophy of Vedanta for practical life. This is one of his most original and significant contributions to world thought. Advaita has to become a sheet anchor of world civilization. From the fullness of his loving heart, he went on speaking about its glorious future with the vigorous enthusiasm of his tremendous personality. The music of his illumined soul was heard in India and it went into the very bloodstream of Indian life. In India, Swamiji's thundering lectures were "rousing calls to a sleeping giant, and in the West they were bombshells." They gave a rude shock to the West, stirring the very depths of its soul. His main objective was to recreate society on the basis of a new, "unshakable, unalterable" concept of man: every life is divine. This gave society a new "ethos of the people," giving the glorious opportunity for individual dignity to create a healthy society based on freedom and justice. His entire scheme of human development was based on this central idea — the divinity of life. He won the heart of the people with his originality, expressing Advaita in novel language and refreshing it with new spiritual vigour.

Swami Vivekananda rescued India from the self-imprisonment of centuries and brought her into the wide world of freedom and life. The dynamic modern world confronted India at every phase of life. This awakened India recognized the necessities and urgencies of modern living. Says Romain Rolland:

> So India was hauled out of the shifting sands of barren speculation wherein she had been engulfed for centuries, by the hand of one of her own *sannyasins*; and the result was that the whole reservoir of mysticism, sleeping beneath, broke its bounds and spread by a series of great ripples into action. . . . This "greater India", this new India. . . is impregnated with the soul of Ramakrishna. The twin star of the Paramahamsa and the hero who translated his thought into action, dominates and guides her present destinies. Its warm radiance is the leaven working within the soil of India and fertilizing it.[11]

Swami Vivekananda, being a spiritual teacher of extraordinary character, was able to teach the people the same eternal message of Vedanta for their everyday life. He attempted to project the undivided view of reality that would bridge the gulf between sacred and secular, between worship and work, between *jnana* and *karma*. Hence, Swamiji taught ordinary people that work is worship.

Swamiji's character was brilliantly summed up by Romain Rolland in two words: equilibrium and synthesis. Indeed, he was a great advocate of equilibrium between reason and faith; matter and spirit; individual and society; science and religion; absolute and relative. A champion of the synthetic view of life, Swamiji accepted the unity of matter and spirit. For him, there is no division between sacred and secular. This message of synthesis made him a prophet of the age. Work and knowledge were fused together. Swamiji demolished the theory of two aspects of reality — absolute and relative — as this theory was a breeding ground of social injustice. He gave us the unitary vision of life. The impact of that life-giving message has been marvellously articulated by his brilliant disciple, Sister Nivedita:

> If the many and the One be indeed the same Reality, then it is not all modes of worship alone but equally all modes of work, all modes of struggle, all modes of creation, which are paths of realization. No distinction, henceforth, between sacred and secular. To labour is to pray. To conquer is to renounce. Life is itself religion. To have and to hold is as stern a trust as to quit and to avoid.[12]

The practical significance of Swamiji's comprehensive view of reality, or unitary vision of reality, made no division between work and worship, sacred and secular. Work at any stage of life done with the real spirit of service to God as manifested in the world, is the real form of worship. Swamiji tried to revive the unitary vision of life as envisioned in the *Gita.*[13]

The Swami threw a flood of light on certain basic tenets of Hinduism. The two doctrines of *karma* and *maya* proved to be a double noose on the neck of the Hindu race for centuries. These theories practically ruined the nation's life with their deadening fatalism and intellectual bankruptcy. *Karma* and *maya,* like two powerful vampires, were sucking the blood of national life, making the Hindu race weak, inactive, isolated and fatalistic. By his magnetic personality, dynamic spirit and inspired attitude, Swamiji gave a new insight into these concepts. It was to the singular credit of the Swami to have interpreted them in a creative manner, bringing back their original significance and vigour, thereby making a very powerful, fresh vehicle for the dynamic movements of national life. He was able to rejuvenate the national life through his soul-stirring message, his robust enthusiasm. To make India well-equipped for her all-round growth, to enable her to rediscover her hidden potential and her glorious past, and to emancipate her mind from pessimism and a narrow mould, Swamiji worked vigorously. He expounded the concept of *karma* and rebirth from a rational point of view, bringing in a new and fresh world of joy and creativity. The theory of *karma* was thus proved to the hilt to be contrary to the prevailing wrong notion of it.

With a rare insight, Swamiji identified the idea of relativity as the substance of *maya,* the Hindu "sphinx." God appears as matter due to *maya*. *Maya* creates division; One appears as many. The world of *maya* will persist so long as the mind, which is itself *maya*, is not purified through spiritual insight. *Maya* will lose its charm, its puzzle will be solved, when the mind is made pure. *Maya* can be transcended.

This saving knowledge, this fresh insight, helped India slowly to liberate her mind from dogmatism and pessimism. "Great convictions are mothers of great deeds," said Swamiji. His fiery *Lectures from Colombo to Almora* and his *Letters* are the predominant source of national rejuvenation. Romain Rolland says, "If India today has definitely taken part in the collective action of organized masses, it is due to the initial shock, to the mighty 'Lazarus, come forth!' of the message from Madras."[14] Swamiji's message was like a transfusion of blood coursing through the national vein, quickening life.

Swamiji was the very embodiment of courage. With a remarkable insight, he equated courage with Reality and interpreted courage, strength, or virility as the most distinguishing attribute of Divinity. This is a completely new interpretation, hitherto unknown to India. We know from our study of the Upanishads[15] that the Divine is fearless; hence, courage stems from that great idea. But the concept of courage is conspicuously absent from our philosophical system and moral vocabularies. Therefore, the word "courage" is not in vogue in our moral tradition. Swamiji projected before us the concept of dynamic Divinity — rather than static Divinity, which hardly evokes enthusiasm in human minds. It may be remembered that Swamiji made strength a pivot on which other virtues turn. He said:

> It is weakness, says the Vedanta, which is the cause of all misery in this world. Weakness is the one cause of suffering. We become miserable because we are weak. We lie, steal, kill and commit other crimes, because we are weak. We die because we are weak. Where there is nothing to weaken us, there is no death nor sorrow.[16]

The *Gita* made courage a central plank to support the moral edifice. In Swamiji's considered opinion, the real message of the Upanishads is strength. He thundered:

> If there is one word that you find coming out like a bomb from the Upanishads, bursting like a bombshell upon masses of ignorance: it is the word fearlessness, and the only religion that ought to be taught is the religion of *fearlessness*.[17]

Newton, as the story goes, discovered the law of gravitation by the fall of an apple: a commonplace fact of experience. Likewise, Swamiji discovered a great mine of strength from our scriptures, which were studied exclusively for gaining freedom from the realm of *maya*. The celebrated verse of the *Gita*[18], according to Swamiji, gives us the essence of the book. Strangely, this great idea, this most inspiring concept contained in that famous verse never received any attention from the known commentators in this regard. Weakness stems from ignorance about our own divinity. The antidote is strength, which is within us all. Hence Swamiji gave strength a special place in the lofty scheme for national growth. He was quite vocal about the great role of strength in shaping the destiny of a nation. When this insight is discussed in philosophy and a powerful philosophical concept of courage is conceived, this idea of strength will be accepted as a moral virtue which is now lacking. It was Swamiji's novel idea to use strength both as a moral quality and as a philosophical concept. Swamiji's humanism is, therefore, based on a very solid rock of pragmatism with strength as its keynote: "The older I grow, the more everything seems to me to lie in manliness. This is my new gospel."[19] This is indeed a new and unique charter of growth. The new era of progress needs new concepts of ethics and morality. Strength that emanates from Soul-consciousness will be the source of morality.

Swami Vivekananda's scheme of social service is based on love. The sure test of real and genuine love is purity, freedom, calmness and happiness. Atman being the only source of bliss,[20] it is the most coveted thing for all. Love is divine and therefore indivisible, infinite and non-dual. It is one with the Supreme Reality.

Unfortunately, this great potential factor in our lives was never harnessed before. In this modern age, Swamiji drew our attention to it and used it as a powerful tool for the social welfare programme he launched. "It is love and love alone that I preach, and I base my teachings on the great Vedantic truths of the sameness and omnipresence of the Soul of this Universe,"[21] he said. In his concept of the religion of service, Swamiji asked people to serve man as God. This loving attitude is conspicuously absent from a religion equated with dogmas, doctrines, rites and rituals. "Religion is being and becoming, it is realization."[22] Again he says, "Religion is the greatest motive power for realizing that infinite energy which is the birth-right and nature of every man."[23] Swamiji infused the powerful element of love into religion, making it no longer a "lifeless mockery."

The dearest object of Swamiji's loving adoration is man. His mission is man-centred; man is the central pillar of his philosophical edifice. Swamiji naturally raised the dignity, divinity, mystery and worth of man to the pinnacle of divine excellence. When he spoke of expressing the divinity within, he pointed to God within each of us. It is not the divine of Semitic religion, seen mainly as external. Swamiji saw each soul struggling to manifest its innate divinity, power and glory.

Reason looms large in Swamiji's philosophical discussion. In his scheme of rationalistic religion, or the philosophy of religion, Swamiji does not posit an external God, or even God immanent in nature. The modern rationalist will deny such postulations. None, however, can deny his own existence, his own being and the obvious feeling of his own existence, his "is-ness." It is not empirical consciousness; it is Pure Consciousness. Therefore, Swamiji satisfies the rationalist with the rationale of religion, that he is Existence itself.

Swami Vivekananda discovered from Advaita Vedanta itself, the real source of human happiness. This superhuman genius can be seen in his new scheme of Practical Vedanta. It was indeed a very difficult task of great magnitude and complexity. Again, it was not the subtle discussion of an academician; it gave millions the bread of life, and tens of thousands of all nations dedicated themselves to implement it. There lies the practical success. Swamiji gave Vedanta a new depth and a new dimension by asserting its tremendous potentiality to create a social revolution leading to the well-being of the masses.

Swamiji laid down a strong foundation for all-round progress based on Practical Vedanta, which is going to be the "ethos of the people" everywhere, in the future. Practical Vedanta can be applied to realize his new definition of religion, of existential philosophy, and of man. Swamiji combined *jnana, bhakti, karma* and *yoga,* to give us an integrated view of life based on such a harmonious balance. He was a staunch Advaitist, yet his brilliant analysis, his rational arguments, and his catholic temper are all very fresh in the field of Vedanta. Truly it has been said, Vivekananda performed the extraordinary feat of breathing life into the purely static monism of Shankara."[24] Really, Swamiji was "the inaugurator of the Neo-Vedantic Movement in India."

7

SWAMIJI AND THE EMANCIPATION OF RELIGION

Religion, Soul, and God — these three words are much misunderstood. However, in spite of misunderstandings and differences, we find some common features in all religions. These common features are: (1) a belief in God who is powerful and benevolent, (2) deep faith in the scriptures and the healthy traditions nurtured by religious culture, (3) a sense of an impelling urge to pray, worship, and render selfless service to God, (4) acceptance of the validity of faith over reason, (5) a general idea of happiness or suffering after death according to our *karma*, and (6) the value of detachment and renunciation to ensure happiness in life and after death. It is generally accepted that peace is within and not without. The dissatisfaction with temporal evanescent pleasures and the inevitability of death confront us. "The day of life sinks inevitably into the night of death. . . . Death is the token of the power of time over us." Hence, the necessity of having a religious faith to feel at ease. Religious faith is like an oasis in the desert of human life.

Religion and God — these two words have lost their original importance; but through meditation and purity of living, we can realize God, the source of abiding peace. That is the highest truth. We are to "deepen ourselves and not merely widen the surface." Solitude, cultivation of spiritual disciplines, renunciation, and love for divine excellences are necessary for having peace through communion with God.

Those who are not faithful are leaning on substitutes for religion: humanism, nationalism, patriotism, science, etc., to escape from the dread of life. Modern fanaticism has been developed around various ideologies that have captured our imagination. This is far more dangerous than religious fanaticism, in view of the technological aid they get for their aggressive attitude. "Man loves his prejudices. . . . Politicians today are wanderers in a western wilderness astray from one true God of their forefathers: to them parochial status occupies the position once occupied by the sectarian church." — Arnold Toynbee. Having lost the spiritual goal and sense of direction from authentic spiritual leaders, people are also worshipping crude and amazing cults. The contemporary climate of popular religion is vitiated by irrational beliefs in institutions, creeds, or dogmas. Inherited faith in such conventional concepts of religion has been drilled into us. Consequently, religion, for most of the so-called educated people, is a regimented system of popular opinion. This sort of religious atmosphere gives rise to cults and ceremonies which keep the unreflective followers in darkness.

In spite of our so-called enlightenment, our ideas of God and spiritual life have remained mostly uninspired and confused. This lamentable lack of a clear concept about the finale of spiritual seeking is the root cause of perversion and the sinister effect of false worship.

Pseudo-religion keeps us away from spiritual development — transformation of character, integration of personality, and genuine love for holiness and purity. The multitude, conditioned through these narrow cults, have passionately embraced these ideas only to destroy themselves and others through intense fanaticism. Evil effects of such practices have been described in a telling manner. "There has been no lack of existential faith in them. In obedience to their supposed commands, thousands have fasted, burned themselves, cast themselves from precipices, endured shame, fought fanatically, and offered their own children as bloody sacrifices." Multitudes of people today are seriously accepting these taboos for psychological satisfaction.

Worshipful tendencies, being innate within us, must manifest themseves in paying homage to either God or Satan. Some contemporary religions, in spite of today's advancement of culture and progressive attitude, are preoccupied with the protection of their churches and dogmas, supported by fanatical militant outfits that are intensely hostile and mercilessly brutal. Other so-called religious people accept the conventional God of "sugar and spice, and everything nice." By them, to use Swamiji's words, God is treated as a "municipal scavenger."

The egocentric character of popular religion lacks the potential of true religion. Popular religion neither enriches our lives, nor deepens our spiritual stature. It neither broadens our outlook, nor does it bring us insight regarding the mystery of God within us. "The perspective is all wrong. Even God becomes a matter of interest to many believers largely for what they can get out of Him. They treat the deity as a kind of valet to do odds and ends for them, a sort of 'cosmic bellboy' for whom they push buttons, and who is expected to come running. 'God for us' is the slogan of their faith instead of 'Our lives for God'. As a result, much current reform appears to be a childish 'auxiliary of selfishness'."

"The anti-centripetal force of a selfish life, when it becomes religious, sweeps the whole cosmos in. God Himself becomes a nursemaid, or our pet, and religion sinks into a comfortable faith that we shall be fondly taken care of, our wishes fulfilled, and our egocentric interests coddled." Again, the infantile concept of spiritual life and the practice of religion has caused much trouble to people. Dogmatic theology produces arrogant and militant fanatics. The antirational and antihumanisitic character of such religion has tarnished the fair image of God, religion, and the immortality of the Soul. History is replete with innumerable examples of flagrant violation of the codes of ethics and morality in the religious pursuit. The enlightened souls, prophets, and authentic messengers of Truth, in all historical religions, have given us the seeds of Truth to cultivate for our spiritual development.

With the passing of time, unfortunately, we have lost the essence of their message. Consequently, the original invigorating impulse of a genuine yearning for holiness, purity, simplicity, and sublimity has become conspicuously absent from our consciousness — our lives overburdened with various taboos, dogmas, and irrational morbid "religious" practices. "Truth gets institutionalized, faith dogmatized, worship socialized, and the noble vocation of religion politicized." As an inevitable consequence, inner spiritual sensitivity becomes fossilized.

Under such tragic circumstances, a few centuries before the renaissance in India, the void caused by degradation in Hinduism provoked Swamiji to say: "What more degradation can there be than that the greatest minds of a country have been discussing about the kitchen for several hundred years whether I may touch you or you may touch me, and what is the penance for this touching."[1] With this preface, it will be our humble endeavour to show how Swamiji emancipated, or rescued the eternal spirit of religion from the debris of fanaticism, irrationalism and antihumanism.

Swamiji was quite aware of the sad state of affairs permeating the religious climate in the world. Religion has been a great healer as well as a cruel killer. This may seem enigmatic to ordinary people, but reflecting persons will conclude that true religion alone brings illumination whereas false religion invariably creates darkness in the human mind. In Swamiji's message, "man" occupies the highest place. Hence, the true welfare of man was his predominant impulse, and a true religion is the only agent for that purpose. Swamiji spelled out clearly the true concept of religion. It has been seen, time and again, that an awakened human being inevitably feels the drag of bondage, and subsequently seeks to achieve total freedom from all restrictions — outer as well as inner. In ancient times it was discovered, after having various miserable experiences to have this supreme freedom, that to live beyond and untouched by negativity was the key which would unlock the mystery of life. Through spiritual illumination, human weakness and the sense of separation are transcended.

One would never think that the true religious quest for absolute freedom is the antithesis of worldly aspirations. True religion does not destroy the zest for life; but rather, it purifies, expands, and heightens our state of consciousness, enabling us to enjoy life more fully. Life cannot be compartmentalized as secular and spiritual. Our spiritual grounding and growth influences our attitudes and behaviour, eliminating much stupidity. Our search for truth can be pursued through the varied experiences of life.

Let us try to comprehend the philosophy of life as envisioned by the Upanishads: Our innermost Self, the Atman, is completely separated from the psychophysical complex, which outwardly envelops it but does not constitute it. Out of this Atman everything comes — matter, life, mind, and reason. They are all sustained by the Atman — the Supreme Reality. It is the only source of happiness. True religion teaches us that the goal of life has to be sought in Atman only. The world is a vale of tears, but through such experiences an ardent seeker has to find that the world is a vale of soul growth too. Swamiji said, "Man is like an infinite spring, coiled up in a small box, and that spring is trying to unfold."[2] Therefore, "Religion is the manifestation of the Divinity already in man. . . . Religion is the search after the highest ideal." The impulse that seeks this ideal is a spiritual impulse. This is religion which culminates in seeking unity in God.

Human mind has to evolve gradually. Therefore, Swamiji never condemned the lower steps of religious discipline. They are necessary steps in spiritual evolution. "To the Hindu, man is not travelling from error to truth, but from truth to truth, from lower to higher truth. To him all the religions, from the lowest fetishism to the highest absolutism, mean so many attempts of the human soul to grasp and realize the Infinite, each determined by the conditions of its birth and association, and each of these marks a stage of progress; and every soul is a young eagle soaring higher and higher, gathering more and more strength, till it reaches the Glorious Sun."[3]

Every religion has two aspects, the ethnic or sociopolitical aspect and the spiritual or universal aspect. We are born to ethnic religion and most of us die in it by clinging to certain creeds or dogmas in the name of religion. Higher religious persuasion in all traditional religions exhibits the primary and secondary aspects of religion, i.e., nonviolence, truth, freedom from lower impulses, purity of mind, renunciation, charity, forgiveness, etc. as the primary aspect, with the secondary aspect of the variable elements which depend upon time, circumstances, and social condition. Consider the kernel and husk, for example. When we think of man's growth in spiritual stature we could equate it with the kernels of ripening corn. When spiritual consciousness deepens and unfolds, the fruits are abundant and the life fuller and more rewarding. Unfortunately, for many, the focus is on the husks — the material outward secondary aspect of religion. Overemphasis on the secondary aspect misdirects our focus and inhibits our vital inner growth. This also creates misunderstandings, hostility, narrowness, and religious warfare within the same group or with other religious groups. Myopic adherence to superficial religious ideas is very harmful to a healthy religious ambience of peace, understanding, cooperation, fraternity, and true purpose. A profound disservice to the essence of religious purpose manifests in such situations. As Swamiji said, "The effect is the cause manifested." Atheists, agnostics, humanists, idolaters, etc., are further along on the spiritual path than narrow, parochial, bigoted, antirational or antihuman individuals or groups. "They are bound to their negative God by conditioning, upbringing, church or party traditions, and by the manipulation of isolated texts of scripture or by morbid conscience. . . . There is a certain masochistic pleasure in being crushed by the juggernaut of a negative God." Again, there is a seeming contradiction in some people's naive attitude toward God. The compassionate and all-merciful God generally invoked by them to improve their lives is also sought after to annihilate their perceived enemies — those not subscribing to their dogmas. Man has justifiably been recognized as a "worshipping animal". Hence, the dire necessity of rescuing religion from false religion.

The most important measures proposed by Swami Vivekananda include an understanding that we are to accept religion as a goal of life to facilitate the attainment of freedom from the bondage of life. We are to shed our infantile concepts of God as a child abandons childish toys and behavior as he matures. Although God is never fully comprehended, we must strive to understand intuitively. He is too great to be described in words fully. He is the substance behind us and nature. He is infinite and in infinite ways He manifests in and through the cosmos.

Swamiji asks, "Is God's book finished? Or is it still a continuous revelation going on? It is a marvelous book, these spiritual revelations of the world. The Bible, the Vedas, the Koran, and all the other sacred books are but so many pages — and an infinite numbers of pages remain yet to be unfolded. I would leave it open for all of them. We stand in the present, but open ourselves to the infinite future. We take in all that has been in the past, enjoy the light of the present, and open every window of the heart for all that will come in the future. Salutations to all the prophets of the past, to all the great ones of the present, and to all that are to come in the future!"[4]

God is beyond the ken of intellect. God is immanent and transcendent. When this broad concept of God is accepted, the real seeker of Truth cannot afford to be loyal to a denominational God. The more we outgrow our prejudices and narrowness, the more we rise above creeds. A sense of respect and accommodative spirit dawns upon us. We begin to see other religions and their tradition with a friendly attitude. "Religion must be studied on a broader basis than formerly. All narrow, limited, fighting ideas of religion have to go. All sect ideas and tribal or national ideas of religion must be given up. That each tribe or nation should have its own particular God and think that every other is wrong is a superstition that should belong to the past. All such ideas must be abandoned."

"As the human mind broadens, its spiritual steps broaden too. The time has already come when any man's recorded thoughts can reach all corners of the earth; by merely physical means, we have come in touch with the whole world; so too must the religions of the world become universal and wide.

"The religious ideals of the future must embrace all that exists in the world that is good and great, and at the same time have infinite scope for future development. All that was good in the past must be preserved; and the doors must be left open for future additions to the already existing store. Religions must also be inclusive and not look down with contempt upon one another because their particular ideals of God are different.

"In my life, I have seen a great many spiritual men, a great many sensible persons who did not believe in God at all — that is to say, not in our sense of the word. And yet, perhaps they understood God better than we can ever do. The personal idea of God or the impersonal, the Infinite, the Moral Law, or the Ideal Man — these all have to come under the definition of religion. And when religions have become thus broadened, their power for good will have increased a hundredfold. Religions, having tremendous power in them, have often done more injury than good, simply on account of their narrowness and limitations."[5] For the good of mankind, it is not desirable to eliminate some objectionable elements, traditional beliefs and practices. Swamiji gave warning against such a naive interpretation of universalism. "You cannot make all conform to the same ideas; that is a fact, and I thank God that it is so. I am not against any sect. I am glad that sects exist, and I only wish they may go on multiplying more and more. Why? Simply because of this: If you and I and and all who are present here were to think exactly the same thoughts, there would be no thoughts to think. We know that two or more forces must come into collision in order to produce motion. It is the clash of thought. Now, if we all thought alike we would be like Egyptian mummies in a museum looking vacantly at one another's faces — no more than that! Whirls and eddies occur only in a rushing, living stream. There are no whirlpools in stagnant, dead water. When religions are dead, there will be no sects; it will be the perfect peace and harmony of the grave. But so long as mankind thinks, there will be sects. Variation is the sign of life, and it must be there. I pray that they may multiply so that at last there will be as many sects as human beings and each one will have his own method, his individual method of thought in religion. My idea, therefore, is that all these religions are different forces in the economy of God, working for the good of mankind; and that not one can become dead, not one can be killed."[6] Reflect upon this. Swamiji further says, "Through high philosophy or low, through the most exalted mythology or the most primitive reasoning, be it through refined rituals or arrant fetishism, every sect, every soul, every nation, every religion, consciously or unconsciously is struggling upward towards God; every vision of truth that man conceives is a vision of Him and of none else."[7]

Swamiji gives his plan of a universal religion. First, Swamiji does not approve of the methods adopted by the Iconoclastic Reformers. Rather, Swamiji asks us to contribute something positively in helping a person in every possible way. Secondly, he invariably exhorts us to practise the principles of religion in order to have vertical growth within us. He recommended different paths of *yoga* for different types of persons. Without inner growth, religion has no value. The very soul of religion is experience. Only the illumined souls of every era could touch the hearts of the people. They were the great souls who profoundly affected mankind. Only those established in divine life radiate joy, peace, and transcend all human weakness.

The most formidable task of Swamiji in this modern age was to focus the image of pure religion of Vedanta with its central principle, the master passion: the chief motivation of seeking self-knowledge for the welfare of humanity. Swamiji did not proclaim a religion of tradition, of rhetoric, of inferential conviction, but of direct experience of the indwelling spirit. He extolled a religion that offers to the intellect an explanation of the universe, a religion that offers to the conscience a law that regulates every action of life, a religion that offers to the heart an absolutely perfect and loving Being as the object of its worship and service.

Swamiji, to whom the invisible world was a matter of direct knowledge and immediate perception, proclaimed the profoundest Truth of one Fundamental Reality which provides, pervades and perpetuates all, a Being who is impersonal as well as personal, transcendental as well as immanent. He is the very substance, the very rock-foundation of the whole Universe. He is deeply embedded within each of us, too. Hence, life is not an aimless voyage; it is from time immemorial not only a wakeful and watchful journey but a rejoicing and truly transporting pilgrimage.

The entire problem of religion is here: how to bring forth change in our impure minds, how to transform the dogma-oriented, parochial, and superstitious religion of tradition into something which can enable us to broaden our spiritual consciousness and deepen our love for the Divine. In this transformation the dross must be eliminated and the essential elements that remain must satisfy our dual allegiance to the demands of reason and of heart as well.

Swamiji introduced a new and fresh image of religion by living the eternal principles of authentic religion in his own life. Swamiji was molded by the shining exemplary life of Shri Ramakrishna. About him Mahatma Gandhi said: "The story of Ramakrishna Paramahamsa's life is a story of religion in practice." That great Master's message was given by Swamiji thus: "Do not care for doctrines, do not care for dogmas, or sects, or churches, or temples or mosques; they count for little compared with the essence of existence in each man, which is spirituality; and the more this is developed in a man, the more powerful is he for good. Earn that first, acquire that and criticise no one, for all doctrines and creeds have some good in them. Show by your lives that religion does not mean words or names or sects but that it means spiritual realization. Only those who have attained to spirituality can communicate it to others, can be great teachers of mankind. They alone are the powers of light."[8]

By experiencing the transcendental Reality behind life and nature and unity in the midst of the manifold, Swamiji, like his Master, could tell us that Infinite Truth has been expressing Itself in infinite ways in infinite time. Each aspect of Truth will culminate in giving us the supreme vision of Reality and therefore each is good in its own place. From this unitary vision, it was possible for him to establish harmony between religion and science, reason and faith, mysticism and logic, polytheism and monotheism. The toleration that he preached and practised was never the toleration of powerlessness, nor the toleration of indifference. It was the toleration of deep and abiding faith in reality based on his actual experience. He did see God in everything. This experience alone begets true toleration. It springs not from inability, not from noninterference, but from dispassion, from equanimity. Swamiji proclaimed that religion has not been the discovery of man but the Self-disclosure of God who has assumed the sacred responsibility for fostering the religious spirit in the bosom of each one of His children. The different religions are only the manifestations of one religion. They are all part and parcel of one Eternal Religion. The apparent difference lies in the forms and the details. The same one God has been revealing Himself to us under different names, at different times and different ages for the benefit of the people in the different stages of evolution. The whole perspective is changed when the eternal spirit is seen in each being and thing. That is the real image of religion which Swamiji practised sincerely and preached untiringly. Religion is not a mere dogma, it is a way of true life. Dogma degenerates into fanaticism and demoralizes a man. Everywhere Swamiji did condemn from the depth of his heart this sort of pseudo-religion. In his famous address at the Parliament of Religions in Chicago, he said, "Sectarianism, bigotry and its horrible descendant, fanaticism, have long possessed this beautiful earth. They have filled the earth with violence, drenched it often and often with human blood, destroyed civilization and sent whole nations to despair. Had it not been for these horrible demons, human society would be far more advanced than it is now. But their time is come; and I fervently hope that the bell that tolled this morning in honour of this convention may be the death-knell of all fanaticism, of all persecutions with the sword or with the pen, and of all uncharitable feelings between persons wending their way to the same goal."[9]

Swamiji's concept of a scientific perspective on religion may appeal to our rational scientific temperament. He says that religion can be approached like any other science by following reason and rational judgement in pursuit of spiritual truth. One can solve the greatest mystery of life in spiritual consummation, through observation, experimentation, and verification.

The name of Ramakrishna -- the greatest modern scientist in the realm of spirituality — may be recalled. Religion, if pursued with a scientific bent of mind, will yield the greatest secrets of life and the source of existence. It will bring incalculable benefits unto humanity. Real spiritual experiences will release stupendous power to usher in an era of real fulfillment of healthy human desires.

In conclusion, we quote Swamiji to get a glimpse of emancipated religion: "All truth is eternal. Truth is nobody's property; no race, no individual can lay any exclusive claim to it. Truth is the nature of all souls. Who can lay any special claim to it? But it has to be made practical, to be made simple, for the highest truths are always simple, so that it may penetrate every pore of human society and become the property of the highest intellects and the commonest minds of man, woman, and child at the same time.[10] . . . .No longer will religion remain a bundle of ideas or theories, nor an intellectual assent; it will enter into our very self. By means of intellectual assent we may today subscribe to many foolish things, and change our minds tomorrow. But true religion never changes. Religion is realization; not talk, nor doctrine, nor theories, however beautiful they may be. It is being and becoming, not hearing and acknowledging; it is the whole soul becoming changed into what it believes. That is religion."[11]

8

UNIVERSAL RELIGION AND SWAMI VIVEKANANDA

Religion is life. "Religious thought is in man's very constitution, so much so, that it is impossible for him to give up religion until he can give up his mind and body, until he can give up thought and life," Swami Vivekananda said.[1] All over the world there is the urge to make religion immensely practical. There is a growing protest against any stale and static religion. We make a great mistake in making it a stone of dogma, instead of the bread of life. In order to gain an insight into the true spirit of religion, we should take an interest in other religions.

It is not proposed, however, that scriptural knowledge is essential in order to understand the spirit of other religions. Knowledge by itself cannot give real insight, which is the gift of genuine spiritual development. "A man may be a very good Christian without Greek and Hebrew, and a very bad Christian with both." The student of comparative religion should devote himself to the task of discovering the unity underlying the different religions.

It should be remembered that comparative religion is not to be considered "competitive religion." This study, taken with an open mind, does not foster any malevolent attitude of competition. In modern times, when we are mingling with other people, religious isolation is impossible. Also, in this modern age, peaceful coexistence is dependent on the recognition of spiritual solidarity. Swami Vivekananda said:

> No civilization can grow, unless fanaticism, bloodshed, and brutality stop. No civilization can begin to lift its head until we look charitably upon one another, and the first step towards that much-needed charity is to look kindly upon the religious convictions of others. Moreover to understand that, not only should we be charitable, but positively helpful to each other, however different our religious ideas and convictions may be.[2]. . . . Religion is the greatest motive power for realizing that infinite energy which is the birthright and nature of

> every man. In making for everything that is good and great, in bringing peace to others, and peace to one's own self, religion is the highest motive power, and therefore ought to be studied from that standpoint. Religion must be studied on a broader basis than formerly.[3] Swami Vivekananda continued: As the human mind broadens, its spiritual steps broaden too. The time has already come when a man cannot record a thought without its reaching all corners of the earth; by merely physical means we have come into touch with the whole world; so the future religions of the world have to become as universal and as wide. The religious ideals of the future must embrace all that exists in the world and is good and great, and, at the same time, have infinite scope for future development.[4]

> The power of religion, broadened and purified, is going to penetrate every part of human life. So long as religion was in the hands of a chosen few, or of a body of priests, it was in temples, churches, books, dogmas, ceremonials, forms, and rituals. But when we come to the real spiritual universal concept, then, and then alone, religion will become real and living; it will come into our very nature, live in our every movement, permeate every pore of our society and be infinitely more a power for good than it has ever been before.[5]

Religion is value oriented. Religious experience, therefore, involves a kind of subjective attitude towards what we look upon as supremely valuable. Religion worth the name anywhere implies a response to a supremely valuable reality which, though divine or supersensuous, is ready to respond to human supplication. A seeker of truth is expected to develop a genuine sense of rapport with the supreme value or absolute value which is not dependent upon any other value, though all other values are absolutely dependent on it. Further, this supreme value, whenever partially experienced, gives us great satisfaction and fulfillment. It is ultimate because it is the final goal of all our actions and pursuits. It fosters a sense of "holiness" around it. This is not necessarily always approached with consuming love. It may bring fear. While engaged in this sort of comparative study, we ought to approach it in a manner that does not hurt the feelings of others. Hence, a special type of mental equipment is urgently needed. A merely biased attitude and argumentative spirit is insufficient, as "grey, cold eyes do not know the value of things." Sympathy is expected of every student of religion. It is not simply a kind of sympathy, but a kind of empathy which alone can help us in this regard.

Scholars of different persuasions have reached a consensus of opinion by their discovery of certain fundamental characteristics shared by all religions. These are:

- Practical utility in bringing harmony into life
- Fellowship engendered due to transformed life
- Religious experience the response to a supremely valuable object or principle
- Involvement of a kind of wholehearted enthusiasm in the religious quest
- Drawing all our attention; pressing every faculty for service
- Awakening our life and compelling us to accept certain duties
- Enabling us to transcend our weakness
- Conviction of the divine power as holiness itself

This sort of study, along with sincere spiritual joy, brings fulfillment. "Many lamps, but one light," this is what mystics feel in all traditions. This reminds us of a Bengali song: "The cows are of many colours but milk has got only one." The Ultimate One is the very perfection of existence, the ideal Reality. Swami Vivekananda said:

> If you go below the surface, you find that unity between man and man, between races and races, high and low, rich and poor, gods and men and men and animals. If you go deep enough all will be seen as only variations of the One, and he who has attained to this conception of Oneness has no more delusion. What can delude him? He knows the reality of everything, the secret of everything. Where is there any more misery for him? He has traced the reality of everything to the Lord, the Centre, the Unity of everything, and that is Eternal Existence, Eternal Knowledge, Eternal Bliss.[6]

To unite all mankind in the acceptance of one universal religion, has been the cherished desire of many wise men and thinkers in all ages. We shall try to give a brief idea of the views of Swami Vivekananda in this regard.

Due to the phenomenal growth of secularism, people of various races, religious beliefs and cultural standards have been living together. The wall of isolation is almost broken. Political stability and economic security are not enough for our common peace. We must discover the common ground of human relationships that transcends all superficial distinctions. In Vedantic language, one Supreme Reality underlies all diversity. Therefore, different religions are varied expressions of the one eternal religion, which is the object of human search through religious practices. We must look upon ourselves as pilgrims to the same temple of Divinity.

In modern times, religion is devalued and, therefore, it has lost its bright image to be adored by the intellectuals. Universal religion seems to be a play of words or an effusion of sentiment. In spite of that, the concept of universal religion has been growing among the thinkers since the advent of Shri Ramakrishna, who is regarded as an apostle of universalism and harmony of religions. There are three main approaches to the problem of a universal religion:

- Universalism through eclecticism and syncretism
- Sectarian religion claiming the privilege of being called universal
- the true concept of universal religion

Eclecticism aims at choosing the best out of every religion and combining them into a consistent whole — a sort of "esperanto" religion. It is like a beautiful flower vase in which different varieties of flowers have been placed together. It may be attractive for the time being, but it is lifeless, having no root in the soil. This method was experimented with in the past, but died. Syncretism wants to bring reconciliation and harmony among the divergent religions by giving emphasis on the similarities among them and neglecting the differences. Akbar's pious attempt to establish a universal religion, *Din-Ilahi,* is a well-known historical example of the syncretic approach. Arnold Toynbee, in modern times seemed to endorse this attitude when he said, "A time may come when the local heritage of the different historic nations, civilizations and religions will have coalesced into a common heritage of the whole human family.... The mission of higher religions is not competitive, they are complementary."[7]

The second approach to this idea of universal religion is the attempt of those religious imperialists who claim their own religion as the best and most fitted to be the universal religion. By this epithet — "universal religion," the adherents mean a religion which is not confined to a particular area but which draws its notions from the whole of humanity. Like warmongers or crusaders, they are bent on destroying all other religions save the one which they think is universal. History is replete with examples of cruelty meted out to the religious for this purpose. This fanatical zeal is not confined to the common masses. Even the high dignitaries and scholars lend support to such movements. The Gifford lectures of Edward Caird (1893) and John Baille (1961-62) are cases in point.

The third approach, in our opinion, is the only sound approach to the problem of a universal religion. As a true disciple of Shri Ramakrishna, Swami Vivekananda laid the path of Universal Religion at the Parliament of Religions in 1893. He made a great impact on Western thinking, especially in the realm of religion. Marie Louise Burke, the well-known research scholar of Swami Vivekananda's life and literature, says this living Vivekananda "gave American ideals Vedantic roots. . . . In regard to the cultural impact of this teaching. . . it is bomb-like in its effect."[8]

In sharp contrast to other views referred to earlier, Swamiji spelled out at the Parliament of Religions, the very first criterion of the universal religion. He said:

> If one religion is true, then by the same logic all other religions are also true. This is authenticated by the fact that "holiness, purity and charity" are not the exclusive possessions of any church in the world and that every system has produced men and women of the most exalted character.[9]

By universality, it is meant that its appeal is not restricted to any particular segment of humanity, to any religious group, nation, race, class, country or age. The individual belonging to any such group is expected to emulate that spirit of universalism in due time:

> The Hindu may have failed to carry out all his plans, but if there is ever to be a universal religion, it must be one which will have no location in place or time; which will be infinite like the God it will preach, and whose sun will shine upon the followers of Krishna and of Christ, on saints and sinners alike; which will not be Brahmanic or Buddhistic, Christian or Mohammedan, but the sum total of these, and still have infinite space for development; which in its catholicity will embrace in its infinite arms, and find a place for, every human being, from the lowest grovelling savage not far removed from the brute, to the highest man towering by the virtues of his head and heart almost above humanity, making society stand in awe of him and doubt his human nature. It will be a religion which will have no place for persecution or intolerance in its polity, which will recognize divinity in every man and woman, and whose whole scope, whose whole force, will be created in aiding humanity to realize its own true divine nature.[10]

Swamiji's spirit of universalism stems from his highest spiritual experience. He saw the divine in the human form and there he spent every ounce of his energy in awakening man's spiritual possibilities. Swamiji gave us a universal message of religion and a comprehensive view of life. He experienced spiritual unity as the root of all diversified objectivity. To discover that unity which underlies all religious doctrines and experiences, is the supreme goal of life. That same unity is getting itself expressed in and through diversity. They are many, but the substance behind diversifications is one and the same. Therefore, Swamiji never approved the idea of theological imperialism. He, on the contrary, pointed out that each traditional religion, when followed properly, will make the seeker broader and more universal. He explained that religion was an effort to go beyond the phenomenon of relativity. He said, "Religion belongs to the supersensuous and not to the sense plane."[11] This spiritual impulse to transcend the human weakness has been responsible for the discoveries of many pathways to divine excellences. Hence, in the economy of spiritual fulfillment, each traditional religion is valuable to its adherents. Swamiji said:

> The second idea that I learnt from my Master, and which is perhaps the most vital, is the wonderful truth that the religions of the world are not contradictory or antagonistic. They are but various phases of one eternal religion. That one eternal religion is applied to different planes of existence, is applied to the opinions of various minds and various races. There never was my religion or yours, my national religion or your national religion; there never existed many religions, there is only the one. One infinite religion existed all through eternity and will ever exist, and this religion is expressing itself in various countries in various ways. Therefore we must respect all religions and we must try to accept them all as far as we can. Religions manifest themselves not only according to race and geographical position, but according to individual powers. In one man religion is manifesting itself as intense activity, as work. In another it is manifesting itself as intense devotion, in yet another, as mysticism, in others as philosophy, and so forth.[12]

This concept of universal religion, which recognizes unity in diversity, is very helpful for our spiritual development because it does not harp on creed or dogma. He was very eloquent about the special mission of each of the traditional religions. He said:

> The fact that all these old religions are living today proves that they must have kept that mission intact; in spite of all their mistakes, in spite of all difficulties, in spite of all quarrels, in spite of all the incrustation of forms and figures, the heart of every one of them is sound — it is a throbbing, beating, living heart. They have not lost, any one of them, the great mission they came for.[13]

Swamiji represented the best spirit of Hinduism and, therefore, to him religion was realization, an experience bringing highest satisfaction. It is not sufficient to record our admiration and recognize their peculiar characteristics of other religions in our study. Practice is the very soul of religion, Swamiji pointed out in the Parliament of Religions:

> May He who is the Brahman of the Hindus, the Ahura Mazda of the Zoroastrians, the Jehovah of the Jews, the Father in Heaven of the Christians, give strength to you . . . The Christian is not to become a Hindu or a Buddhist, nor a Hindu or a Buddhist to become a Christian. But each must assimilate the spirit of the others and yet preserve his individuality and grow according to his own law of growth. . . . The Parliament of Religions . . . has proved . . . that holiness, purity and charity are not the exclusive possessions of any church in the world, and that every system has produced men and women of the most exalted character . . . Upon the banner of every religion will soon be written in spite of . . . resistance, "Help and not Fight," "Assimilation and not Destruction," "Harmony and Peace and not Dissension."[14]

This attitude of catholicity and sincere appreciation was never academic and scholastic in him. He found this method of reciprocity and sympathetic understanding very rewarding and enriching. In one of his famous letters, Swamiji expressed the vital need of such a reciprocal approach:

> Therefore I am firmly persuaded that without the help of practical Islam, theories of Vedantism, however fine and wonderful they may be, are entirely valueless to the vast mass of mankind. We want to lead mankind to the place where there is neither the Vedas, nor the Bible, and the Koran. Mankind ought to be taught that religions are but the varied expressions of THE RELIGION, which is Oneness, so that each may choose that path that suits him best. For our own motherland a junction of the two great systems, Hinduism and Islam — Vedanta brain and Islam body — is the only hope.[15]

Unlike the other two opinions, this third proposition does not require the necessity of creating a universal religion. As for this third view, a universal element can be found in every traditional religion. Every religion has two aspects, the ethnic or sociopolitical, and the spiritual or universal. We are born to ethnic religion and most of us die in it by clinging to certain creeds and dogmas in the name of religion. When real thirst after genuine spiritual experience comes into our life, only then do we enter into the higher phase of religion, one of pure spiritual adventure. Here religion means the entire scheme of self-improvement geared to the experience of ultimate truth. Disciplines are observed with a view to develop integrity of character, harmony of life, joy in fellowship and sincere longing for the vision of truth within and without. This higher religious impulse comes from within. When our life is truly awakened to this quest, moral consciousness quickens and we feel spiritual progress in our lives. This is verifiable truth. It culminates in that plenary experience which enriches life, broadens our views, and purifies us with Divinity. Then we truly enjoy life and can radiate peace of joy. Vivekananda said, "This is the real science of religion. As mathematics in every part of the world does not differ, so the mystics do not differ."

The scientific temper of the human mind cannot remain satisfied with superficial, dogma-ridden, ethnic religion. Swami Vivekananda, lamenting over this great loss of the human resources due to our stagnation in ethnic religion, remarked:

> My ideal indeed can be put into a few words and that is: to preach unto mankind their divinity and how to make it manifest in every moment of life. . . . Religions of the world have become lifeless mockeries. What the world wants is character. The world is in need of those whose life is one burning love, selfless. That love will make every word tell like a thunderbolt.

Then Swami Vivekananda also said:

> My Master used to say that these names as Hindu, Christian, etc., stand as great bars to all brotherly feelings between man and man. We must break them down first. They have lost all their good powers and now stand only as baneful influences under whose black magic even the best of us behave like demons.[16]

The spiritual insight of Swamiji discovered the seeds of a universal element in every religion worth the name. He pointed out:

> And that universal religion about which philosophers and others have dreamed in every country already exists. It is here. As the universal brotherhood of man is already existing, so also is universal religion. Which of you, that have travelled far and wide, have not found brothers and sisters in every nation? I have found them all over the world. Brotherhood already exists; only there are numbers of persons who fail to see this and only upset it by crying for new brotherhoods. Universal religion, too, is already existing. If the priests and other people that have taken upon themselves the task of preaching different religions simply cease preaching for a few moments, we shall see it is there. They are disturbing it all the time, because it is to their interest.[17]

Four fundamental ideas of universal religion, as envisioned by Swamiji, are being studied: acceptance of the plurality of religion, uniqueness of each religion, interreligious dialogue, and an acceptance of a common standard of validity. Swamiji visualized the attainment of spiritual culture based on mutual respect and acceptance. Plurality of religion, to him, was not a hindrance but an opportunity to develop maturity. Instead of hostility, we can have spiritual fraternity without giving up our individuality. Swamiji said:

> I believe that they (religions) are not contradictory, they are supplementary. Each religion, as it were, takes up one part of the great universal truth, and spends its whole force in embodying and typifying that part of the great truth. It is, therefore, addition, not exclusion. That is the idea. System after system arises, each one embodying a great idea, and ideals must be added to ideals. And this is the march of humanity.[18]

The second point of Swamiji is the acknowledgement of the special features of each religion. Each religion has, to Swamiji, a special trait, a central theme. The dominant values in Christianity are love and fellowship. Buddhism places special emphasis on high moral qualities. It extols renunciation, compassion, nonviolence and rationality. The dominant characteristic of Islam is its spirit of equality and brotherhood. Hinduism lays special emphasis on spiritual practice in order to have direct, intuitive experience of the divine. The attitude of acceptance rather than tolerance stems from the philosophy of Vedanta extolling the unity of spiritual consciousness. Swamiji had the unique capacity to appreciate the special merit of each religion. His motto was: Each is great in his own place. Each race, similarly, has a peculiar bent, each race has a peculiar *raison d'être*, each race has a peculiar mission to fulfill in the life of the world.[19] It is well-known that Swamiji's training under Shri Ramakrishna gave him the master quality and habit "of seeing every people from their strongest aspect."[20]

Swamiji believed that every religion has a unique mission in the world apart from its special features. We have given his views in this respect earlier. The third principle of universal religion as envisioned by Swamiji is the wholehearted acceptance of the spirit of other religions. This admiration will motivate us for assimilation and, thereby, enrichment of the total personality will take place. Swamiji set the tone of this accommodative spirit in the Parliament.

Regarding the fourth point — an acceptance of one non-changing, common standard of validity — Swamiji extolled the beauty and rationality of Vedanta. In the world there is nothing more mysterious than the human being. Vedanta unravelled this great mystery at the very dawn of human history. Hindus discovered the great truth through their intuitive knowledge that man is divine, infinite powers are lying deeply embedded within him; the supreme goal of religion is to manifest this divine power through the practice of the religious discipline. The truths declared by Vedanta are the ultimate unity of existence, the immortal self of man, harmony of religions and the attainment of freedom through spiritual intuitive experience. Without the recognition of the spiritual oneness of mankind, the dream of universal religion will never be accomplished. This is the common ground where all people coming from different backgrounds can meet and profit.

Vedanta alone can provide this standard of validity. Vedanta is not one of the many faiths, but the common basis of them all. It deals with eternal principles which underlie the various other faiths and their practices. It teaches not one particular aspect or concept of God, but several; it prescribes not one particular spiritual discipline or method of worship, but many. It recommends different religious courses for the seekers of different capacities. The goal is one and the same, but the various paths are recommended. "All roads lead to Rome," said Swamiji in the Parliament.

> As the different streams having their sources in the different places all mingle their waters in the sea, so, O Lord, the different paths which men take through different tendencies, various though they appear, crooked or straight, all lead to Thee.[21]

This acceptance of religious plurality as a law of life, acknowledgement of the recurring themes of each religion, and the constant dialogue with a view to assimilate the values of others, with the scientific and rational philosophy of Vedanta being used as a common basis of all religions, was the scheme of universal religion envisioned by Swamiji. Needless to say, a rational mind will find his principles relevant. Despite all their differences, religious people should live together like one family.

Swamiji initiated the idea of having interreligious dialogue in the Parliament and now it is the spirit of the age. Swamiji gave prophetic articulation for all thinking people. His words formed the blueprint and the manifesto of universal religion aimed at harmony and peace through interreligious dialogue. Therefore, universal religion demands the happy coexistence of other religions:

> 'Our watchword, then,' Swamiji said, 'will be acceptance, and not exclusion. Not only toleration, for so-called toleration is often blasphemy, and I do not believe in it. I believe in acceptance. Why should I tolerate? Toleration means that I think that you are wrong and I am just allowing you to live. Is it not a blasphemy to think that you and I are allowing others to live? I accept all religions that were in the past, and worship with them all; I worship God with everyone of them, in whatever form they worship Him. I shall go to the mosque of the Mohammedan; I shall enter the Buddhistic temple where I shall take refuge in Buddha and in his Law. I shall go into the forest and sit down in meditation with the Hindu, who is trying to see the Light which enlightens the heart of every one.

Not only shall I do all these, but I shall keep my heart open for all that may come in the future. Is God's book finished? Or is it still a continuous revelation going on? It is a marvellous book — these spiritual revelations of the world. The Bible, the Vedas, the Koran, and all other sacred books are but so many pages, and infinite numbers of pages remain yet to be unfolded. I would leave it open for all of them. We stand in the present, but open ourselves to the infinite future. We take in all that has been in the past, enjoy the light of the present, and open every window of the heart for all that will come in the future. Salutations to all the prophets of the past, to all the great ones of the present, and to all that are to come in the future.'[22]

Mere pious wishes or utopian attitude, or possessing a critical yet sympathetic attitude will not usher in such an enlightened attitude as expressed by Swamiji. Inner life has to be quickened through intense spiritual practice in order to be universal. The major religions of the world should be united to wage a relentless war against the common enemy of all "religions" worth their names: materialism, positivism, love and loyalty to nationalism, humanism and secularism. The present attitude of posing oneself as a universalist based on study or so-called refinement of character cannot reach the goal. Different religions should not engage themselves in the destructive purposes of killing one another theologically. It is a great waste and breeds cynicism. The spirit of rivalry and an aggressive attitude will only force the people to shun religion and will never make them friendly. Therefore, the high task of establishing spiritual fraternity depends on the development of the inner life of the follower, more so than the so-called intellectual discussion of the academicians bereft of spiritual experience. "Blessed are the pure in heart for they shall see God" within as well as without.

9

HARMONY OF RELIGIONS AND SWAMI VIVEKANANDA

In all religions, the mystics realized God in the deepest recess of their hearts. Their own illuminated lives testified to the sincerity of their inner convictions. Hence, genuine religious life is always held in high esteem.

What is religion? Down the ages in all countries we find people — maybe an insignificant minority — searching for something which alone can provide them with total fulfillment. We are basically weak and feel impelled to overcome our limitations. The search to attain spiritual rapport with the Divine Infinity is always within us. Religion, with its emphasis upon this communion with reality, points the way to fulfillment.

Religion truly observed should involve our whole being in the search of that identity. Spiritual consciousness changes our life. Spiritual manifestation of the divine potentiality in human personality is the essence of religion. When divine spirit dominates our life, we always stand wholly chastened. We become divine.

Indian mystics discovered two basic universal spiritual principles: the spiritual oneness of all things, and the divine nature of man. The conception of the unity of existence behind the multiplicity not only resolves all seeming contradictions and differences, it also enriches life in every way. The conception of the divinity of man led to the conviction that the goal of life was spiritual experience through the purification of mind. The central principle of the microcosm is not different from the central principle of the macrocosm. The ever-changing world is held by one eternal, self-existent, self-manifest reality, popularly addressed as God. "That science is the greatest which makes us know Him who never changes. No search has been dearer to this human heart than that which brings to us light from God" said Swami Vivekananda.[1] This search for God is religion. "If conformity is the law of the universe, every part of the universe must have been built on the same plan as the whole. So we naturally think that behind the gross material from which we call this universe of ours, there must be a universe of finer matter, which we call thought, and behind that, there must be a Soul, which makes all this thought possible, which commands, which is the enthroned king of this universe. That soul which is behind each mind and each body is called *Pratyagatman*, the individual Atman, and that Soul which is behind the universe as its guide, ruler, and governor is God."[2]

He also said "From whom all beings are projected, in whom all live and unto whom they return; that is God."[3] "The sum total of this Universe is God Himself. Is God then matter? No, certainly not, for matter is that God perceived by the five senses; that God as perceived through the intellect is mind; and when the spirit sees, He is seen as spirit. He is not matter, but whatever is real in matter is He."[4]

In the evolution of spiritual life, the concept of God also undergoes change. Weak persons cannot grasp the concept of a transcendental and invisible God. In the primitive stage, God is conceived as extra-cosmic, living outside the world, in the faraway regions, who governs the affairs of the world. In this way, gradually the idea comes of a Personal God. This cannot be the most satisfying concept for advanced thinkers and the idea of an Impersonal God dawns upon them. Devotion finds its fulfillment in a Personal God. Seekers of truth following the path of knowledge find an Impersonal God. God in Hinduism has two aspects, Personal and Impersonal. But the distinction between them does not make a difference. The Personal and Impersonal are the same Being, in the same way as milk and its whiteness, or the diamond and its lustre are inseparable in our thought. It is impossible to conceive of the one without the other. To the Hindu, though God is one, He or She has various manifestations in many gods and goddesses. God is infinite, so are the infinite expressions of Him or Her. "We have seen that it began with the Personal, the extra-cosmic God. It went from the external to the internal cosmic body, God immanent in the Universe, and ended in identifying the Soul itself with that God, and making one Soul, a unity of all these various manifestations, in the universe."[5]

But an intellectual approach, however satisfying it may be, alone can never give us that satisfaction. The soul of religion is practice. Swamiji said, "Religion is realization; not talk, nor doctrine, nor theories, however beautiful they may be. It is being and becoming, not hearing nor acknowledging; it is the whole soul becoming changed into what it believes."[6]

"Religion is the manifestation of the divinity already in man," said Swamiji. This spark within us compels us to seek the divine and, therefore, its compulsive urge can never be totally ignored. It does give us inspiration and motivation for spiritual struggle. It is a real source of inspiration and that is why the religions of the world have tremendous vitality and dynamism. As Swamiji forcefully remarked, "Not one of the great religions of the world has died; not only so, each of them is progressive."[7]

The truth of religion is verifiable. It culminates in that plenary experience which enriches life, broadens our views, and purifies our vision. When we become universal, our thoughts and actions are in tune with Divinity. Then we truly enjoy life and can radiate peace and joy unto others. Swamiji said, "This is the real science of religion. As mathematics in every part of the world does not differ, so the mystics do not differ."[8]

Though different in names and forms, religions have certain ideals and hopes in common. "One infinite religion existed all through eternity and will ever exist, and this religion is expressing itself in various countries in various ways."[9] The supreme fact that can be gleaned from all these different religions is ". . . that there is an ideal Unit Abstraction, which is put before us, either in the form of a person, or an Impersonal Being, or a Law, or a Presence, or an Essence."[10]

Only with the realization of spiritual oneness can universal love and sympathy develop. The spiritual oneness of humanity is the source of ethics, too. Swamiji remarked, "The infinite oneness of the Soul is the eternal sanction of all morality, that you and I are not only brothers — every literature voicing man's struggle towards freedom has preached that for you — but that you and I are really one. This is the dictate of Indian philosophy. This oneness is the rationale of all ethics and spirituality."[11]

"We have always heard it preached, 'Love one another'. . . Why should I love my brother? Because he and I are one. There is this oneness, this solidarity of the whole universe. . . . That universal sympathy, universal love, universal bliss, that never changes, raises man above everything."[12] Essentially, the goal of all religions is of the same nature. Through all religions, people have been searching for this "real" in the midst of temporal things. "This has been the search throughout the history of the human mind. In the very oldest times, we often find glimpses of light coming into men's minds. We find man, even then, going a step beyond this body, finding something complex which is not this external body, although very much like it, much more complete, much more perfect, and which remains even when this body is dissolved."[13] "It is a significant fact that all religions, without one exception, hold that man is a degeneration of what he was," said Swamiji.

Our spiritual hunger stems from our divine heritage. Perfection is our real nature — our soul; we aspire to this quality. This alone provides the clue to the real strength behind our weak and fragile body-mind complex. Indian philosophy extols the beauty of our divinity, which animates, sustains and enlivens the psychophysical organism. This point has been beautifully dealt with in Swamiji's illuminating discourse, *The Real and the Apparent Man* in his *Jnana Yoga.* This spiritual "warfare" to attain perfection and complete freedom from bondage of life is a common phenomenon in all religions, and Swamiji mentioned it as the first impulse toward becoming religious. "In spite of the almost hopeless contradictions of the different systems, we find the golden thread of unity running through them all, and in this philosophy this golden thread has been traced, revealed little by little to our view, and the first step to this revelation is the common ground that all are advancing toward freedom."[14] This urge to attain freedom is the only hope for human progress. Had there been no such impulsion toward freedom, toward the divine, toward the eternal, we would be lost in the maze of life. This is a basic urge. "This idea of freedom you cannot relinquish.

Your actions, your very lives will be lost without it. Every moment nature is proving us to be slaves and not free. Yet, simultaneously rises the other idea, that still we are free. At every step we are knocked down, as it were, by *maya,* and shown that we are bound; and yet at the same moment, together with this blow, together with this feeling that we are bound, comes the other feeling that we are free. Some inner voice tells us that we are free."[15] In this battle of life, a few fortunate souls are winners who command our respect and worship. This tradition of showing honour to these God-men is a common characteristic of all religions.

Spiritual life is like traveling in an unknown land; at every step we require the helpful guidance of those who have gone there. We cannot form any idea of an Omnipotent God and, therefore, we are told by the experts to resort to forms (material images) of divinity. Ritual, repetition of holy names, faith in the sacred word, etc., are also advocated by them. Symbols are used by all traditions to express the invisible by the help of concrete representations. Swamiji said, "From time immemorial symbols have been used by all kinds of religions. In one sense we cannot think but in symbols; the whole universe is a symbol and God is the essence behind." Again, we find through observation and study that these methods are also common in other traditions. "So we find, that in almost every religion, these are the three primary things which we have in the worship of God — forms or symbols, names, God-men."[16]

The experience of the illumined souls codified in holy books is respected in all religions. These sacred scriptures are very helpful in all faiths. Having found many similarities in the practice of religion in different religions, Swamiji remarked, "Between all great religions of the world there are many points of similarity; and so startling is this likeness, at times, as to suggest the idea that in many particulars the different religions have copied from one another.

"This act of imitation has been laid at the door of different religions; but that it is a superficial charge is evident from the following facts:

"Religion is fundamental in the very soul of humanity; and as all life is the evolution of that which is within, it, of necessity, expresses itself through various peoples and nations.

"The language of the soul is one, the languages of nations are many; their customs and methods of life are widely different. Religion is of the soul and finds expression through various nations, languages, and customs. Hence it follows that the difference between the religions of the world is one of expression and not of substance; and their points of similarity and unity are of the soul, are intrinsic, as the language of the soul is one, in whatever peoples and under whatever circumstances it manifests itself. The same sweet harmony is vibrant there also, as it is on many and diverse instruments."[17]

In each religion we find there are three divisions; namely, Holy Books containing philosophy, mythology and ritual. Swamiji gave a masterly exposition of it in *The Ideal of a Universal Religion.* He said, "First, there is the philosophy which represents the whole scope of that religion, setting forth its basic principles, the goal and the means of reaching it. The second part is mythology, which is philosophy made concrete. It consists of legends relating to the lives of men, or of supernatural beings, and so forth. It is the abstraction of philosophy concretized in the more or less imaginary lives of men and supernatural beings. The third part is the ritual. This is still more concrete and is made up of forms and ceremonies, various physical attitudes, flowers and incense, and many other things that appeal to the senses. In these consists the ritual. You will find that all recognized religions have these three elements. Some lay more stress on one, some on another."[18]

A distinctive trait of Vivekananda's teachings is the comprehensiveness of his idealism. He vividly saw the divine image in human beings. In his charter of Universalism there was no cleavage between faith and reason, between action and contemplation. He was a loving friend to all. "Take man where he stands and from there give him a lift. . . . Our duty is to encourage every one in his struggle to live up to his own highest ideal, and strive at the same time to make the ideal as near as possible to the truth. . . .[19] "All the men and the women, in any society, are not of the same mind, capacity, or of the same power to do things; they must have different ideals, and we have no right to sneer at any ideal."[20]

Swamiji experienced spiritual unity as the ultimate ground of all diversities. Each religion has been searching to reach this goal through divergent forms and methods. Swamiji said, "If you go below the surface, you find that Unity between man and man, between races and races, high and low, rich and poor, gods and men, and men and animals. If you go deep enough, all will be seen as only variations of the One, and he who has attained to this conception of Oneness has no more delusion. What can delude him? He knows the reality of everything, the secret of everything. Where is there any more misery for him: what does he desire? He has traced the reality of everything to the Lord, the Centre, the Unity of everything, and that is Eternal Existence, Eternal Knowledge, Eternal Bliss."[21]

To his penetrating insight there was no sharp division in fundamental points between one segment of humanity and another. Romain Rolland very beautifully articulated this point of his universal spirit thus: "His intuition of unity of the human race did not stop at the arbitrary divisions of races and nations."[22]

Unity in variety and not uniformity being the pattern for world culture, one expression of life does not militate against another as long as the main idealism is not abandoned. Swamiji visualized the future trend of the world situation and boldly gave his message of universalism: "One atom in this universe cannot move without dragging the whole world along with it. There cannot be any progress without the whole world following in the wake, and it is becoming every day clearer that the solution of any problem can never be attained on racial, or national, or narrow grounds. Every idea has to become broad till it covers the whole of this world; every aspiration must go on increasing till it has engulfed the whole of humanity, nay, the whole of life, within its scope."[23]

Modern trends of lifestyle testify to this truth, told to us a long time ago. "We want today that bright sun of intellectuality joined with the heart of Buddha, the wonderful infinite heart of love and mercy. This union will give us the highest philosophy. Science and religion will meet and shake hands. Poetry and philosophy will become friends. This will be the religion of the future, and if we can work it out, we may be sure that it will be for all times and peoples."[24]

"Just as a physicist, when he pushes his knowledge to its limits, finds it melting away into metaphysics, so a metaphysician will find that what he calls mind and matter are but apparent distinctions, the reality being One.

"The more advanced a society is in spirituality, the more is that society or nation civilized. No nation can be said to have become civilized only because it has succeeded in increasing the comforts of material life by bringing into use lots of machinery and things of that sort. The present-day civilization of the West is multiplying day by day only the wants and distresses of men. On the other hand, the ancient Indian civilization, by showing people the way to spiritual advancement, doubtless succeeded, if not in removing once for all, at least in lessening, in a great measure, the material needs of men. In the present age, it is to bring into coalition both these civilizations that Bhagavan Shri Ramakrishna was born. In this age, as on the one hand people have to be intensely practical, so on the other hand they have to acquire deep spiritual knowledge."[25]

Religion is not other-wordly; it is all-inclusive. It touches upon every aspect of life. Modern man is alienated from himself, divided from his fellow beings, and separated from his Maker — God. Religion, as Swamiji explained, can heal the wounds of life. Even secular scholars like Dr. C. G. Jung, in his work, *Modern Man in Search of a Soul*, expressed his view in these terms: "It is safe to say that every one of them (patients) fell ill because he had lost that which the living religion of every age had given to their followers and none of them was really healed who did not regain a religious outlook." Hence, secular scholars are convinced that real religion does play a vital role to make us mentally healthy. Religion is revelation. It is spiritual experience that elevates our life, broadens our outlook, gives strength to our character. It demands nothing less than the ultimate unification of life under its own supreme control.

Its primary aim is all-inclusive and coextensive with the whole of life. Whatever brings "real" significance, the only life divine that can attain real celebrity and glory in our life is religion. It includes and covers morality, art, science and philosophy, but transcends them all. Religious experience, if genuine, will grant us synthetic vision. This type of vision gave a peculiar glow to Swamiji's life. Being endowed with it, he was elevated far above others and was able to declare to humanity ideals of religious harmony which were bequeathed to him as a sacred legacy by Shri Ramakrishna. Harmony of religions is indispensable. It is very vital for peaceful coexistence. All narrowness and prejudice stem from the puerile attitude toward religion. Spiritual values of religion are the saving values of life.

"No civilization can grow, unless fanaticism, bloodshed and brutality stop. No civilization can begin to lift up its head until we look charitably upon one another; and the first step towards that much needed charity is to look charitably and kindly upon the religious convictions of others. Nay, more, to understand that, not only should we be charitable, but positively helpful to each other, however different our religious ideas and convictions may be. And that is exactly what we do in India as I have just related to you. It is here in India that Hindus have built and are still building churches for Christians and mosques for Mohammedans. That is the thing to do. In spite of their hatred, and in spite of their brutality, in spite of their cruelty, in spite of their tyranny, and in spite of the vile language they are given to uttering, we will and must go on building churches for the Christians and mosques for the Mohammedans until we conquer through love, until we have demonstrated to the world that love alone is the fittest thing to survive and not hatred, that it is gentleness that has the strength to live on and to fructify and not mere brutality and physical force."[26]

"Religion is the greatest motive power for realizing that infinite energy which is the birthright and nature of every man. In building up character, in making for everything that is good and great, in bringing peace to others and peace to one's own self, religion is the highest motive power and, therefore, ought to be studied from that standpoint. Religion must be studied on a broader basis than formerly.

"As the human mind broadens, its spiritual steps broaden too. The time has already come when a man cannot record a thought without its reaching to all corners of the earth; by merely physical means, we have come into touch with the whole world; so the future religions of the world have to become as universal, as wide.

"The religious ideals of the future must embrace all that exists in the world and is good and great, and, at the same time, have infinite scope for future development. All that was good in the past must be preserved; and the doors must be kept open for future additions to the already existing store. Religions must also be inclusive, and not look down with contempt upon one another, because their particular ideals of God are different.

"The power of religion, broadened and purified, is going to penetrate every part of human life. So long as religion was in the hands of a chosen few or of a body of priests, it was in temples, churches, books, dogmas, ceremonials, forms, and rituals. But when we come to the real, spiritual, universal concept, then, and then alone, religion will become real and living; it will come into our very nature, live in our every movement, permeate every pore of our society, and be infinitely more a power for good than it has ever been before," said Swamiji.[27]

Synthesis or harmony is the distinguishing feature of Swamiji's philosophy of religion. Swamiji, like his teacher, Shri Ramakrishna, not merely expounded the theory of the harmony of religions, but lived it. Their lives also represented a Parliament of Religions. Nowhere have we seen such harmonious blending of plurality of religions. Before the advent of Shri Ramakrishna, the religious climate was full of tension. The followers of different faiths in India and abroad were at loggerheads with one another. Shri Ramakrishna made experiments with many different religions. He emphatically declared, "To realize God is the Goal of human life."

Shri Ramakrishna also said, "Each religion is a pathway to God." Amplifying, he said further, "So many religions are so many paths to the temple of God. Let all men and women sincerely follow their own religions as true, but never think that only their religions are true and all others are false. All religions are true, they lead to the same God." Thus Shri Ramakrishna laid the foundation of harmony of religions. About this prophet of the harmony of religions, one venerable monk remarked, "In his life one finds an unsurpassed record of God-intoxication, spotless purity and surging love for humanity. And then with his mind broad as the sky, strong as adamant and pure as crystal, he plumbed the depths of spirituality, collected the treasures of the entire wisdom of the past, tested their worth and reinvested them with a fresh hallmark of truth. From his lips the world hears the voice of the ancient prophets, in his life it discovers the meaning of the scriptures. Through his life and teachings man has got an opportunity of learning the old lessons afresh.

"By his deep and extensive spiritual experience of the entire range of Upanishadic truths, Ramakrishna surely heralded an epoch-making Hindu renaissance, which is expected to bring in its train a general spiritual upheaval all over the world. He discovered the wonderful spirit of Catholicism within the sealed bosom of Hinduism and released it through his own realizations to spread all over the globe and liberalize all communal and sectarian views. His advent marks a new era in the evolution of religion, when all sects and all communities, keeping intact the individual characteristics of their faiths, will transcend the limitation of narrow and sectarian outlook and thus pave the path for a universal Brotherhood."[28]

We are all at different stages of evolution and, therefore, our mental constitution is bound to vary. Accepting this fact of variation, Swamiji said, "You cannot make all conform to the same ideas: that is a fact, and I thank God that it is so. . . . Now, if we all thought alike, we would be like Egyptian mummies. . . . Variation is the sign of life and it must be there."[29]

SHRI RAMAKRISHNA (1836–1886)

He saw God in everything and experienced directly that all religions are true and lead to the same goal through different paths.

THE HOLY MOTHER, SHRI SARADA DEVI (1853–1920)

She gave Swami Vivekananda her blessings, knowing that it was Shri Ramakrishna's wish that he should undertake the journey to America.

Swamiji himself had spelled out his idea of Universal Religion when he said, "What then do I mean by the ideal of a Universal Religion? I do not mean any one universal philosophy, or any one universal mythology, or any one universal ritual held alike by all; for I know that this world must go on working, wheel within wheel, this intricate mass of machinery, most complex, most wonderful. What can we do then? We can make it run smoothly, we can lessen the friction, we can grease the wheels, as it were. How? By recognizing the natural necessity of variation. Just as we have recognized unity by our very nature, so we must also recognize variation."[30]

Shri Ramakrishna's thesis that, "As many faiths, so many paths," is likely to be misunderstood unless we accept one God as the sole support and substance of the manifold. Swamiji said in clarification of that great idea of Shri Ramakrishna, "We must learn that truth may be expressed in a hundred thousand ways, and that each of these ways is true as far as it goes. We must learn that the same thing can be viewed from a hundred different standpoints, and yet be the same thing. Take for instance the sun. Suppose a man standing on the earth looks at the sun when it rises in the morning; he sees a big ball. Suppose he starts on a journey towards the sun and takes a camera with him, taking photographs at every stage of his journey, until he reaches the sun. The photographs of each stage will be seen to be different from those of the other stages; in fact, when he gets back, he brings with him so many photographs of so many different suns, as it would appear; and yet we know that the same sun was photographed by the man at the different stages of his progress. Even so is it with the Lord. Through high philosophy or low, through the most exalted mythology or the grossest, through the most refined ritualism or arrant fetishism, every sect, every soul, every nation, every religion, consciously or unconsciously, is struggling upward, towards God; every vision of truth that man has is a vision of Him and of none else. Suppose we all go with vessels in our hands to fetch water from a lake. One has a cup; another a jar, another a bucket, and so forth, and we all fill our vessels. The water in each case naturally takes the form of the vessel carried by each of us. He who brought the cup has the water in the form of a cup; he who brought the jar — his water is in the shape of a jar, and so forth; but, in every case, water, and nothing but water, is in the vessel. So it is in the case, religion; our minds are like these vessels, and each one of us is trying to arrive at the realization of God. God is like that water filling these different vessels, and in each vessel the vision of God comes in the form of the vessel. Yet He is One. He is God in every case. This is the only recognition of universality that we can get."[31]

According to Swamiji's interpretation, Vedanta "alone can become the universal religion of man and no other is fitted for that role." Vedanta upholds the unity of existence, oneness of God, and identity of man with the Divine. It is rational, universal and also practical. "One infinite religion existed all through eternity and will ever exist, and this religion is expressing itself in various countries in various ways." This eternal religion is the subject-matter of Vedanta and it has, necessarily, no founder and, therefore, is timeless. The conception of Absolute Thought and Being, popularly known as God, is not an empty logical abstraction. Mystics experienced the Truth and broadcast it. Human mind can develop a suprasensuous and suprarational faculty, intuition, which is far superior to intellect and can unravel the facts otherwise inaccessible to mere intellect. Ramakrishna and Vivekananda are the latest mystics in modern times to authenticate the Truth.

Another speciality of Vedanta is that it endorses various courses, grades, according to the mental constitution of the seeker and his situation in life. Another important feature of Vedanta is its comprehensiveness. It accepts life as a whole. There is no inherent dichotomy between secular and spiritual, reason and faith, science and religion. Swamiji had the firm conviction that Advaita Vedanta was most invigorating, most rational, and totally in conformity with modern science. Unity in variety, not dull uniformity, is the pattern of world culture. All facets of life have a place in the economy of spiritual growth. Swamiji advocated toleration, liberalism and rational temper to work out the peaceful coexistence of various religions.

Swamiji, being an Advaitin (monist), developed a unitary vision which enabled him to see the expression of One in and through many. Hence, synthesis or harmony is the special characteristic of his view. "Every religion is only evolving a God out of the material man, and the same God is the inspirer of all of them."

"Religions do not come from without but from within. . . . As long as man thinks, this struggle must go on, and so long man must have some form of religion. Thus we see various forms of religion in the world. It is a bewildering study; but it is not, as many of us think, a vain speculation. Amidst this chaos there is harmony, throughout these discordant sounds there is a note of concord; and he who is prepared to listen to it will catch the note."[32] Hence, Swamiji said, "Real religion is one; all quarrel is with the forms, the symbols, the 'illustrations'."[33]

To a monist, toleration and sympathy are a religion in themselves. Endowed with such a width of vision and depth of understanding, a universalist like Swamiji alone could articulate, "I accept all religions that were in the past . . . and will come in the future."[34]

10

SWAMI VIVEKANANDA'S IMPACT ON THE WORLD'S PARLIAMENT OF RELIGIONS – I

On Monday, September 11, at 10 a.m., 1893, the Parliament of Religions opened its historic deliberations at the Art Institute in Chicago. The august convention was an adjunct of the World's Columbian Exposition, which had been organized to celebrate the four hundredth anniversary of the discovery of America by Christopher Columbus. It was a great assembly consisting of the most notable persons of the world; a huge crowd of humanity varying from seven thousand to ten thousand in number. All accredited religious organizations were invited. More than one thousand papers were read by the delegates. "The exposition was designed to demonstrate western man's material progress, especially in science and technology. It was agreed, however, that all forms of progress must be represented, and there were congresses devoted to such varied themes as women's progress, the public press, medicine and surgery, temperance, commerce and finance, music, government and legal reform, economic science, and strange as it may sound to us nowadays — Sunday rest. And since, to quote the official language of the committee, 'faith in a Divine power has been, like the sun, a light-giving and fructifying potency in Man's intellectual and moral development', there had also to be a Parliament of Religions."

Swamiji spoke in the afternoon session. His well-known address, "Sisters and Brothers of America," instantly moved the entire audience. They found in him a "real brother." Swamiji thanked the youngest of the nations in the name of the most ancient monastic order in the world, the Vedic order of *sannyasins*. He also introduced Hinduism as "the Mother of Religions, a religion which has taught the world both tolerance and universal acceptance." From the Hindu scriptures he quoted two verses illustrating the Hindu spirit of toleration. He told the audience how ancient India had sheltered the religious refugees such as the Jews and the Parsees (descendants of the Zoroastrians who emigrated to India in the eighth century). In conclusion he fervently appealed for the speedy abolition of sectarianism, bigotry, and fanaticism. The response was spontaneous and prolonged applause. The Swami won the hearts of the audience by that brief speech noted for its spirit of universality, its fundamental ring of sincerity, earnestness, and broad-mindedness. During the entire session of the Parliament which ended on the twenty-seventh of September, the Swami spoke about a dozen times. His celebrated paper on Hinduism was unique for various reasons. Whereas the other delegates had spoken of their ideal or their own sect, Swami Vivekananda had spoken about the universal character of religious truth, and the sameness of the goal of all religious experiences. In his first address he gave utterance to the demand of the modern world to end the era of isolation, division, and indifference. Humanity refused to remain in darkness; it was ready for mutual understanding and cooperation. The vast mass of humanity found in him a true representative of Hinduism proper, one who could boldly state the universal principle of religion, oneness of humanity, the non-duality of the Godhead, harmony of religions, and the divinity of the Soul. In that Parliament "America discovered Vivekananda and made a gift of him to India and the World."

Shri Ramakrishna had tremendous faith in Narendra (Swamiji); he also knew through his divine intuitive knowledge that Narendra would "remove the miseries and suffering of humanity." Shri Ramakrishna also wrote on a piece of paper, "Narendra will teach others." Shri Ramakrishna's mandate was successfully executed by Swamiji in the East and the West, and their unique message of man's undying divinity and strength, and the essential spirituality of life, did render positive and constructive help to all, in all spheres of life — physical, mental, moral and spiritual. Theirs was a message for the whole person.

Swamiji's historic appearance in the Parliament was a part of his divine mission of removing the spiritual blindness of people, making them conscious of their own innate divine heritage and giving them the supreme opportunity of being exposed to the invigorating spiritual thoughts contained in the Vedanta. In him the modern West met the ancient India for mutual benefit. History does not record a single instance of any other illumined soul of Swamiji's stature who ever walked on the soil of the U.S.A.

"He was one of the greatest souls that had visited the earth for many centuries. An incarnation of his Master, of Krishna, Buddha, Christ and all other great souls (he was). . . . No person stood out with such magnificent individuality. . . . Compared to his gigantic intellect they (university professors) were mere children. . . . This great Hindu cyclone has shaken the world" — thus articulated the Californians who heard him during his second visit.[1]

In spite of his stupendous success at the Parliament of Religions, Swamiji literally had to face another world, a world of hatred, coldness, calumny and curse. He also had to face a world of solid opposition from the die-hard enemies of his mission to emancipate religion from dogmatism and the sense of fear. Apart from the fanatical Christian missionaries, charlatans, curiosity-mongers, and other religious cranks gave stiff opposition. Leon Landsberg, later Swami Kripananda, one of the Swami's housekeepers and disciples, gave a pen-picture of the Swami's deplorable situation of that period: "The Americans are a receptive nation. That is why the country is a hotbed of all kinds of religious and irreligious monstrosities. There is no theory so absurd, no doctrine so irrational, no claim so extravagant, no fraud so transparent, but can find its numerous believers and a ready market. To satisfy this craving, to feed the credulity of the people, hundreds of societies and sects are born for the salvation of the world, and to enable the prophets to pocket $25 to $100 initiation fees. Hobgoblins, spooks, *mahatmas*, and new prophets were rising every day. In this bedlam of religious cranks, the Swami appeared to teach the lofty religion of the Vedas, the profound philosophy of Vedanta, the sublime wisdom of the rishis. The most unfavourable environment for such a task!"[2]

By nature a self-absorbed mystic, friendly to all, Swamiji unconsciously became a "warrior prophet" with the passage of time. One disciple of Swamiji wrote later about this change: "When Swamiji first started lecturing he was dreamy and meditative, often so wrapped in his own thoughts as to be hardly conscious of his surroundings. The constant friction of alien thoughts, the needless questioning, the frequent sharp conflict of wits in the Western World, awoke a different spirit, and he became as alert and wide awake as the world in which he found himself." The cruel, unscrupulous, and mean crusaders found in him a remarkable specimen of a mild Hindu resisting the attack of the multitudes almost single-handedly with the help of his vast intellect, deep sympathy and strength of character. Swamiji wrote to Alasinga on 17th August, 1896, "It is hard work, my boy, hard work! I had to work till I am at death's door and had to spend nearly the whole of that energy in America, so that Americans may learn to be more broader and more spiritual."[3]

This knowledge was imparted in a manner which evoked the admiration of impartial observers. The famous Indologist, Professor A. L. Basham, says, "It is a very friendly, unaggressive counter-attack, as one would expect. Slowly, but nonetheless surely, Hindu ideas, or ideas of an Indian character, are beginning to be heard even among earnest and apparently orthodox Christian people, among Jews and among unbelievers with no religion at all."[4]

We quote Burke to get an idea of the opposition and Swamiji's method of tackling the situation. She writes, "Almost a whole nation had barked after Swamiji, but he stood on unperturbed, chastising where it was necessary with one or two well-directed blows, awakening and quickening the minds of thousands, and bestowing his blessings upon friends and foes alike. Both America and Swamiji had changed from a year and a half's contact with each other. The eyes of the country have been opened to a new vista of thought, and the living seed of spirituality had been firmly planted in the souls of the people."[5] The same author gives us a pen-picture of his "prophetic-mission". "During his travels he was, consciously or unconsciously, fulfilling the function of a divine prophet to America — scattering the seeds of spirituality wherever he went and bestowing his blessing upon innumerable men and women. As he himself later wrote to Swami Ramakrishnananda: 'I am careering all over the country. Wherever the seed of his power will fall, there it will fructify — be it today, or in a hundred years.' Throughout his life, wherever he was and whatever he was outwardly doing, he permanently lifted the consciousness of all with whom he came in contact. It was truly said of him: 'Vivekananda is nothing if not a breaker of bondage.' His very presence was a profound blessing, and we shall miss the full significance of his activities and teachings if we forget that above all he was a prophet, born — if his Master is to be believed — for the good of mankind."[6]

It should not be understood that Swamiji was a loner in America. His thoughts were deeply understood by some and there were hosts of genuinely liberal minded, sympathetic Americans who did give positive support to his cause. The young nation, by and large, was very receptive to his mission.

The image of real India was put onto the map of the world, and her spiritual treasures were scattered everywhere in the West by her ablest exponent. Hindu thoughts and ideas became as familiar to many as those of Huxley and Spencer. Helen Huntington recorded her opinion about Swamiji's capability in presenting to the West a religion of universality, unfailing charity, self-renunciation and the purest sentiments conceivable by the human intellect. "It had no bad odour of creed and dogma, and therefore it was uplifting, purifying, infinitely comforting and altogether without blemish, based on the love of God and man, and on absolute chastity." She wrote: "He has met all phases of society on equal terms of friendship and brotherhood; his classes and lectures have been attended by the most intellectual people and advanced thinkers of our cities; and his influence has already grown into deep, strong undercurrent of spiritual awakening. No praise or blame has moved him to either approbation or expostulation . . . He is altogether such a man as 'kings delight to honour'". She writes again: "It will always be a marvel to us that an oriental could take such a firm hold on us occidentals, trained as we have been by long habit of thought and education to opposing views."[7]

One of the best known women poets and writers of America, Mrs. Wheeler Wilcox, described the Swami's illuminating talks as fresh water in a long-parched throat. Being fully refreshed and strengthened on hearing Swamiji, she wrote to the *New York American* of May 26, 1907: "When any philosophy, any religion, can do this for human beings in this age of stress and strain, and when, added to that, it intensifies their faith in God and increases their sympathies for their kind and gives them a confident joy in thought of other lives to come, it is a good and great religion." "We need to learn the greatness of the philosophy of India. We need to enlarge our narrow creeds with the wisdom religious. But we want to imbue them with our own modern spirit of progress, and to apply them practically, lovingly and patiently to human needs. Vivekananda came to us with a message . . . 'I do not come to convert you to new belief,' he said. 'I want you to keep your own belief; I want to make the Methodist a better Methodist; the Presbyterian a better Presbyterian; the Unitarian a better Unitarian. I want to teach you to live the truth, to reveal the light within your own soul.' He gave the message that strengthened the man of business, that caused the frivolous society woman to pause and think; that gave the artist new aspirations; that imbued the wife and mother, the husband and father, with a larger and holier comprehension of duty."[8]

This impact of Swamiji's spiritual ministry was stated by Christopher Isherwood as follows: "At this point it is perhaps advisable to remark that a knowledge of Vedanta did not, of course, enter the Western world for the first time in 1893, with Swami Vivekananda. Schopenhauer, Emerson, Thoreau, and their circle; Max Mueller and his fellow orientalist — to name only a few of the Swami's many forerunners — had all studied, discussed and publicized the philosophy long before that date. What Vivekananda did bring to the West was the living example of a man wholly dedicated to the practice of Vedanta — an example infinitely more inspiring and convincing than any book, as Emerson himself would have been the first to admit."[9]

Swamiji electrified the intellectual world by his very presence and by his masterly presentation of Hinduism. Swamiji's presentation at the Parliament was the catalyst for opening the eyes and ears of the world to understand, appreciate and recognize the oldest spiritual tradition of mankind, sprung from the sages and seers of India. Instead of speaking in a humble and apologetic tone, like an affectionate father he expressed his thoughts boldly and fearlessly. He cogently pointed out the elements of universalism in all faiths and very clearly dispelled the myth of superiority of any faith over other faiths. Contemporary newspapers reported, "His eloquent and graceful manner pleased his listeners who followed him from beginning to end with the closest attention." They described him as "gentle in manner, deliberate in movement and extremely courteous in every word."

Beneath the glittering opulence of the West, Swamiji found an undercurrent of materialism and its inevitable baneful consequences of boredom, anguish and depression. To Nivedita he said, "Social life in the West is like a peal of laughter, but underneath it is a wail. It ends in a sob."[10] He wrote to Alasinga Perumal on August 31, 1894: "The whole world requires light. It is expectant! India alone has light, not in magic mummeries and charlatanism, but in the teaching of the glories of the spirit of real religion."[11]

Swamiji's main idea of preaching this message of Vedanta was to highlight six important points. These ever recurring themes of his teachings were: the divinity of life, whose highest manifestation is seen in the human soul; the oneness of existence; non-duality of the Godhead; harmony of religions; intuitive experience of truth in this life; and a reverential attitude towards other faiths and religious prophets. This message was new to the West, but he delivered that saving wisdom in a manner of one having a divine mandate. His brilliant eloquence, logical arguments, psychological approach, scientific temper, mystical insight and above all his stupendous personal magnetism created a spell on the audience. The unique response he received throughout his spiritual ministrations in the West speaks highly of the American audience.

Cultured Americans basically kept their spirit of open-mindedness and free-thinking since the days of the Pilgrim Fathers. The young adventurous nation was touched by Swamiji's strange but rational message of the divinity of the human soul. "Here was a message which brought the glad tidings of the noblest birthright of man — his own divinity and the inevitability of salvation. By making a unique juxtaposition of a mere five words he created a 'spiritual history'. Four of these words were taken from India and one from the West. 'Ye divinities on earth —

sinners!' With these words, he struck the mightiest blow on the whole structure of 'soul-degenerating, cowardice-producing negative, pessimistic thoughts' and set in motion a new wheel of *dharma,* of spiritual energism, freedom, conquest and creativity, of mastery over nature — inner and outer — of fearlessness, strength, love, and service — in one word, true universalism. . . . For the whole history of Western civilization the threat of damnation has yawned its earthquake chasms beneath everyone's feet without exception, and no one has felt safe from it. This religious terrorism was above all what the West needed to be saved from. . . . Light was badly needed in the West, a genuine spiritual sunrise, not a false phosphorescent marsh glow."[12]

Some found in him "a colossal figure," "a man of fire and flame," one "who truly walked with God," and "a marvellous combination of sweetness and irresistible force, verily a child and a prophet in one."

Swamiji's message of Vedanta highly benefited both the East and the West. "The rationale and passion for human understanding and solidarity was never before or after more convincingly presented in any world forum. In a world habituated to listening to dogmatic voices of 'either or', or patronizing condescension of existing varieties of thoughts, his indeed was a refreshing and wonderfully inspiring message."[13]

Swami Vivekananda was commissioned by Shri Ramakrishna. Being captivated by his unique love, he dedicated his life for the cause of human enlightenment through spiritual regeneration. He heightened the glory of human life, deified the world and human existence, quickened the receptive mind with a new promise, and enlarged the spiritual consciousness of the average person. This awakener of the soul became a fit conduit of God's love for man. Shri Ramakrishna used his body and mind for this divine purpose. Swamiji himself acknowledged that.

Swamiji was conscious of his Master's presence within himself. He wrote from America to his brother monks in India: "While I am on earth, Shri Ramakrishna is working through me." He was very categorical in his statement on this point. "If there has been anything achieved by me by thought, word, or deed, if from my lips has fallen one word that has helped anyone in the world, I lay no claim to it, it was his."[14]

What Swamiji spoke came from the inmost depths of his illumined soul, from his strong conviction and deep spiritual insight. These facts are to be seriously taken into account while trying to understand the mystery of spontaneous oration. This explains why his common words — "Sisters and Brothers of America" — created an unprecedented spontaneous spiritual upsurge of emotion in the minds of an audience of seven thousand members and raised them to their feet.

Swamiji had witnessed a Parliament of Religions almost every day at Dakshineswar in the life of his Master. The Parliament in Chicago was anticipated by Shri Ramakrishna long before its appearance. The impact of his spiritual ministry can be found in the growing literature of the West having a distinct Vedantic overtone. Of the innumerable writings, we will quote just one here: "Vivekananda speaks to humanity. They (prophets) cannot whisper if they would, and he did not attempt to do so. A great voice is made to fill the sky. The whole earth is its sounding box." In this statement Romain Rolland emphatically painted the image of Swamiji as a universalist. The universal message of Vedanta can be the only antidote to the modern malady of the West. Romain Rolland says: "I am bringing to Europe, as yet unaware of it, the fruit of a new autumn, a new message of the soul, the symphony of India, bearing the name of Shri Ramakrishna. . . . It is my desire to bring the sound of the beating of that artery (the Upanishads) to the ears of fever-stricken Europe which has murdered sleep. I wish to wet its lips with the blood of immortality."[15]

This life-giving, eternal message has entered into the very heart of human consciousness, and is striving to awaken the drooping soul of man. Swamiji, the colossus of Divinity, raised both East and West by his two strong hands and enabled them to find the rock of divine consciousness under their feet. Both hemispheres are being highly benefited. The Parliament was arranged by some providential power to bring forth a new, spiritually oriented civilization to help humanity to find fulfillment in life. We quote Burke to highlight the impact of Swamiji's presence at the Parliament: "The Parliament of Religions can perhaps be likened to a huge boulder dropped into the middle of a shallow pond, causing upheaval on all sides. Even without Swamiji the Parliament would have created no little confusion, for it was a shock to people to discover Oriental priests were not grotesquely masked medicine men; but with Swamiji's appearance the effect was galvanizing and permanent. Something had happened in America that could never be talked away, although many an effort was made to do just that."[16]

The West has lately witnessed a very startling trend — a pronounced tendency for many persons of all ages to look to the East for serious enlightenment and spiritual wisdom. Colin Wilson wrote in his famous book, *The Outsider*, "Ramakrishna, at the opposite extreme, could plunge to a depth of imaginative ecstasy which few Westerners have ever known, except those mediaeval saints who also were able to give up their mind as he did to contemplation and serenity. "This book was one of the famous books after the Second World War. The young author used to keep a copy of *The Gospel of Sri Ramakrishna* with him. In this context, we are reminded of Arnold Toynbee's remark. He envisioned the great future of Ramakrishna's message. He said, "In history books written fifty or a hundred years from now, I do not think Shri Ramakrishna's name will be missing."[17] That many people in the West are being attracted to Ramakrishna in increasing numbers is the natural conclusion one arrives at when one notices how the books about him are becoming more available in different languages in the West. Younger generations nowadays have been searching for ways and means to experience something deeper in themselves, something which is unknown in the psychological literature of the West. In flower magazines, medical journals, health magazines and other publications, Ramakrishna and Vivekananda are quoted with, or without, attribution. The immense popularity of interfaith dialogue, interest in other religions, attitude of friendliness and mutual respect for other faiths, increasing sense of cosmopolitanism, intensity of feeling about ecological imbalance, dominant worshipful attitude towards Mother Earth, and many allied themes unmistakably show the direct or indirect impact of Swamiji's cosmic vision of the future civilization. The love for global peace and respect for nonviolence are becoming very pronounced among the common people of the world. The church has been forced to eschew her old undignified and derogatory vocabulary from her sermons. The concept of a loving God as well as the motherhood of God compels us to think that Ramakrishna's message is being accepted. This is a revolution of consciousness as critical of the traditional ethos as it is completely different in its solution.

This change has been commented upon as follows: "Describing this revolution in intellectual concepts, George Leonard has labelled it 'the transformation.' Chronicling its colourful social fashions, Tom Wolfe has termed it 'The Third Great Awakening.' Capturing its vital cultural significance, Theodore Roszak claims we can see 'where the Wasteland ends,' and William Irwin Thompson says we are 'at the edge of history'."[18]

One impetus towards this new consciousness is provided by the contemporary religious literature having a distinct Vedantic flavor. Scholars are becoming increasingly convinced that the scientific temperament of the modern mind prefers the Indian to the Judeo-Christian world view. Tillich, asked at the end of his life, "Sir, do you pray?" replied, "No I meditate." The growing number of meditation centers, the practice of vegetarianism, the belief in *karma* and reincarnation and even the concept of the *avatar* are all very familiar today. About Swami Vivekananda's contribution to this trend, Ann Myren writes: "It can certainly be said that meditation was his gift to America. Historically, whenever a very great soul comes and gives his power to the people of a nation, those people become transformed and their transformation causes a deep current of spirituality in the society. He founded societies, and left groups of people who followed his teachings and practices of meditation. Look what has happened in the last twenty years with regard to meditation in American society. There was little widespread knowledge of these practices in 1960; today there are many different groups trying to help people toward a spiritual way of life. Meditation has become an accepted practice by a wide variety of spiritual seekers, psychologists, and persons who simply want a little tranquillity in their lives. The great spiritual treasure of meditation was brought to this country by Swami Vivekananda. And it is only now that we are beginning to see the emergence of a society which has become ready for the liberal and strength-giving teachings of Swami Vivekananda."[19]

The concept of a loving God, the wide latitude granted in choosing any discipline for spiritual growth, and the quest for spiritual experience in religious life, have attracted people towards Hinduism. We quote a letter from an unknown American. He states: "Although I am unlearned in philosophy, science and religion, two things I know: I love Shri Ramakrishna and Shri Ramakrishna loves me. Actually what else need one know? Shri Ramakrishna entered my life just as I had come to what I believed was the end of a long and almost futile search for God. In every way known to me, I had searched for Him. But I could not harmonize all the creeds, doctrines and ideas. A fundamentalist background which consigns most of humanity to the flames of hell almost swamped the little light I had and caused me untold mental suffering. Finally, in desperation, I wept and called for help. Shri Ramakrishna came."[20]

This corroborates Ramakrishna's repeated assurance that God loves the devotee.

In conclusion, we quote some eminent authorities: "As I see it, (Vivekananda's) gigantic mission in America (and also, of course, in England) was to alter at its deepest source the whole thought-current of the western people — and this without in any way disturbing their inherent greatness — their long-evolving capacity for rational thought, their powers of scientific analysis, their innate ability to invent and to explore, to brave any storm and hurdle any obstacle, their passion for freedom, their capacity for compassion, their yearning for truth. Swamiji knew there was only one way to save these priceless, long developing human qualities from erosion, and that was to root them in the unshakeable, adamantine truth of Advaita Vedanta. Nothing else could hold them firm — and nothing else can hold them firm — against the terrible blows this present age is dealing them and will continue to deal them."[21]

"The swing of a highly materialistic culture toward spiritual values and goals is, of course, not a usual event. More often, a culture that has lost its hope and enthusiasm simply dies. But I do not think this will be the case with America, for not only is America inherently great, America also has been greatly blessed. If a seed of spirituality has been planted in the heart of a nation, then times of inner erosion can act as awakeners of that seed; it will surely stir and sprout. Such a seed was planted in the heart of America some eighty years ago by the towering prophet of this age — Swami Vivekananda. That is the wonderful hope."[22]

Writes Jacob Needleman in his book, *The New Religions*, "When considering the Indian influence in America, a special place must be reserved to the Vedanta Societies throughout the country. Historically, the Vedanta Society was the first Eastern religious tradition that took roots on our soil, having been brought here late in the nineteenth century by Swami Vivekananda, the chief disciple of the great Indian Master, Shri Ramakrishna. Intellectually, the influence of this form of Vedanta has been enormous."

Dr. Floyd H. Ross, Professor of World Religions in the University of Southern California, wrote in *Vedanta and the West,* "Under the leadership of men trained in the spirit of Vivekananda and Ramakrishna, the Ramakrishna Centers are living examples of how timeless truths of the past have value when they are continuously relived and reinterpreted in the present . . . The Ramakrishna Centers in the West are playing their own part quietly in helping to prepare the way for the united pilgrimage of mankind toward self-understanding and peace."

SWAMI ABHEDANANDA (1866–1939),
Leader of The Vedanta Society of New York, from 1897 to 1910.

"In Swami Vivekananda I found the ideal of Karma Yoga, Bhakti Yoga, Raja Yoga and Jnana Yoga; he was like the living example of Vedanta in all it's different branches."

11

SWAMI VIVEKANANDA'S IMPACT ON THE WORLD'S PARLIAMENT OF RELIGIONS - II

It is said that ideas are the most mysterious things in a mysterious world. They appear in human consciousness in a strange manner, without ever giving any prior indication of their emergence. They are really independent of time and space and therefore not subject to human calculations or control. They are extremely powerful forces and are equally contagious. Assertive minds are moulded by these ideas. These living and life-giving ideas are found to flourish, according to their innate nature, in a suitable environment, drawing nourishment from the subsoil of the cultures, and withering away in hostile mental climates. Swamiji says: "These universal thought waves seem to recur every five hundred years, when invariably the great wave typifies and swallows up the others. It is this which constitutes a prophet. He focuses in his own mind the thought of the age in which he is living and gives it back to mankind in concrete form. Krishna, Buddha, Christ, Mohammed, and Luther may be instanced as the great waves that stood up above their fellows (with a probable lapse of five hundred years between them). Always the wave that is backed by the greatest purity and the noblest character is what breaks upon the world as a movement of social reform."[1]

Great men and women, being possessed by these inconceivable "living ideas" do appear in time and place like thickly set constellations. In Periclean Athens, in the Italian Renaissance, in Elizabethan England and in the Indian Renaissance of the nineteenth century, we find how these living ideas got themselves embodied and brought forth bumper crops in different aspects of human life. Zeitgeist or Time-Spirit creates these ideas, nurtures them and ultimately takes them away. Involved universal intelligence unfolds itself; evolution presupposes involution. "This universal intelligence is what we call God."[2] The sixth century BC was a golden age in human history.

Lao-tse, Confucius, Buddha, Mahavira, Zarathushtra and Pythagoras were living at that time. This has been called by Karl

Jaspers the "axial period" in human history. This marked the emergence of rational thinking and understanding out of the mythical imagination of ancient periods.

Great ideas appear in life silently. H. G. Wells says: "The beginnings of such things are never conspicuous. Great movements of the racial soul come at first like a thief in the night, and then suddenly are discovered to be powerful and worldwide. Religious emotion — stripped of corruptions and freed from its priestly entanglements — may presently blow through life again like a great wind, bursting the doors and flinging open the shutters of individual life and making many things possible and easy that in these days of exhaustion seem almost difficult to desire."

Albert Camus is of the opinion that they come into the world gently as doves. Under the compelling, receptive emotions generated by new ideas, Columbus and Vasco da Gama undertook hazardous adventures in uncharted oceans, having no idea of the tremendous impact of such voyages. Gandhiji was forcibly pushed out of the railway compartment at 9 p.m in 1893 at Pietermaritzburg (South Africa). That singular incident was a turning point of his life and the apostle of nonviolence emerged in history in due time. When George Fox (1624-1691), starting a career as a cobbler's apprentice, received "a voice of God" at the age of twenty, history was created. "Perhaps, the most remarkable incident in modern history," writes Carlyle, "is not . . . the Battle of Austerlitz, Waterloo, Peterloo, or any other battle; but an incident passed carelessly over by most historians, and treated with some degree of ridicule by others; namely, George Fox's making of himself a suit of leather. This man was one of those to whom, under purer or ruder form, the Divine Idea of the Universe is pleased to manifest itself, and who are, therefore, rightly accounted prophets, God-possessed." The celebrated Quaker movement thus came into being. When Swamiji spoke only five words, "Sisters and Brothers of America," at the Parliament of Religions, history was created at that supreme moment of spontaneous fraternity. The unknown monk "absolutely took the Parliament by storm." These five words were nothing, but the power behind them mattered everything.

"It was the power of the sovereign quality of his being, transmuted by illumination, that passing through those sound waves quickened every soul like a flash of lightning. And they all responded instantaneously. They did not know what he was going to speak. But they surely felt that, at last, here was one who truly was the brother of everybody." This was a literal fulfillment of Shri Ramakrishna's prophecy: "Naren shall shake the world to its foundations."[3] This is corroborated by Marie Louise Burke: "His entrance onto the scene of the West was dramatic and impressive. Through hindsight it almost seems to have been planned by a master planner in response to the profound need of the age."[4]

There is one most important point to be noted here. Unlike others mentioned earlier, Swamiji had a strong conviction of his role in the Parliament and its tremendous impact in the regeneration of the entire humanity.

In every civilized society there is a small group of people who rebel against orthodoxy. Liberal ideas haunt and agitate their minds, and they take the risk of being unpopular for their views. They give expression of their own convictions and thereby make friends as well as enemies. These pure-minded, devout and conscientious individuals speaking from the depth of their souls, with passage of time, invariably find sympathy from people in distant futures. Since the period of the Renaissance in Europe, new winds of liberal thought began to blow everywhere and Eastern spiritual ideas and thoughts began to percolate into the United States of America through that group which constituted the "Transcendental Movement" of the 1830's. They were mentally nurtured by Indian scriptures tinged with the spirit of liberalism. "They brought into their vision a curious blending of both cultures, Indian and American, and developed an eclectic attitude to life."[5] They were really speakers as well as writers of extraordinary abilities and of still more exceptionally sincere thoughts and ideas.

After many centuries of orthodoxy, New England had been riven by sterile controversies. The people were eager to hear new thoughts in religion and these transcendentalists brought the ideas which were "a new morning for even the rudest undergraduates in Harvard Hall." They sincerely believed that their message would further the cause of civilization. Emerson, Thoreau and Walt Whitman are well-known to the world of Transcendentalists. Of these Transcendentalists, Theodore Parker (1810-1860), was "a religious Titan" who had ". . .the largest regular congregation on the American continent. The great hall of Boston could seat four thousand people, and at his regular discourses every part of it was filled."[6] This is indicative of the new enthusiasm for liberalism.

The new biblical study with its emphasis on "scientific history" and rationalism produced a work in 1881, the *Revised Version of the New Testament.* It was a great achievement in giving articulation "of a more frank and open dealing with scriptural criticism. . . . It was exceedingly cautious and conservative; but it had the vast merit of being absolutely conscientious."

One can easily and unmistakably find "ethical progress in theological methods." The *Chicago Times* and the *Chicago Tribune* both printed the entire text, while 200,000 copies of this book were sold in New York in less than a week.

Again, the study of comparative religion was gaining considerable appreciation and it was revealed that non-Christian religions were being studied as a subject of academic interest. "Comparative religion as an historical science was involved in each of the foregoing matters to a certain extent, notably in such questions as the relation of Hebrew religion to its ancient neighbours, or the Apostle Paul's indebtedness to Greek thought and the oriental mystery cults. In these pursuits many of the major disciplines for studying the history of religions were first developed. But it was the Western discovery of the great "higher religions" of the Orient, above all Hinduism and Buddhism, that raised the more difficult questions, because these highly philosophical religions possessed an intrinsic appeal for an age already imbued with idealistic philosophy and pantheistic theology. In Emerson's *Brahma*, Americans savoured the forbidden fruit in their parlours."[7]

James Freeman Clarke's liberal treatment of *Ten Great Religions* was quite a success and had twenty-one editions after its publication in 1871. William James' (1842-1910) Gifford Lectures, were published in 1902 as *The Varieties of Religious Experience* and this book created such an interest that within a dozen years it had been reprinted twenty-one times.[8] Each of these several new thoughts gave a serious jolt to the traditional thinking of popular Christianity. Robert G. Ingersoll, the son of a Congregational minister, was a great orator and used his skill in undermining the authority of orthodoxy by questioning the basic tenets of Christian belief.

Colonel Bob Ingersoll created a good deal of embarrassment among the Christians through his book, *The Mistakes of Moses*, and other publications. The scholars criticized Christianity for lack of intellectual basis. They became more anticlerical, antireligious and materialistic under the stress of conflict. Darwinian biology, the new trend of biblical studies, and the scientific temper of the age seriously affected the image of traditional Christianity. J. W. Draper wanted to focus this incompatibility of science and religion in his book, *History of the Conflict between Religion and Science* (1874). This study was undertaken by A. D. White in his *History of the Warfare of Science with Theology in Christendom* in two volumes (1896). When the proposed Parliament of Religions was talked about, it naturally did not receive approval from all quarters. The protagonists of conservatism did not share the view of liberal minded people in supporting the cause of a Parliament of Religions. Years later one prime evangelist, Billy Sunday, "looked back on the Parliament as one of the biggest curses that ever came to America." "In 1892 the Presbyterian General Assembly called the anticipated Parliament uncalled for, misleading and hurtful."[9]

In spite of all these reactionary forces working against the spirit of the Parliament, it was a grand success. "The fact that orthodoxy has allowed people of conflicting faiths to express themselves in the same city, without attempting to cut off their heads, or burn them alive speaks volumes for the progress of liberalizing thought."[10] The nineteenth century was plagued by uncertainty and confusion. The people had no fixed goal and therefore they were subject to hope and fear, faith and doubt, optimism and cynicism. People of that century were living in an age which was not inspired by the spiritual insight of the illumined ones and consequently they were bewildered by the dazzling success of their intellectual ability and their dismal failure in the realm of spiritual affairs. This is highlighted by Einstein: "Perfection of means, confusion of the goal, is the characteristic of the age."

This dichotomy between the two worlds — spirit and matter — demanded a synoptic comprehension of Truth embracing both the worlds. To overstep the limited area of human knowledge and embrace Truth in its totality and entirety, has been the supreme longing of philosophers in all ages and climes. To this supreme task Vedanta as interpreted by Swamiji provided the best solution in bringing harmony, making the mind free from nagging confusion and giving the modern people a philosophy of life that can satisfy them intellectually, emotionally and spiritually.

The Parliament of Religions was held in Chicago in 1893 as an adjunct of the World's Columbian Exposition to celebrate the fourth centenary of the discovery of America by Columbus in 1492. This very noble conception of having a Parliament of Religions was the brainchild of Mr. Charles Carroll Bonney, an eminent lawyer. Mr. Bonney developed a cosmopolitan attitude in theology and "believed that there were common essentials by which everyone may be saved in all religions." The demand for a cosmopolitan outlook was in the air. This was highlighted by Rev. Dr. W. R. Alger of New York in his speech at the Parliament: "All over the world the hatred of the professors of religion for one another is irreligion injected into the very core of religion. That is fatal."[11]

The immense popularity of religious liberalism having strong emphasis on the humanitarian impulse, may be gathered from the tremendous enthusiasm shown by the public. "More than seven thousand persons were crowded into the halls of Washington and Columbus."[12] It was a grand and unique Parliament of humanity where religious leaders, eminent philosophers, scientists, and common people assembled. It was indeed a unique phenomenon in the history of the world.

The manner in which this penniless, forlorn monk became the most successful spokesman of Universalism in the Parliament suggests the hand of the inscrutable destiny. Hinduism in the *Bhagavad Gita* gives us a clear picture of the deep mystery of Divine Incarnation.[13] God manifests Himself in a human form wherever *dharma* (righteousness) declines and irreligious impulses prevail: "He did so in the Western world with an appropriate flourish, setting the stage for His appearance there — or, more accurately, for the appearance of His Prophet — 'I had no desire to go to join the Parliament, but Shri Ramakrishna has come to me and insists that I go.' He said, 'You have come to do my work. You will have to go. Know for certain that the Parliament of Religions has been arranged for you'."[14]

Sister Nivedita wrote to Miss MacLeod in 1904 about this communion. Having received the direct command of Shri Ramakrishna, the prophet of religious harmony, Swamiji himself told one of his brother disciples, Swami Turiyananda, at Mount Abu, "The Parliament of Religions is being organized for this (pointing to himself). My mind tells me so. You will see this verified at no distant date."[15] Today it is known to all of us how true was his prediction. Swamiji addressed the Parliament highlighting the broadness of the Vedic religion which has taught the world both tolerance and universal acceptance. And he quoted two well-known verses from the scriptures of Hinduism which are very significant on this point: "As the different streams having their sources in different places all mingle their water in the sea, so, O Lord, the different paths which men take through different tendencies, various though they appear, crooked or straight, all lead to Thee!" And the other: "Whosoever comes to Me, through whatsoever form, I reach Him; all men are struggling through paths which in the end lead to Me." The keynote of his very first address articulated the spirit of the Parliament — its spirit of Universalism — and this made a deep impact on the vast audience and soon after, the vast multitudes outside. "It was like a tongue of flame," says Romain Rolland; "among the gray wastes of cold dissertation it fired the souls of the listening throng."

The reason for the unprecedented and spontaneous oration on his first historic speech has been cited thus: "It was inspired by Swamiji himself and by something unspoken that came through his words, making them not sentiment but fact and recalling some long-forgotten sense of spiritual unity in the hearts of the people — a recollection that would henceforth work in its secret but ineluctable away to change the face of civilization and bring about a true harmony of religions. If for nothing else — and actually there was little else — it was for this, as Swamiji had said, that the Parliament was convened. But few at the time were aware of it."[16]

We may also give here the remark of Christopher Isherwood: "The other delegates to the Parliament were prominent men, admirably representative of their respective creeds. Vivekananda, like his Master, was unknown. For this very reason, his magnificent presence created much speculation among the audience. When he rose to speak, his first words, 'Sisters and Brothers of America,' released one of those mysterious discharges of enthusiasm which seem to be due to an exactly right conjunction of subject, speaker and occasion. People rose from their seats and cheered for several minutes. Vivekananda's speech was short, and not one of his best; but, as an introduction, it was most effective. Henceforward, he was one of the Parliament's outstanding personalities."[17]

We also present the view of Miss Monroe, the then Editor of *Poetry, A Magazine of Verse.* While writing her reminiscences of the Parliament of Religions and of Swamiji in her autobiography entitled *A Poet's Life*, she has impartially stated: "The Congress of Religions was a triumph for all concerned, especially for its generalissimo the Reverend John H. Barrows of Chicago's First Presbyterian Church, who had been preparing it for two years. When he brought down his gavel upon the 'World's First Parliament of Religions,' a wave of breathless silence swept over the audience — it seemed a great moment in human history, prophetic of the promised new era of tolerance and peace. On the stage with him, at his left was a black-coated array of bishops and ministers representing the various Protestant and Roman Catholic Churches; at his right a brilliant group of strangely costumed dignitaries from afar and a monk of the orange robe from Bombay. It was the last of these, Swami Vivekananda, the magnificent, who stole the whole show and captured the town. Others of the foreign groups spoke well. . . But the handsome monk in the orange robe gave us in perfect English a masterpiece. His personality, dominant, magnetic; his voice, rich as a bronze bell; the controlled fervour of his feeling; the beauty of his message to the Western World he was facing for the first time — these combined to give us a rare and perfect moment of supreme emotion. It was human eloquence at its highest pitch."[18] "'This resounding success of the Swami even in this opening session of the Parliament, made him one of the most popular figures in the whole assembly, and at the subsequent sessions,' wrote the *Northampton Daily Herald* on April 11, 1894, 'Vivekananda was not allowed to speak until the close of the programme, the purpose being to make people stay until the end of the session . . . thousands would wait for hours to hear a fifteen minutes' talk from this remarkable man'."[19]

The liberal-minded people were touched by Swamiji's purity of life and his deep conviction of the oneness of humanity. His stupendous personality invigorated, strengthened and awakened the intellect and morale in the congregation. His magnificent eloquence, genuine love for all humanity and his universal outlook made a deep impact on them. Swamiji's speeches did impart to many their own verdure and freshness, impelling them to think in terms of universalism and respect for other faiths. About Swamiji's famous *Paper on Hinduism*, Burke's comment is given: "If some of the ideas which it contained had been presented before, they had never before been presented with such sublime eloquence, nor with the full force behind them of a divine mission. There was actually no ground left for the evangelizing Christians to stand on, for not only Swamiji's paper but Swamiji himself gave proof that Hinduism was a religion that soared to the highest reaches of the Divine — and attained them."[20]

During the entire historic sessions of the Parliament consisting of seventeen days, Swamiji was acclaimed by a consensus of opinion as an "orator by divine right." In the course of his enlightening addresses, Swamiji extolled the dynamic message of Hinduism with its characteristic emphasis on universalism before the entire humanity. He said, "From the high spiritual flights of the Vedanta philosophy of which the latest discoveries of science seem like echoes, to the low ideas of idolatry with its multifarious mythology, the agnosticism of the Buddhists and the atheism of the Jains, each and all have a place in the Hindu's religion . . . Science is nothing but the finding of unity. As soon as science would reach perfect unity, it would stop from further progress, because it would reach the goal . . . and the science of religion [would] become perfect when it would discover Him who is the one life in a universe of death, Him who is the constant basis of an ever-changing world, One who is the only Soul of which all souls are but delusive manifestations. Thus is it, through multiplicity and duality, that the ultimate unity is reached. Religion can go no further. This is the goal of all science. . . . As we find that somehow or other, by the laws of our mental constitution, we have to associate our ideas of infinity with the image of the blue sky, or the sea, so we naturally connect our idea of holiness with the image of a church, a mosque or a cross. . . . The Hindus have associated the ideas of holiness, purity, truth, omnipresence, and such other ideas with different images and forms . . . if a man can realize his divine nature with the help of an image, would it be right to call that a sin? Nor, even when he has passed that stage, should he call it an error. To the Hindu, man is not travelling from error to truth, but from truth to truth, from lower to higher truth. To him all the religions, from the lowest fetishism to the highest absolutism, mean so many attempts of the human soul to grasp and realize the Infinite, each determined by the conditions of its birth and association, and each of these marks a stage of progress; and every soul is a young eagle soaring higher and higher, gathering more and more strength till it reaches the Glorious Sun. . . . To the Hindu, then, the whole world of religions is only a travelling, a coming up, of different men and women, through various conditions and circumstances, to the same goal . . . The Lord has declared to the Hindu in His incarnation as Krishna: 'I am in every religion as the thread through a string of pearls. Whenever thou seest extraordinary holiness and extraodinary power raising and purifying humanity, know thou that I am there'. . . If there is ever to be a universal religion, it must be one which will have no location in place or time; which will be infinite, like the God it will preach, and whose sun will shine upon the followers of Krishna and of Christ, on saints and sinners alike; which will not be Brahminic or Buddhistic, Christian or Mohammedan, but the sum total of all these, and still have infinite space for development; which in its catholicity will embrace in its infinite arms, and find a place for, every human being, from the lowest grovelling savage not far removed from the brute, to the highest man, towering by the virtues of his head and heart almost above humanity, making society stand in awe of him and doubt his human nature. It will be a religion which will have no place for persecution or intolerance in its polity, which will recognize divinity in every man and woman, and whose whole scope, whose whole force, will be centred in aiding humanity to realize its own true, divine nature. Offer such a religion and all nations will follow you.

"May He who is the Brahman of the Hindus, the Ahura Mazda of the Zoroastrians, the Buddha of the Buddhists, the Jehovah of the Jews, the Father-in-Heaven of the Christians, give strength to you to carry out your noble idea.

"The Christian is not to become a Hindu or a Buddhist, nor a Hindu or a Buddhist to become a Christian. But each must assimilate the spirit of the others and yet preserve his individuality and grow according to his own law of growth. If the Parliament of Religions has shown anything to the world it is this: it has proved to the world that holiness, purity and charity are not the exclusive possessions of any church in the world, and that every system has produced men and women of the most exalted character. In the face of this evidence, if anybody dreams of the exclusive survival of his own religion and the destruction of others, I pity him from the bottom of my heart, and point out to him that upon the banner of every religion will soon be written, in spite of resistance: 'Help and not Fight', 'Assimilation and not Destruction', 'Harmony and Peace and not Dissension'."[21]

In Swamiji we find the best spirit of a synthesist. He envisioned a new age in which a new type of humanity, having universal ideas and aspirations, will live together amicably. The East and the West will meet and learn from each other without misgiving, always remembering the great values of each culture. In the remarks of Christopher Isherwood: "No Indian before Vivekananda had ever made Americans and Englishmen accept him on such terms — not as a subservient ally, not as an avowed opponent, but as a sincere well-wisher and friend, equally ready to teach and to learn, to ask for and to offer help." He stood impartially "between the East and the West praising their virtue but condemning the defects of both cultures. Who else could represent in his own person Young India of the Nineties in synthesis with Ancient India of the Vedas? Who else could stand forth as India's champion against poverty and oppression, and yet sincerely praise American idealism and British singleness of purpose? Such was Vivekananda's greatness."[22]

The impact of Swamiji's presence in the Parliament has been assessed by Marie Loiuse Burke: "The descriptions we have of Swamiji at the Parliament of Religions show him as colourful and dynamic, dominating the scene with the force of his personality and the utter purity of his message. He was in the full vigor of his youth, ready to face the entire world and to sacrifice his life for the poor, the ignorant, the oppressed of his motherland. And there was yet another reason for his phenomenal popularity. Never before had the people of America seen one in whom spiritual truths had been fully realized. Though the fact that Swamiji was not consciously known by the thousands who flocked to hear him speak, who waited interminable hours for even a few words by him and who applauded when he simply crossed the platform, the people through some inner knowledge unerringly recognized him for what he was and, from start to finish, instinctively sensed that his very presence conferred a blessing. *Darshan* was unheard of in America, but here at the Parliament was a spontaneous and unconscious manifestation of the attraction of the human soul to the spiritually great."[23] She further adds: "It is undeniable that the American people had not been merely intellectually impressed by the nobility and supreme wisdom of Eastern doctrines which hitherto, in the words of Dr. Alfred Momaric, 'they had been taught to regard with contempt', but they had been touched by and had responded to the tremendous power of living spirituality that Swamiji embodied. Something far more important and more far-reaching had taken place than a mere intellectual appreciation of Eastern religions. It was as though the soul of America had long asked for spiritual sustenance and had now been answered."[24]

12

HUMAN DEVELOPMENT THROUGH WORK

The desire for happiness is a universal one, but the conception of happiness is not. The so-called prosperity of outer life does not hide our emptiness and depression. We have improved many things but not the mind that really enjoys them. We work very hard and work has become an addiction to us. We are workaholics. Our daily preoccupation with work does not give us any time for thoughts of spiritual interest. A thousand thoughts throng in our mind and make us very unhappy. The practical advantages derived from our work no longer are available to serve our purpose but to tyrannize over us. "Things are in the saddle and ride mankind."

Acharya Shankara, the Indian mystic of the 9th century, compared the frothy and superficially learned people to men who get lost in a forest of long and flourishing verbiage. T. S. Elliot echoes the same sentiment in this famous quotation: "Knowledge of speech, but not of silence; knowledge of words, and ignorance of the Word." Hamlet gave eloquent expression in his three-word answer to Polonius' question as to what he was reading: "Words, words, words." As we are lost in the wake of words, so we are equally confused in the midst of enervating and irritating work.

Work, only if done in a spirit of *yoga*, does give an insight about our inner natures. Work, like an X-ray machine, provides us with an X-ray report of our hidden mind. Goethe's famous saying is worth remembering here: "Genius develops in solitude, character in struggling with the world." Work renders service to society. Desire stands behind thought, thought leads to action. Desire is the root of all activities. Laws relating to desire, thought and action, taken together, make up the law of *karma.*

Swami Vivekananda said in this context, "All the actions that we see in the world, all the movements in human society, all the works that we have around us, are simply the display of thought, the manifestation of the will of man. Machines or instruments, cities, ships or men-of-war, all these are simply the manifestation of the will of man; and this will is caused by character, and character is manufactured by *karma*. As is *karma* so is the manifestation of the will."[1] The individual soul consists of will, knowledge and action. The entire superstructure of modern civilization has been developed by the people who envisioned it, willed it and worked for it. We are the product of our own *karma*.

We read in the Upanishad, "One becomes noble through righteous work and ignoble through unrighteous work."[2] We, being the chief architects of our fate, are assured of our highest success, the realization of truth, through our own work geared to achieve this goal. In this short essay, we shall discuss the impact of work on the formation of excellence in human character.

The two words, *karma* and work, are not synonymous. Mechanical work done by inanimate objects is not *karma*. *Karma* is strictly volitional action. Work done by a living agent with the expectation of enjoying the fruits of labor is *karma*. *Karma* is ever associated with self-determination. No volitional action is ever done without having self-consciousness.

The word *karma* has a double meaning: action, and its effects. Swamiji said, "All action is *karma*. Technically, this word also means the effects of actions. In connection with metaphysics, it sometimes means the effects, of which our past actions were the causes."[3] Each *karma* produces a twofold result; one is immediate, the other is remote. Apart from that, each *karma* — physical, verbal, or mental — be it good or evil, leaves on the mind an impression. The character of such impressions depends on the nature of the *karma*; one's character is determined by the impression acquired by his own *karma*. Each person is responsible for his own *karma*. It may be remembered that the human being has the freedom of selecting his course of *karma*. One's future depends absolutely on this. As we sow, so we reap. This is the exacting law of *karma*. With regard to human life, this law is universally valid. Each cause has its corresponding effect. Nature guides the destiny of the subhuman species, whereas the progress of human life is entirely dependent on the strength of righteous life. Hence merit-producing *karma* is so very important. The main struggle in spiritual development is to overcome the obstacles of unrighteous *karma* done in the past.

Karma yoga is the path of action by which the seeker of God gets fulfillment. When the seeker earnestly follows the path of *karma yoga*, God-vision comes. Therefore, every sincere seeker is aware of the consequences of his *karma* and this strong conviction about the inviolable moral law of *karma* guides his conduct. This is explained by Swami Vivekananda, "Every thought that we think, every deed that we do. . . . This is law of *karma*."[4]

Karma yoga converts our work into a powerful means for our spiritual growth. Swamiji said that every *karma* — physical, verbal or mental — leaves an indelible mark on one's character. Man is responsible for his own *karma*. This law rules out fatalism in human life. Work or duty by itself is neither good nor bad, it is the attitude of the mind that determines the effect of *karma* on our character. Hence mind is the source of all bliss as well as the root of all evils. To elucidate this idea, Swamiji said, "If I tell a lie, or cause another to tell one, or approve of another doing so, it is equally sinful. If it is a very mild lie, still it is a lie. Every vicious thought will rebound, every thought of hatred which you may have thought, in a cave even, is stored up, and will one day come back to you with tremendous power in the form of some misery here. If you project hatred and jealousy, they will rebound on you with compound interest. No power can avert them; when once you have put them in motion, you will have to bear them. Remembering this will prevent you from doing wicked things."[5]

"We are what our thoughts have made us, so take care of what you think. Words are secondary. Thoughts live, they travel far. Each thought we think is tinged with our own character. . . ."[6]

Yoga, according to the *Gita*, is the art or skill in the performance of an action.[7] The fruits of action, which are inevitable, can be avoided through *yoga*. The law of *karma* is the counterpart, in the moral world, of the law of cause and effect and the law of conservation of energy in the physical world. This law of *karma* rules out fatalism, accidentalism, and madness in nature. We are conditioned by our past *karma*. This conscious activity of today becomes the unconscious habit of the future. In this way, our entire life-style, habits, character, and mode of thinking, are determined by our actions. Every action produces two kinds of effects. One is the remorse effect that visits us as the fruit of action after a long period and shapes our destiny; the other effect produces a tendency (*samskara*) in our mind. Through good living, it is quite possible to root out the evil ideas from our mind, but the fruits of action do visit us. "For every man shall bear his own burden," said St. Paul.[8]

Swami Vivekananda in his famous *Karma Yoga* gave us a very rational interpretation of this law. He said, "When persons do evil actions, they become more and more evil, and when they begin to do good, they become stronger and stronger and learn to do good at all times."[9] In the same section, after having given a very rational exposition of this law, Swamiji said further, ". . . just as light waves may travel for millions of years before they reach any object, so thought waves may also travel hundreds of years before they meet an object with which they vibrate in unison. It is quite possible, therefore, that this atmosphere of ours is full of such thought pulsations, both good and evil. Every thought projected from every brain goes on pulsating, as it were, until it meets a fit object that will receive it. Any mind which is open to receive some of these impulses will take them immediately. So, when a man is doing evil actions, he has brought his mind to a certain state of tension and all the waves which correspond to that state of tension, and which may be said to be already in the atmosphere, will struggle to enter into his mind. That is why an evildoer generally goes on doing more and more evil. His actions become intensified. Such also will be the case with the doer of good; he will open himself to all the good waves that are in the atmosphere, and his good actions also will become intensified. We run, therefore, a twofold danger in doing evil: first, we open ourselves to all the evil influences surrounding us; secondly, we create evil which affects others, maybe hundreds of years hence. In doing evil we injure ourselves and others also. In doing good we do good to ourselves and to others as well; and, like all other forces in man, these forces of good and evil also gather strength from outside."[10]

Here we may mention that Hinduism, unlike Buddhism and Jainism, does acknowledge the intervention of a gracious God, who is never bound by any law. God is "what makes impossible possible." Devotees do rely upon the redemptive power of God and get themselves relieved of the painful effects of the past *karma*.

To keep our mind from unspiritual thought, we are to be ever vigilant. "Enjoyment is the million-headed serpent that we tread underfoot," said Swamiji. Due to our impulsive nature, we very often indulge in sense enjoyments. Even if they are subtle enjoyments, still they are very dangerous. Hence, Swamiji said, "Think of the power of words! They are a great force in higher philosophy as well as in common life. Day and night we manipulate this force without thought and without inquiry. To know the nature of this force and to use it well is also a part of *karma yoga*."[11]

Karma yoga encompasses the whole of life and moral character plays a vital role in the forces of this *yoga*. Karma is ever associated with self-determination. Our moral action produces certain modifications in our moral life. *Karma* does not bind us exclusively. We have full freedom to enjoy our divine life by following the spirit of *karma yoga*. Swamiji said, "The only way to come out of bondage is to go beyond the limitations of law, to go beyond where causation prevails."

The human being is a conscious agent of his destiny. Hence the doctrine of *karma* is not fatalistic. Swami Vivekananda was one of the greatest champions of the Soul force. He invariably extolled the beauty, majesty, dignity, mystery and potentiality of the Soul lying dormant in all of us. About the sole responsibility of the individual, Swamiji said, "Each one of us is the maker of his own fate. This law knocks on the head at once all doctrines of predestination and fate and gives us the only reconciliation between God and man. We, we, and none else, are responsible for what we suffer. We are the effects, and we are the causes. We are free therefore. If I am unhappy, it has been of my own making, that very thing shows that I can be happy if I will. If I am impure, that is also of my own making, and that very thing shows that I can be pure if I will. The human will stands beyond all circumstance. Before it — the strong, gigantic, infinite will and freedom in man — all the powers, even of nature, must bow down, succumb, and become its servants. This is the result of the law of *karma*."[12]

Virtue purifies our mind and brightens our intellect. Therefore, a virtuous person is able to practise discrimination. Due to his sound judgement and contemplative life, Swamiji gave us an inspiring idealism and practical suggestions to develop our potentiality, work efficiency and moral temperament. He said, "*Karma* in its effects on character is the most tremendous power that man has to deal with. Man is, as it were, a centre, and is attracting all the powers of the universe towards himself, and in this centre is fusing them all and again sending them off in a big current."[13] Society is highly benefited by those people who are pure, loving, unselfish and persons of strong character. Swamiji was never tired of telling us that work held the golden key for our success in life.

Following the precepts of the *Bhagavad Gita*, he told us that life and work always go together. One cannot exist without the other. He further made it crystal-clear that every action of an individual would leave a deep mark on his character. In this manner our actions influence our character and vice versa. This observation impelled him to warn us against carelessness and its disastrous consequences. Every action produces two kinds of results, one cosmic and another individual. The *samskaras*, i.e., the impressions left in the mind, fashion our character. This was Swamiji's opinion: "As pleasure and pain pass before his soul they leave upon it different pictures, and the result of these combined impressions is what is called man's 'character.' If you take the character of any man, it really is but the aggregate of tendencies, the sum total of the bent of his mind; you will find that misery and happiness are equal factors in the formation of that character. Good and evil have an equal share in moulding character, and in some instances misery is a greater teacher than happiness."[14] Hence, our future entirely depends on the quality of the mind that does good work and enables us to have strong character. Swamiji wanted us to cultivate a good moral character through our ceaseless work directed to achieve grand success in spiritual life.

Swamiji gave us a rational and scientific analysis of mind. "*Samskara* can be translated very nearly as 'inherent tendency.' Using the simile of a lake for the mind, every ripple, every wave that rises in the mind, when it subsides, does not die out entirely, but leaves a mark and a future possibility of that wave coming out again. This mark, with the possibility of the wave reappearing, is what is called *samskara*. Every work that we do, every movement of the body, every thought that we think, leaves such an impression on the mind-stuff and even when such impressions are not obvious on the surface, they are sufficiently strong to work beneath the surface, subconsciously. What we are every moment is determined by the sum total of these impressions on the mind. What I am just at this moment is the effect of the sum total of all the impressions of my past life. This is really what is meant by character; each man's character is determined by the sum total of these impressions."[15]

Work or *karma* by itself is a neutral power. Our inner attitude, our motive and purpose do play a great role in shaping the destiny of our life. Good work elevates our soul, and the bad denigrates its image. Good impulses impel us to involve ourselves in creative activities leading to spiritual development. Therefore, to break the sinister influence of unhealthy impulses, we are required to generate a strong will to counteract the evils of lower tendencies of the mind.

The old Adam in us remains subdued to a great extent when we engage ourselves ceaselessly to keep it under control. Swamiji observed that, "When a man has done so much good work and thought so many good thoughts that there is an irresistible tendency in him to do good, in spite of himself and even if he wishes to do evil, his mind, as the sum total of his tendencies, will not allow him to do so; the tendencies will turn him back; he is completely under the influence of the good tendencies. When such is the case, a man's good character is established."[16]

Eternal vigilance being the price of high success in spiritual life, we are to be alert. Knowledge helps us in our daily living. Knowledge about our inner nature can save us from misery and unhappiness. In this context, Swamiji said, "If good impressions prevail, the character becomes good; if bad, it becomes bad. If a man continuously hears bad words, thinks bad thoughts, does bad actions, his mind will be full of bad impressions; and they will influence his thought and work without his being conscious of the fact. In fact, these bad impressions are always working and their result must be evil, and that man will be a bad man; he cannot help it. The sum total of these impressions in him will create the strong motive power for doing bad actions. He will be like a machine in the hands of his impressions, and they will force him to do evil. Similarly, if a man thinks good thoughts and does good works, the sum total of these impressions will be good; and they, in a similar manner, will force him to do good even in spite of himself."[17] This is the fundamental law of our inner nature and that law shapes our destiny. Hence good living is so imperative. To enable us to follow the rugged path of spiritual disciplines we are to follow Swamiji's guidelines. He said, "The mind, to have non-attachment, must be clear, good, and rational. Why should we practise? Because each action is like the pulsations quivering over the surface of the lake. The vibration dies out, and what is left? The *samskaras*, the impressions. When a large number of these impressions are left on the mind, they coalesce and become a habit. It is said, 'Habit is second nature.' It is first nature also and the whole nature of man; everything that we are is the result of habit. That gives us consolation, because if it is only habit, we can make and unmake it at any time. The *samskaras* are left by these vibrations passing out of our mind, each one of them leaving its result. Our character is the sum total of these marks, and according as some particular wave prevails one takes that tone. If good prevails, one becomes good; if wickedness, one becomes wicked; if joyfulness, one becomes happy. The only remedy for bad habits is counter habits; all the bad habits that have left their impressions are to be controlled by good habits. Go on doing good, thinking good thoughts continuously; that is the only way to suppress base impressions. Never say any man is hopeless, because he only represents a character, a bundle of habits, which can be checked by new and better ones. Character is repeated habits and repeated habits alone can reform character."[18]

Swamiji coined a phrase, "secret of work." One of the secrets of work consists in nonattachment to the work itself. Another secret is self-restraint. Swamiji put tremendous emphasis on this self-restraint as a very important factor in the development of human growth. With reference to the effect of such restraint, Swamiji said, "Unselfishness is more paying, only people have not the patience to practise it. It is more paying from the point of view of health also. Love, truth, and unselfishness are not merely moral figures of speech, but they form our highest ideal, because in them lies such a manifestation of power. In the first place, a man who can work for five days, or even for five minutes, without any selfish motive whatever, without thinking of future, of heaven, of punishment, or anything of the kind, has in him the capacity to become a powerful moral giant. It is hard to do it, but in the heart of our hearts we know its value, and the good it brings. It is the greatest manifestation of power — this tremendous restraint; self-restraint is a manifestation of greater power than all outgoing action. A carriage with four horses may rush down a hill unrestrained, or the coachman may curb the horses. Which is the greater manifestation of power, to let them go or to hold them? A cannonball flying through the air goes a long distance and falls. Another is cut short in its flight by striking against a wall, and the impact generates intense heat. All outgoing energy following a selfish motive is frittered away; it will not result in development of power. This self-control will tend to produce a mighty will, a character which makes a Christ or a Buddha. Foolish men do not know this secret; they nevertheless want to rule mankind. Even a fool may rule the whole world if he works and waits. Let him wait a few years, restrain that foolish idea of governing; and when that idea is wholly gone, he will be a power in the world. The majority of us cannot see beyond a few years, just as some animals cannot see beyond a few steps. Just a little narrow circle — that is our world. We have not the patience to look beyond, and thus become immoral and wicked. This is our weakness, our powerlessness."[19] Hence, Swamiji firmly believed that through the path of work or *karma yoga* one can gradually and systematically harness his potential energy and attain a high degree of character development. Work, education and religion are the avenues of character development. Like education and religion, work, too, is a method of gaining spiritual knowledge by gradually removing the obstacles of the mind. How can one gain this knowledge through work? Swamiji threw light on this point, "Now this knowledge, again, is inherent in man. No knowledge comes from outside; it is all inside. What we say a man 'knows,' should, in strict psychological language, be what he 'discovers' or 'unveils'; what a man 'learns' is really what he 'discovers,' by taking the cover off his own soul, which is a mine of infinite knowledge.

"All knowledge, therefore, secular or spiritual, is in the human mind. In many cases it is not discovered, but remains covered, and when the covering is being slowly taken off, we say, 'We are learning,' and the advance of knowledge is made by the advance of this process of uncovering. The man from whom this veil is being lifted is the more knowing man, the man upon whom it lies thick is ignorant, and the man from whom it has entirely gone is all-knowing, omniscient. There have been omniscient men, and, I believe there will be yet; and that there will be myriads of them in the cycles to come. Like fire in a piece of flint, knowledge exists in the mind; suggestion is the friction which brings it out. So with all our feelings and our laughter, our curses and our blessings, our praises and our blames — every one of these we may find, if we calmly study our own selves, to have been brought out from within ourselves by so many blows. The result is what we are. All these blows taken together are called *karma* — work, action. Every mental and physical blow that is given to the soul, by which, as it were, fire is struck from it, and by which its own power and knowledge are discovered, is *karma*, this word being used in its widest sense. Thus we are all doing *karma* all the time. I am talking to you: that is *karma*. . . . We walk: *karma*. Everything we do, physical or mental, is *karma*, and it leaves its marks on us."[20]

The development of a strong moral character, however important it may be, cannot be the end of life. It lays the foundation, but one has to go beyond the realm of morality. Swamiji said, "There is still a higher stage to attain after one has reached the aforesaid condition of unalterable good tendencies of the mind, and that is to be had with an ardent desire for liberation." Swami Vivekananda claimed that even total *mukti* or freedom can be achieved through unselfish work without having faith in God. He remarked, "By work alone men may get to where Buddha got largely by meditation or Christ by prayer."[21] Swamiji said, "The *karma yogi* need not believe even in God, may not ask what his soul is, nor think of any metaphysical speculation. He has got his own special aim of realizing selflessness; and he has to work it out himself."[22]

Swamiji advocated the philosophy of "work for work's sake." It is an independent and direct path of final liberation. In his opinion, loving service, selfless love expressed through work for the welfare of the children of God, was an admirable form of Divine worship. Swamiji earnestly believed that work was worship, if done properly. Swamiji always emphasized that spiritual practices and selfless service are complementary ideals of the Vedanta and the worshipful attitude of work was equated with *jnana*, *bhakti* and *yoga*. His categorical statement was, ". . . spiritual ideal is for life and this must be lived in all spheres, private, social and international." Swamiji further said, "Build up your character and manifest your real nature, the Effulgent, the Resplendent, the Ever-Pure and call It up in everyone you see."[23]

Swamiji added new dimensions to this *yoga*. He widened the scope of this *yoga* by incorporating the ideal devotion to serve God in man. This attitude of a matured devotee, this excellent social expression of Divine love was a unique feature of his *bhakti yoga*. For the first time, he showed that genuine devotion and loving service are complementary ideals of the Vedanta. It is for this magnificent universal ideal that Swamiji offered his dedicated life at the feet of God, who appears as man, and in reality, Vivekananda himself was a new incarnation of his model of devotion and an illustrious exemplar of such *bhakti yoga*.

13

SWAMI VIVEKANANDA ON BHAKTI YOGA

It is interesting to note that Shri Ramakrishna started his spiritual journey as a sincere devotee of the Divine Mother. Due to his tremendous thirst for the vision of the Mother, he continued his sole quest with an unabated zeal to experience that eternal fountain of bliss and immortality. His intense devotion, deep faith and whole-souled prayer, welling forth from the depth of his pure heart, carried him through and gave a fillip to that "possessed life." At last, his excruciating pain and agony were suddenly over, and the joy, peace and enlightenment of divine consciousness were experienced. This sort of great success takes place in the lives of the earnest seekers in all countries. This is due to abiding faith and absolute dependence on God. It should be noted that without the help of anyone, having not much scriptural knowledge, and observing no prescribed method of *sadhana,* Shri Ramakrishna stormed the citadel of divinity solely armed with deep faith and great longing to experience the vision of the Mother.

He saw an infinite, effulgent ocean of consciousness all around him without any trace of matter. This example of Shri Ramakrishna unquestionably puts emphasis on the genuine aspiration alone which brought realization to him. Again, devotion is a fusion of self-effort and self-surrender. We are struck with wonder at the profound vision Shri Ramakrishna achieved through sheer, earnest longing. The complete sincerity and childlike simplicity that come to a genuine seeker due to intense restlessness, the felt want for inner bliss, the craving for absolute peace which is not available in ordinary life — these are the first stirrings of a "possessed soul."

This was incontrovertible proof, at least to Shri Ramakrishna, that the other name of God is Love, the ultimate reality of the universe. God's love may be likened, as Shri Ramakrishna observed, to a magnet. It attracts a devotee to Him as a magnet attracts iron. Devotion is a self-forgetfulness; therefore, steadfast devotion and unconditional loving surrender are regarded as indispensable means to God-realization or the discovery of one's identity with the Divine.

These conditions are fulfilled in Swami Vivekananda's life. He was a devotee par excellence. Here is one instance of his burning passion for God. This is what he related once:

> I went to my study at my grandmother's. As I tried to read I was seized with great fear, as if studying was a terrible thing. My heart struggled within me. I burst into tears; I never wept so bitterly in my life. I left my books and ran away. I ran along the streets. My shoes slipped from my feet — I did not know where. I ran past a haystack and got hay all over me. I kept on running along the road to Cossipore.[1]

The Master himself made a remarkable statement about Swamiji's devotion. At Cossipore, Shri Ramakrishna affectionately stroked his face and hands, and said, "Your face and hands show that you are a *bhakta*. But the *jnani* has different features; they are dry."[2]

M., the chronicler of the *Gospel of Sri Ramakrishna*, giving his first account of young Narendranath, whom he saw at the Kali Temple, wrote, "His eyes were bright, his words were full of spirit, and he had the look of a lover of God."[3] Swamiji himself once told one of his disciples, "I am all *jnana* without; but within my heart, it is all *bhakti.*"

The intelligent and perceptive reader, having a real insight into Swamiji's *Complete Works,* will discover in him an outstanding devotee of a different character. Devotion to God, who is immanent in creation, was the singular object of his life and, therefore, this attitude of devotion was very much pronounced in his entire personality and activities. He saw God in the world and, therefore, he exhorted us to deify the world. He was a monist out and out, but his whole attitude towards the world was very different:

> Swamiji had the head of Shankara and the heart of Sri Chaitanya, the eyes of a monist and the hands of a monotheist, the tenacity of a scholar and the tenderness of a lover, the devotion of a theist

and the spirit of service of a humanist. His was a humanistic monism.[4]

Swamiji was an illumined soul of a high order and his discipleship under Shri Ramakrishna gave him the rare privilege to develop a synthetic view of reality and life. He clearly experienced "the oneness of the macrocosm with the microcosm." The impact of his personal realization, added to his exposure to Shri Ramakrishna, gave a distinctive colour and a convincing voice of authority throughout his spiritual ministry. This modern exemplar of Vedanta will be best remembered for his genius in developing a synthetic view of life, as well as for his extraordinary capacity to help people irrigate the parched lands of life with the life-giving water of Vedantic wisdom formerly used by the mystics only. Devotion to God was given a new turn by him to usher a new spiritual culture based on the holistic approach enabling us to see and serve God in the world.

Swamiji was a modern exponent of Vedanta. Rooted firmly in the life-giving message of Vedanta, and with the help of his rare insight, Swamiji came to the rescue of the common people struggling for existence. Soul is one with God and, therefore, the very purpose of devotion is to find our own individual life in the universal life. With this maturity, the devotee realizes the presence of God in all affairs of life and thereby he becomes an instrument of social welfare.

Swamiji in his *Bhakti Yoga*, after reviewing all the fundamental concepts of devotion, finally was captivated by the beauty of the great prayer articulated by Prahlada. His great heart was very much touched by the majesty of this lofty prayer. *The Vishnu Purana* records the prayer as follows:

> That deathless love which the ignorant have for the fleeting objects of the senses — as I keep meditating on Thee — may not that love slip from my heart.[5]

From this idea of *bhakti*, Swamiji wants us to worship God through our activities. By following the precept of this *yoga* — which is the easiest of all *yogas*, as he said frequently — one can direct one's natural impulse of love to God who is immanent in the world. God or infinite love being the only source of our love impulse, it can be easily focused on God through this *yoga.* Our love is nothing but the manifestation of Divine Love within us. It can be purified, magnified and perfected through this *yoga.* Therefore, Swamiji equated devotion with the Godward movement of our thoughts, words and deeds. He wanted us to direct this impulse to higher levels.

In this context, we may remember his famous lecture, *God In Everything*, delivered in London on October 27, 1896. In that lecture he said,

> What Vedanta seeks to teach . . . is the deification of the world, . . . giving up the world as we think of it, as it appears to us. Deify it, it is God alone. We read at the commencement of one of the oldest Upanishads, 'Whatever exists in this universe is to be covered with the Lord.'[6]

So Swamiji accepted Prahlada as a model of devotion and exhorted us to cultivate an intimate, loving relationship with God. He said:

> *Bhakti* is not destructive, it teaches us that not one of the faculties we have has been given in vain, that through them is the natural way to come to liberation. *Bhakti* does not kill out our tendencies, it does not go against nature, but only gives it a higher and more powerful direction. How naturally we love the objects of the senses! We cannot but do so, because they are so real to us. . . . And when the same kind of love that has before been given to sense-objects is given to God, it is called *bhakti.*[7]

Real devotion welling forth from the depths of the pure heart possesses the entire being of the devotee. Swamiji did not approve of devotion originating from any weakness, sin or fear. He says, "The central idea of ours is that there is no thought of fear. It is always love of God."[8]

Devotion involves unconditional faith in God, who is regarded as the ground of our being. The devotee prefers a personal aspect of God to an Impersonal one, as the very nature of devotion can be fruitful only in relation to a Personal God. Maturity in spiritual life gives us an insight that the Brahman of the *jnanis* is also the God of the devotee. Brahman is both Personal and Impersonal. The devotee has to offer his or her devotion to Brahman as seen "through the mist of the senses." Personal God is neither different from Brahman nor inferior to Him. Swamiji said:

> It has always to be understood that the personal God worshipped by the *bhakta* is not separate or different from Brahman. All is Brahman, the one without a second; only Brahman, as Unity or Absolute, is too much of an abstraction to be loved and worshipped; so the *bhakta* chooses the relative aspect of Brahman, that is *Ishwara*, the Supreme Ruler.[9]

So ultimately the same goal is reached by the devotee and the *jnani*. Divinity is not a mere nameless and formless entity. On the other hand, it is a living consciousness capable of assuming a tangible personal form.

So the devotee's Personal God is not "purely anthropomorphic, who like a great potentate in this world is pleased with some or displeased with others."[10] Devotees worship a Personal God as they love one another. Momentary religious enthusiasm is no good. It may be only a beginning. Without the development of a strong moral character, it is not possible to sustain genuine devotion enabling us to love all and hate none. The *Gita* delineates the essential qualifications of a devotee.[11] The real characteristics of a devotee are purity, love and loyalty to the chosen diety. The words 'loyalty' and 'faith' are very confusing, as the fanatics of all religions have tarnished the fair image of religious life due to their immaturity, narrowness and hatred. For this reason Swamiji said, "The fanatical crew in Hinduism or Islam or Christianity have always been almost exclusively recruited from these worshippers on the lower planes of *bhakti*."[12] Faith in and loyalty to God, if genuine, will expand our spiritual consciousness.

Swamiji always and invariably gave the highest importance to the development of moral character, which alone can protect a devotee from all sorts of weakness. "Character is repeated habit, and repeated habit alone can reform character" which can face the most difficult situations. It can never be built overnight. "Upon ages of struggle a character is built." It "has to be established through a thousand stumbles."[13]

Devotion, to be real and abiding, is never a cheap sentiment or emotion. A real devotee wants to overcome his or her weakness by being close to God. This urge to transcend one's limitations through sincere devotion is a spiritual compulsion. There is place for genuine emotion in the growth of a devotee but everything has to be judged from the standpoint of real spiritual evolution. To use the words of Christ, "By their fruits ye shall know them." In a genuine devotee aspiring after divine life, the "love of the pleasure of the senses and of the intellect is all made dim and thrown aside and cast into the shade by the love of God Himself," said Swamiji. Swamiji never spared the pseudo-devotees and gave timely warning to the real seekers of God against the pitfalls of sentimentalism:

> The effusion of sentiment which is not attended by a corresponding transformation of character, which is strong enough to destroy the craving of lust and gold by awakening in the heart an enthusiasm for the vision of God, is neither deep nor of any real value in the realm of spirituality. Physical contortions, tears, horripilations, and even momentary trances which result from this wrong emotion are, in reality, hysterical. These should be controlled by a determined effort . . . If that fails, one should take a nutritious diet or even consult a doctor. For unconsciously you are feigning these things. It is only in the rare individuals of gigantic spirituality that those emotions, overflowing the walls of restraint and appearing as trance or the shedding of tears, etc. are genuine. But ignorant people do not realize this and think that these outward symptoms, of themselves, indicate deep spiritual fervour. So instead of practising restraint, devotion and renunciation, they studiously cultivate these effusions with the result that their weakened nerves respond in this way to the slightest religious stimulus. If this is allowed to go on unchecked, the result is physical and mental disaster. Of one hundred persons who take up the spiritual life, eighty turn out to be charlatans and

> fifteen become insane. Only the remaining five may be blessed with a vision of real truth. Therefore beware.[14]

Bhakti in its lower form indulges in emotional display, what Swamiji called sentimental nonsense. Devotees give vent to their emotional outbursts through ritual, symbols, songs and dances. Said Swamiji, "People having no self-control indulging in such songs! Even the slightest impurity is a great hindrance to the conceptions of these ideals. It is a joke!" Swamiji never denounced these rituals, symbols, songs and dances summarily but accepted them in right places and said, "Without it there would be nothing but intellect here (pointing to his forehead) and dry thought." These are part and parcel of *bhakti yoga.* Matured devotees transcend them and keep their mind on God. They deepen their spiritual life through various means. Swamiji said:

> It is necessary always to remember that forms and ceremonies, though absolutely necessary for the progressive soul, have no other value than taking us on to that state in which we feel most intense love for God.[15]

With the quickening of spiritual life, devotion assumes the form of *para-bhakti.* In that phase of spiritual evolution, all weakness gets burnt up. Swamiji said:

> That love of God grows and assumes a form which is called *para-bhakti* or supreme devotion. Forms vanish, rituals fly away, books are superseded; images, temples, churches, religions and sects, countries and nationalities — all these little limitations and bondages fall off by their own nature from him who knows this love of God. Nothing remains to bind him or fetter his freedom. A ship, all of a sudden, comes near a magnetic rock, and its iron bolts and bars are all attracted and drawn out, and the planks get loosened and freely float on the water. Divine grace thus loosens the binding bolts and bars of the soul, and it becomes free. So in this renunciation auxiliary to devotion, there is no harshness, no dryness, no struggle, nor repression nor suppression. The *bhakta* does not have to suppress any single one of his emotions, he only strives to intensify them and direct them to God.[16]

Bhakti has two stages: *gauni-bhakti* or preparatory devotion, and *para-bhakti* or *prema-bhakti.* The former is for beginners when love for God demands external support, and the latter is for the matured devotee whose love for God is spontaneous. *Bhakti* when matured is called *para-bhakti.* When love is purified and well-regulated, God reveals Himself in the pure mind of the devotee and gradually the enlightened devotee realizes the illusoriness of worldly happiness. Love helps a devotee to find his or her higher Self. Swamiji defined *bhakti* as the irresistible teleological demand in us to expand and reach God. Love is a psychological phenomenon and its systematic cultivation helps evolve human personality. In the beginning it is crude, narrow, instinctive, and emotional. In its higher phases, the devotee is impelled by the inexorable teleological urge in him or her to attain that supreme perfection. All emotional vestiges are burnt up in the pure fire of true love. At this point there is no difference between *bhakti* and *jnana.* Swamiji delineated the evolutionary passage of this idea as follows:

> We are passing through all these different loves — love of children, father, mother, and so forth. We slowly exercise the faculty of love; but in the majority of cases we never learn anything from it, we become bound to one step, to one person. In some cases men come out of this bondage. Men are ever running after wives and wealth and fame in this world; sometimes they are hit very hard on the head, and they find out what this world really is! No one in this world can really love anything but God. Man finds out that human love is all hollow. Men cannot love though they talk of it. A finite subject cannot love, nor a finite object be loved: when the object of the love of a man is dying every moment, and his mind also is constantly changing as he grows, what eternal love can you expect to find in the world? There cannot be any real love but in God: why then all these loves? These are mere stages. There is a power behind, impelling us forward, we do not know where, to seek for the real object, but this love is sending us forward in search of it. Again and again we find out our mistake. We grasp something, and find it slips through our fingers, and then we grasp something else. Thus on and on we go, till at last comes light; we come to God,

the only one who loves. His love knows no change and is ever ready to take us in."[17]

Swamiji visualized the noble character of a devotee in whom "knowledge, and love and *yoga* are harmoniously fused." This is *para-bhakti*, when the devotee is being "possessed by God" and constantly meditates on Him as the needle of the compass. *Bhakti yoga* is followed by a certain type of devotee whose heart is tender, sensitive and overflowing with faith. He is not interested in dry, intellectual, hair-splitting talks, but finds peace in worshipping God, the fountain of love. Love expands one's consciousness and quickens the faculty of reason, and ultimately transforms the life — and this is the eventual goal of all paths.

The popular notion that devotion is inferior to knowledge is irrelevant. Down the ages, this misconception has been the cause of a good deal of misunderstanding among the various sects in India. Being a prophet of the synthetic attitude toward reality and life, Swamiji never indulged in such meaningless arguments. His discipleship under Shri Ramakrishna and his own spiritual wisdom enabled him to appreciate the beauty and strength of each path. He had no difficulty in reconciling them. Swamiji provided the rationale of his matured synthetic view as follows: "There is not really so much difference between knowledge (*jnana*) and love (*bhakti*) as people sometimes imagine. We shall see, as we go on, that in the end they converge and meet at the same point."[18]

Swamiji has given guidelines for a person seeking fulfillment in this path. The devotee has to find a genuine teacher. The teacher should live a holy life, follow the spirit of the scriptures, and accept students out of unselfish love. The student, on the other hand, is expected to cultivate the spirit of renunciation, deep faith and sincerity. The earnestness to follow the instruction given to him is very important. Apart from that, the teacher instructs the students in a specific way. The student is asked to repeat and meditate on a sacred *mantra*, a word-symbol. When followed with deep faith and earnestness, this practice produces peace and enlightenment. Of all the sound-symbols, the most universal is "OM," the matrix of all sounds. "OM represents the whole phenomena of sound-producing." "OM" has become the one very sacred symbol for the Hindus. God's "highest name is OM."[19] Repetition of the holiest of the holy "word" quickens one's progress in spiritual life.

As regards the spiritual teacher, Swamiji gave the highest place to the incarnations of God, who can redeem millions through their grace. In them we find the manifestation of the redemptive power of God. They are also epoch-makers. Our history testifies to that. About incarnations, Swamiji said:

> Higher and nobler than all ordinary ones are another set of teachers, the *Avataras* of *Ishwara*, in the world. They can transmit spirituality with a touch, even with a mere wish. The lowest and the most degraded characters become in one second saints at their command. They are the Teachers of all teachers, the highest manifestations of God through man. We cannot see God except through them. We cannot help worshipping them; and they are the only ones whom we are bound to worship.
>
> No man can really see God except through these human manifestations. If we try to see God otherwise, we make for ourselves a hideous caricature of Him and believe the caricature to be no worse than the original.[20]

To reach the goal, Swamiji advised the devotee to intensely practise the traditional *navavidha bhakti* (ninefold devotional discipline), to earnestly develop certain qualities of mind, such as discrimination and renunciation, and to discharge one's duties with the worshipful attitude of an offering to God.

Purity of mind leads to success in spiritual life and, therefore, moral virtues are to be practised with all sincerity. By consistent endeavour, the beginner is able to mount the higher ladder of devotional life which is known as *para-bhakti,* the supreme, selfless devotion for God. The progress of a devotee takes place gradually through the following stages:

- *Shraddha* — deep and abiding faith in oneself, faith in the power of truth and goodness. This positive attitude is the impelling force behind the practice of the discipline of the devotee.

- Natural happiness in the thought of God.
- Intense longing for God.
- Living only for the sake of God, having all other desires fully burnt up.
- Complete forgetfulness of one's identity and consequently having a God-centred mind. This is also known as complete resignation to God.

This sort of growth of mind is brought about by eliminating selfishness through the purification of love. This stage is called *para-bhakti*, the supreme love. Swamiji often compared love to a triangle having three angles. The first angle of the triangle of love is absolute unselfishness, the second and third being fearlessness and the absence of rivalry. Love is a power coming from God, given to all of us to bind God with the silken thread of sweet devotion. After passing through earlier stages of *vaidhi-bhakti* (the stage of obedience to regulations, which are like fences to protect the tender plant of love), the qualified devotee develops *para-bhakti* which leads to the consummation of *bhakti*, when the ego is lost in divine ecstasy. This is the pure "gold" of love from which all weakness has been eliminated.

To deepen this love, the devotee constantly remembers God, his or her Beloved. This path does not demand the absolute renunciation prescribed in *jnana yoga*. The devotee is to redirect his or her passions and emotions towards the chosen ideal. This path is the least violent. All the emphasis is on the whole-souled devotion to God and this enables the devotee, almost automatically, to practise detachment. The devotee develops, slowly and patiently, a particular attitude toward the object of adoration. This is known as *bhava*. It is an attitude of a devotee in the form of a persistent relationship with God. *Bhava* is strictly personal and confidential. Spiritual *sadhana* demands that one should focus the mind on God and develop a specific relationship with him. This is very important as it controls the entire lifecurrent of the devotee.

Having gone through preliminary disciplines, the devotee has to set his or her mind on actual practice followed in this lower stage (*gauni-bhakti*). In the practice of this path, the devotee invariably accepts various symbols of God, such as rituals, images, *mantras*, divine forms, and spectacular natural phenomena like the sun, the moon, the sky, etc. These are helpful for contemplation on God and to deepen one's devotion. They are known as *pratikas*. Swamiji holds that when a devotee worships God through *pratikas*, it leads to *bhakti* and *mukti*. Here, the image — *pratima* or *pratika* — is used as a substitute or a suggestion thereof for God. The devotee does not worship the image as image, but he worships God in and through the image.

Image worship becomes idolatry when worship is done to propitiate the deity for various selfish desires. An image is helpful to concentrate the mind on God. Swamiji discusses also the importance of *ishta-nistha*, "steadfast devotion to the chosen ideal." Here Swamiji upholds the glory of Vedanta, which is all-inclusive. He says:

> Every sect of every religion presents only one ideal of its own to mankind, but the eternal Vedantic religion opens to mankind an infinite number of doors for progress into the inner shrine of divinity, and places before humanity an almost inexhaustible array of ideals, there being in each of them a manifestation of the Eternal One. With the kindest solicitude, Vedanta points out to aspiring men and women the numerous roads hewn out of the solid rock of the realities of human life, by the glorious sons, or human manifestations, of God, in the past and in the present, and stands with out-stretched arms to welcome all — to welcome even those that are yet to be — to that Home of Truth and that Ocean of Bliss, wherein the human soul, liberated from the net of *maya*, may transport itself with perfect freedom and with eternal joy.[21]

Swamiji also gave importance to prayer, *japa*, etc., to develop devotion.

Bhakti yoga, when practised, will lead the devotee to reach the highest goal of life, and thereby the devotee will love the whole universe, which is looked upon as the body of God. When devotion is fully matured, when divine love fully "possesses" the devotee, his or her ideas, ideals, and attitude to the world undergo a thorough change. The divine intoxication is so overwhelming and captivating that a real devotee rejects even the idea of liberation and keeps himself or herself engaged in the loving service of God. This is exemplified in Swamiji's own life.

Love, according to Swamiji, is a divine gift. God is the Love that implants the seed of love in the heart of all beings, with the expectation to be bound by their love. God is the Love that lifts up the lowly to the reach of the lofty. The love that we experience in our individual and social life stems from the same source. The entire universe, to a real devotee, is saturated with divine Love. Hence the Love within is finding expression without. The devotee feels the all-encompassing love for everything, as he or she sees that "God alone has become everything." This acme of spiritual growth is the highest consummation of pure devotion. As Swamiji said:

> We all begin with love for ourselves, and the unfair claims of the little self make even love selfish. At last, however, comes the full blaze of light, in which this little self is seen to have become one with the Infinite. Man himself is transfigured in the presence of this light of Love, and he realizes at last the beautiful and inspiring truth that Love, the Lover, and the Beloved are one.[22]

Rooted in Vedanta, Swamiji chalked out a programme for human welfare in the concept of divinity of a person. When this Soul-force is aroused, life is transformed. Swamiji was an incarnation of manliness, fearlessness, and strength that stemmed from his own spiritual experience of the immortality of the Self. Therefore, Swamiji always and incessantly extolled the beauty of the Self. Unlike other saints and sages of the world, he gave maximum importance to the cultivation of Soul-force for a devotee. Devotion, to be real and sustaining, must grow from Soul-consciousness, the fountain of Love.

14

SWAMI VIVEKANANDA, A MYSTIC

The advancement of science and technology, the uncertainty about the goal of life, the zeal for sensuous enjoyment and the lack of spiritual vision have made us restless, insecure and depressed. The complexity of modern living, a deep-rooted horror of being confined to the abhorrent ego — our insulated puny self — have made us cynics. We are alienated from our spiritual heritage, from nature and from ourselves. A false concept of philosophy that interprets the universe to be soulless, a machine made of matter, governed by natural laws having no spiritual element behind it, cannot be accepted as a sane philosophy. Science and technology have their own spells on our mind; disbelief has its own fascination, glamour of superficial life its own enchantment. But are we really happy? Fear, hopelessness, and insecurity have gripped our minds. This tragic sense of futility in the midst of plenty finds an eloquent expression in the writing of Bertrand Russell who was but a mouthpiece of the age. Said Russell, "Brief and powerless is Man's life; on him and all his race the slow, sure doom falls pitiless and dark. Blind to good and evil, reckless of destruction, omnipotent matter rolls on its relentless way; for Man, condemned today to lose his dearest, tomorrow himself to pass through the gate of darkness, it remains only to cherish, ere yet the blow falls, the lofty thoughts that ennoble his little day; disdaining the coward terrors of the slave of Fate, to worship at the shrine that his own hands have built; undismayed by the empire of chance, to preserve a mind free from the wanton tyranny that rules his outward life; proudly defiant of the irresistible forces that tolerate, for a moment, his knowledge and his condemnation, to sustain alone, a weary but unyielding Atlas, the world that his own ideals have fashioned despite the trampling march of unconscious power."[1]

But there are people who refuse to accept this mood of depression, this inexorable fate of doom. The desire to believe is inveterate in us and the tendency of self-enquiry is evident. In human history we invariably find a deep and abiding faith in

God — the supreme creative force, behind and in the universe, Who manifests Himself as infinite energy in Nature, as vitality in life, as moral conscience in human beings, as the sole source of Truth, beauty and order — brings prosperity as well as spiritual growth. To search for the meaning of life is natural in us. "Man is declared," says Plato, "to be that creature who is constantly in search of himself, a creature who at every moment of his existence must examine and scrutinize the condition of his existence. He is a being in search of meaning." An urge to self-transcendence is common with us along with self-assertion. In our desperate struggle to attain spiritual freedom we do need a living faith. Authentic mystics can implant faith in us through their illumined lives. They are the greatest benefactors of humanity. Arnold Toynbee in his *Civilization on Trial*, has endorsed this view.[2] Fear imprisons, paralyses, and disheartens us but a living faith liberates and inspires us. These mystics alone create that deep faith in transcendental truth, bestow incorporeal bliss and help transform our consciousness steeped in fear, doubt and hopelessness.

Mysticism should not be equated with misty, foggy, vague or sloppy occultism. Mysticism is essentially a moral discipline and therefore spiritual in its character; it is always in search for God who is within as well as without. There is no contradiction between rationalism and mysticism; the methods being different. In the former, intellect and reason dominate; in the latter, there is no conscious reasoning or inference. The perception of God is immediate and spontaneous to the mystic. It is gained, as it were, in a flash — "unannounced and unheralded." The mystic invariably gets the vision of truth that the whole Universe is within himself; he is but a microcosm of the macrocosm. Genuine mystics always sternly disapprove of false mysticism, which encourages the acquisition of occult powers, name and fame without seeking the highest goal of life. Indian mystics condemn these miraculous powers as hindrances and obstacles to final union with God. From Patanjali to Shri Ramakrishna, this attitude is universal. Ramakrishna's attitude is well-known on this point. True mystical experience or rather "mystical consciousness" gives us an "integrated thought," "a meaningful whole." It is the outcome of a true vision of truth — stemming from the depth of a pure heart. "Mysticism is the art of union with reality. The mystic is a person who has attained that union in a greater or lesser degree; or who aims at and believes in such attainment."[3] Russell wants to include many thinkers genuinely devoted to have an inkling of intellectual comprehension of truth. "Mysticism is, in essence, little more than a certain intensity and depth of feeling in regard to what is believed about the universe . . ."[4]

Swami Vivekananda was a mystic par excellence. He experienced *nirvikalpa samadhi*. His intuitive experience of reality transcended all determinations, and was above the distinction of subject and object. The consciousness of duality is completely absent in this state and the individual gets himself lost in the universal Self and enjoys undifferentiated bliss. The mystic is very rare. In this world we find "a small group of men who teach religion from experience. They are called mystics, and mystics in every religion speak the same tongue and teach the same truth. This is the real science of religion."[5] From our modern cynicism and insecurity, Swami Vivekananda, a modern mystic, can redeem us. Humanity is sure to get an insight of a living faith, a healthy value of living and the assurance of supreme enlightenment from him. The mystic Vivekananda opens a new vista of saving wisdom to the fear-stricken people of the modern world. Through his spiritual experience, he saw only divinity in the world of matter. In his famous lecture, *God In Everything* (delivered in London, on October 27, 1896) Swamiji said, "The whole world is full of the Lord. Open your eyes and see Him. This is what Vedanta teaches. Give up the world which you have conjectured, because your conjecture was based upon a very partial experience, upon very poor reasoning, and upon your own weakness. Give it up; the world we have been thinking of so long, the world to which we have been clinging so long, is a false world of our own creation. Give that up; open your eyes and see that as such it never existed; it was dream, *maya*. What existed was the Lord Himself. It is He who is in the child, in the wife, and in the husband; it is He who is in the good and in the bad; He is in the sin and the sinner; He is in life and in death."[6] Again he says, "We are the children of the Almighty, we are the sparks of the infinite; divine fire. How can we be nothing? We are everything, ready to do everything, we can do everything, and man must do everything. This faith in themselves was in the hearts of our ancestors, this faith in themselves was the motive power that pushed them forward and forward in the march of civilization; and if there has been degeneration, if there has been defect, mark my words, you will find that degradation to have started on the day our people lost this faith in themselves. Losing faith in one's self means losing faith in God. Do you believe in that good Providence working in and through you? If you believe that this omnipresent One, the *Antaryamin*, is present in every atom, is through and through, *ota-prota*, as the Sanskrit word goes, penetrating your body, mind, and soul, how can you lose heart?"[7]

In this short essay we shall study various mystical experiences of Swamiji for our own benefit. His great life, experiences, and teachings may help remove the cobwebs of die-hard ignorance. In his enlightened vision the objective world was transfigured in such a manner that divinity alone was seen in and through the world of matter.

Swamiji was an adept in meditation. He was *dhyana-siddha* even from his very birth. At four or five he was found "motionless in deep meditation." One evening he was meditating or rather keeping himself engaged in this "pastime" along with a few friends. Noticing a big cobra, others immediately took to their heels. Even the loud shouting of his friends could not disturb him in the least. The snake suddenly glided away. Later, on enquiry, Naren said, "I knew nothing of the snake or of anything else; I was feeling inexpressible bliss." Every night he used to fall asleep in a strange manner. No sooner had he closed his eyes than he saw between his eyebrows "a wonderful spot of light changing hues, which would expand and burst and bathe his whole body in a flood of white radiance. As his mind became preoccupied with this phenomenon, his body would fall asleep. It was a daily occurrence which he would court by lying down on his chest; as soon as drowsiness overtook him, the light appeared." His pronounced simplicity was revealed at his enquiry of this experience. He took it for granted that it was very natural with everyone. In later years, Ramakrishna asked him about it. "Naren, my boy, do you see light when you go to sleep?" This natural experience continued throughout his life in some form or other. About this experience, Sister Nivedita has given us the following information: "In later life, he would often mention this question and digress, to describe the light he saw. Sometimes it would come as a ball, which a boy was kicking towards him. It would draw nearer. He would be on one side with it, and all would be forgotten. Sometimes it was a blaze, into which he would enter."[8] From Swamiji we get the information that he began to meditate at an early age. Sister Nivedita told, "When he was only eight years old, sitting at play, he had developed the power of entering into *samadhi*."[9] About this art of meditation Swamiji gave us an inkling in his speech, delivered in California on January 5, 1900. "I know very little of this science (of the mind), but the little that I gained I worked for thirty years of my life, and for six years I have been telling people the little that I know. It took me thirty years to learn it; thirty years of hard struggle. Sometimes I worked at it twenty hours during the twenty-four; sometimes I slept only one hour in the night; sometimes I worked whole nights; sometimes I lived in places where there was hardly a sound, hardly a breath; sometimes I had to live in caves. Think of that. And yet I know little or nothing; I have barely touched the hem of the garment of this science. But I can understand that it is true and vast and wonderful."[10]

It was *maharshi* Devendranath Tagore, who told him, "All the marks of a *yogi* are manifested in you; you will win quick success if you practise meditation." Narendranath did practise secretly every night; sometime this practice lasted the whole night. In later years Swamiji gave indication of his early days to his English disciple, Mr. Sturdy: "In my childhood I used to feel that same power was growing within me, that it was spreading within and beyond me, making me restless, unable to keep quiet. . . ."[11] Narendranath had one notable experience, maybe during this period. Due to his sincere regular meditative habit he saw a vision of "a luminous figure." Later, Swamiji thought it was the Lord Buddha. Questioned about this experience of visions, Swamiji narrated the following to Sarat Chandra Chakravarty, his disciple: "While at school, one night I was meditating within closed doors and had a fairly deep concentration of mind. How long I meditated in that way, I cannot say. It was over, and I still kept my seat, when from the southern wall of that room a luminous figure stepped out and stood in front of me. There was a wonderful radiance on its visage, yet there seemed to be no play of emotion on it. It was the figure of a *sannyasin* absolutely calm, shaven-headed, and staff and *kamandalu* (a *sannyāsin's* wooden water-bowl) in hand. He gazed at me for some time and seemed as if he would address me. I too gazed at him in speechless wonder. Then a kind of fright seized me, I opened the door, and hurried out of the room. Then it struck me that it was foolish of me to run away like that, that perhaps he might say something to me. But I have never met that figure since. Many a time and often have I thought if again I saw him, I would no more be afraid but would speak to him. But I met him no more."[12] Swamiji also gave hints of the quality of the mind prone to such experience. "When the mind is purified, when one is free from the attachment for lust and gold, one sees lots of visions, most wonderful ones! But one should not pay heed to them. The aspirant cannot advance further if he sets his mind constantly on them. Haven't you heard that Shri Ramakrishna used to say, 'Countless jewels lie uncared for in the outer courts of my beloved Lord's sanctum'? We must come face to face with the Atman; what is the use of setting one's mind on vagaries like those?"[13] In 1877, Narendranath had to take his mother, brother, and one sister to Raipur. The party took a train up to Nagpur and thereafter engaged a bullock-cart to reach Raipur. It was indeed a great ordeal to travel in a bullock-cart for more than a fortnight through deep forests filled with wild animals. In spite of the many trials and tribulations of such a hazardous journey, the young Narendranath was fascinated by the scenic beauty of the forest. His innocent mind was filled up with devotion of God who created this magnificent beauty. He told later: "What I saw and felt when going through the forest has forever remained firmly imprinted on my memory, particularly a certain event of one day. We had to travel by the foot of the Vindhya mountains that day. The peaks of the ranges on both sides of the road rose very high in the sky; various kinds of trees and creepers bending under the weight of fruits and flowers produced wonderful beauty on the mountainsides. Birds of various colours, flying from tree to tree, filled the quarters with sweet notes. I saw all these and felt an extraordinary peace in my mind. The slow-moving bullock-cart arrived at a place where two mountain peaks coming forward as though in love, locked themselves in an embrace over the narrow forest path. Observing carefully below the meeting-points I saw that there was a very big cleft from the crest to the foot of the mountain on one side of the path; and filling that cleft, there was hanging in it an enormous honeycomb, the result of the bees' labour for ages. Filled with wonder, as I was pondering over the beginning and the end of that kingdom of bees, my mind became so much absorbed in the thought of the infinite power of God, the controller of the three worlds, that I completely lost my consciousness of the external world for some time. I do not remember how long I was lying in the bullock-cart in that condition. When I regained normal consciousness, I found that we had crossed that place and come far away. As I was alone in that cart, no one could know anything about it."[14]

Narendranath first came to know about Ramakrishna — his future spiritual teacher — through his college principal, William Hastie. While explaining Wordsworth's *Excursion*, Hastie exhorted his students to see Ramakrishna Paramahamsa who enjoys such trances like that of the "Wanderer" depicted by the poet. Narendranath met Shri Ramakrishna at Dakshineshwar. On his second visit, he had an experience of extraordinary character, when he was touched by Ramakrishna. About this Narendranath said: ". . . The touch at once gave rise to a novel experience within me. With my eyes open I saw that the walls, and everything in the room, whirled rapidly and vanished into naught, and the whole universe together with my individuality was about to merge in an all-encompassing mysterious void!"[15] Narendranath was captivated by the loving and sweet personality of Ramakrishna. Intimacy grew between them as time rolled on. One day at Dakshineshwar, Ramakrishna was trying to impart the highest teaching of Advaita Vedanta — the identity of the individual soul with Brahman. Narendranath remained unconvinced and left the room. Even Narendranath spoke derisively while talking with Hazra about it. Sensing Narendranath's criticism, Ramakrishna touched him in a semiconscious state. The effect of the touch was given by Narendranath as follows: "The magic touch of the Master that day immediately brought a wonderful change over my mind. I was astounded to find that really there was nothing in the universe but God! I saw it quite clearly, but kept silent to see whether the impression would last; but it did not abate in the course of the day. I returned home, but there too, everything I saw appeared to be Brahman. I sat down to take my meal, but found that everything — the food, the plate, the person who served, and even myself — was nothing but that. I ate a morsel or two and sat still. I was startled by my mother's words, 'Why do you sit still? Finish your meal,' and then began to eat again. But all the while, whether eating or lying down, or going to college, I had the same experience and felt myself always in a sort of trance. While walking the streets, I noticed cabs plying, but I did not feel inclined to move out of the way. I felt that the cabs and myself were of one stuff. There was no sensation in my limbs, which seemed to be becoming paralyzed. I did not relish eating, and felt as if somebody else were eating. Sometimes I lay down during a meal; after a few minutes I got up and again began to eat. The result would be that on some days I would take too much, but it did no harm. My mother became alarmed and said that there must be something wrong with me.

She was afraid that I might not live long. When there was a slight change in this state, the world began to appear dream-like. While walking in Cornwallis Square, I would strike my head against the iron railings to see if they were real or only a dream. This state of things continued for some days. When I became normal again, I realized I must have had a glimpse of the Advaita state. Then it struck me that the words of the scriptures were not false. Thenceforth I could not deny the conclusions of the Advaita philosophy."[16]

In spite of all these experiences and many more, cruel misfortune dogged him and doubts assailed him. After the death of his father, Narendranath had an experience which is given below. "The summer was over, and the rains set in. The search for a job still on. One evening, after a whole day's fast and exposure to rain I was returning home with tired limbs and a jaded mind; overpowered with exhaustion and unable to move a step forward, I sank down on the outer plinth of a house by the roadside. I can't say whether I was insensible for a time or not. Various thoughts crowded in on my mind, and I was too weak to drive them off and fix my attention on anything in particular. Suddenly I felt as if by some divine power the coverings of my soul were being removed one after another. All my former doubts regarding the coexistence of divine justice and mercy, and the presence of misery in the creation of a Blissful Providence, were automatically solved. By a deep introspection I found the meaning of it all and was satisfied. As I proceeded homewards I found there was no trace of fatigue in the body, and the mind was refreshed with wonderful strength and peace. The night was well-nigh over."[17]

The vicissitudes of life followed him like a shadow and impelled him to seek the aid of Ramakrishna in solving the pecuniary needs of the family. On being requested by Ramakrishna to pray to mother Kali, Narendra went thrice in the same night for this favour but each time he was wonderstruck to see the living Divine Mother. This experience is given by Narendranath as follows: "Reaching the temple, as I cast my eyes on the image, I actually found that the Divine Mother was living and conscious, the perennial fountain of Divine Love and Beauty. I was caught in a surging wave of devotion and love. In an ecstasy of joy I prostrated myself again and again before the Mother and prayed, "Mother, give me discrimination! Give me renunciation! Give me knowledge and devotion! Grant that I may have the uninterrupted vision of thee!" A serene peace reigned in my soul. The world was forgotten. Only the Divine Mother shone within my heart."[18]

In the days at Cossipore, Narendranath pestered Ramakrishna for *nirvikalpa samadhi* and it was granted to him. Narendranath had this experience at least on three other occasions — on the shore of Lake Michigan; at Camp Percy, in New Hampshire; and at Thousand Island Park. In his itinerant days in North India Narendranath sat for meditation at Kakrighat, which is about fourteen and a half miles from Almora. About his deep spiritual experience he told Swami Akhandananda thus: "Oh, Gangadhar! I have just passed through one of the greatest moments of my life. Here under this peepul tree one of the greatest problems of my life has been solved. I have found the oneness of the macrocosm with the microcosm. In this microcosm of the body everything that is there (in the macrocosm), exists. I have seen the whole universe within an atom."[19] In his notebook he noted in Bengali the gist of that Supreme experience. "In the beginning was the Word etc. The microcosm and the macrocosm are built on the same plan. Just as the individual soul is encased in the living body, so is the universal soul in the Living *prakriti* (Nature) — the objective universe. Shiva (i.e. Kali) is embracing Shiva: this is not a fancy. This covering of the one (Soul) by the other (Nature) is analogous to the relation between an idea and the word expressing it: they are one and the same; and it is only by a mental abstraction that one can distinguish them. Thought is impossible without words. Therefore in the beginning was the Word etc. This dual aspect of the Universal Soul is eternal. So what we perceive or feel is this combination of the Eternally Formed and the Eternally Formless."[20]

"After his (Shri Ramakrishna's) leaving the body, I associated for some time with Pavhari Baba of Ghazipur. There was a garden not far distant from his Ashrama where I lived. People used to say it was a haunted garden, but as you know, I am a sort of demon myself and have not much fear of ghosts. In the garden there were many lemon trees which bore numerous fruits. At that time I was suffering from diarrhoea, and there no food could be had except bread. So, to increase the digestive powers, I used to take plenty of lemons. Mixing with Pavhari Baba, I liked him very much, and he also came to love me deeply. One day I thought that I did not learn any art for making this weak body strong, even though I lived with Shri Ramakrishna for so many years. I had heard that Pavhari Baba knew the science of *hatha yoga*. So I thought I would learn the practices of *hatha yoga* from him, and through them strengthen the body. You know, I have a dogged resolution, and whatever I set my heart on, I always carry out. On the eve of the day on which I was to take initiation, I was lying on a cot thinking; and just then I saw the form of Shri Ramakrishna standing on my right side, looking steadfastly at me, as if very much grieved. I had dedicated myself to him, and at the thought that I was taking another *guru* I was much ashamed and kept looking at him. Thus perhaps two or three hours passed, but no words escaped from my mouth. Then he disappeared all on a sudden. My mind became upset seeing Shri Ramakrishna that night, so I postponed the idea of initiation from Pavhari Baba for the day. After a day or two again the idea of initiation from Pavhari Baba arose in the mind — and again in the night there was the appearance of Shri Ramakrishna as on the previous occasion. Thus when for several nights in succession I had the vision of Shri Ramakrishna, I gave up the idea of initiation altogether, thinking that as every time I resolved on it, I was getting such a vision, then no good but harm would come from it."[21]

We are recounting another incident which, of course, took place in Chicago: "When I began lecturing in Chicago and other cities, I had to deliver every week some twelve or fifteen or even more lectures at times. This excessive strain on the body and mind would exhaust me to a degree. I seemed to run short of subjects for lectures and was anxious where to find new topics for the morrow's lecture. New thoughts seemed altogether scarce. One day, after the lecture, I lay thinking of what means to adopt next. The thought induced a sort of slumber, and in that state I heard as if somebody standing by me was lecturing — many new ideas and new veins of thought, which I had scarcely heard or thought of in my life. On awaking I remembered them and reproduced them in my lecture. I cannot enumerate how often this phenomenon took place. Many, many days did I hear such lectures while lying in bed. Sometimes the lecture would be delivered in such a loud voice that the inmates of adjacent rooms would hear the sound and ask me the next day, 'With whom, Swamiji, were you talking so loudly last night?' I used to avoid the question somehow. Ah, it was a wonderful phenomenon."[22]

Through deep meditation, Swamiji's personality was transfigured, spiritual radiance suffused his being. "Describing the Swami (Vivekananda) . . . before his (Vivekananda's) departure for America, Swami Abhedananda spoke of him as a soul on fire. He found him tortured with emotions and seething with ideas relating to the spiritual regeneration of the Hindus. The Swami's restlessness frightened Abhedananda. He was like a hurricane. The Swami told his brother-disciple, 'I feel such a tremendous power and energy, it is as though I should burst'."[23]

Swamiji proceeded to Kanyakumari in December, 1892. After worshipping the deity, Kanyakumari (virgin girl), he swam some two furlongs of shark-infested waters in the ocean and reached the two rocks "sanctified by the blessed feet of the Divine Mother." Here he sat down on the last stone of India and was lost in meditation for three days (perhaps from Dec. 24 to Dec. 26). He had a "rare type" of spiritual experience of incalculable value. He became "condensed India" and got divine inspiration to embark upon the journey to the West. "He gazed over the waters through a mist of tears. His heart went out to the Master and to the Mother in prayer. From this moment his life was consecrated to the service of India, but particularly to the service of her outcast

Narayanas, her starving Narayanas, her millions of oppressed Narayanas. To him, in this hour, even the direct experience of Brahman in the *nirvikalpa samadhi*, and the bliss attending it, became subservient to the overwhelming desire to give himself utterly for the good of the Indian people. His soul was caught up in the vision of Narayana Himself, the Lord of the Universe, transcendent, yet immanent in all beings — whose boundless love makes no distinction between high and low, pure and vile, rich and poor. To him religion was no longer a special province of human endeavour: it embraced the whole scheme of things — the Vedas, the sages, asceticism and meditation, the Supreme Vision, and the people, their lives, their hopes, their misery and poverty and sorrows. He saw that religion, without concern for the poor and suffering, was so much dry straw. Yes, indeed, at Kanyakumari the Swami became the patriot and prophet in one."[24] His whole being was deeply absorbed in the contemplation of the divine and thus enabled him to have a strong vision. The soul being the only source of strength and living faith, Swamiji, in times of sheer weakness and exhaustion, used to assert his soul-force to remove the fatigue. In one of his lectures in California, Swamiji said, "Many times I have been in the jaws of death, starving, footsore, and weary; for days and days I had no food, and often could walk no farther; I would sink down under a tree, and life would seem to be ebbing away. I could not speak, I could scarcely think, but at last the mind reverted to the idea: 'I have no fear nor death; never was I born, never did I die; I never hunger nor thirst. I am It! I am It! The whole of nature cannot crush me; it is my servant. Assert thy strength, thou Lord of lords and God of gods! Regain thy lost empire! Arise and awake and stop not!' And I would rise up, reinvigorated; and here I am today, living! Thus, whenever darkness comes, assert the reality, and everything adverse must vanish. For, after all, it is but a dream. Mountain-high though the difficulties appear, terrible and gloomy though all things seem, they are but *maya*. Fear not, and it is banished. Crush it, and it vanishes. Stamp upon it, and it dies."[25]

At one time, "when he was walking on foot in Kutch, he passed through a desert. His utter exhaustion due to extreme heat, his parched throat and surely his hunger, as it was a no man's land, tempted him to search for water. The sight of a village and the tempting sight of water made him walk many miles only to be deceived. Soon he came to his senses and saw that the village and the water are all a mirage and he thought of the deceptiveness of *maya*." In his series of lectures on *maya* in the West, he used this illustration of *maya* from his practical experience.[26] At moments such as these, Swamiji's very appearance became an epitome of "fearlessness." Later in his life he told his disciples, ". . . the other day, I was guest of Babu Priyanath Mukherjee at Baidyanath. There I had such a spell of asthma that I felt like dying. But from within, with every breath arose the deep-toned sound, 'I am He, I am He.' Resting on the pillow, I was waiting for the vital breath to depart, and observing all the time that from within was being heard the sound of 'I am He, I am He!' I could hear all along — The Brahman, the one without a second, alone exists, nothing manifold exists in the world."[27]

Expansion of heart is indicative of spiritual growth and therefore we find the all-encompassing heart among the spiritual luminaries. When we are able to transcend our self-centeredness, cosmic, spiritual energy is released to make us compassionate. That Swamiji became a second Buddha in modern times can be noticed unmistakably in the following statement of Swami Turiyananda who saw Swamiji at Mount Abu in May, 1893: ". . . I vividly remember some remarks made by Swamiji at that time. The exact words and accents, and the deep pathos with which they were uttered, still ring in my ears. He said, 'Haribhai, I am still unable to understand anything of your so-called religion.' Then with an expression of deep sorrow on his countenance and intense emotion shaking his body, he placed his hand on his heart and added, 'But my heart has expanded very much, and I have learnt to feel. Believe me, I feel intensely indeed.' His voice was choked with feeling; he could say no more. For a time profound silence reigned, and tears rolled down his cheeks." In telling of this incident Swami Turiyananda was also overcome. He sat silent for a while, his eyelids heavy with tears. With a deep sigh he said, "Can you imagine what passed through my mind on hearing the Swami speak thus? 'Are not these,' I thought, 'the very words and feelings of Buddha?' . . . . I could clearly perceive that the sufferings of humanity were pulsating in the heart of Swamiji: his heart was a huge cauldron in which the sufferings of mankind were being made into a healing balm."[28] Swami Turiyananda relates another incident indicative of the Swami's profound love for all men. This incident occurred at Balaram Bose's home. . . . Swami Turiyananda said: "I came to see Swamiji and found him walking alone on the veranda lost in such deep thought that he did not perceive my arrival. I kept quiet, lest I should interrupt his reverie. After some time, Swamiji, with tears rolling down his cheeks, began to hum a well-known song of Mirabai. Then, with his face in his hands and leaning on the railings, he sang in anguished tones, 'Oh, nobody understands my sorrow! Nobody understands my sorrow!' The sad strains, and Swamiji's dejection, seemed to affect even the objects around him! The whole atmosphere vibrated with the sad melody: 'No one but the sufferer knows the pangs of sorrows.' His voice pierced my heart like an arrow, moving me to tears. Not knowing the cause of Swamiji's sorrow I was very uneasy. But it soon flashed upon me that it was a tremendous universal sympathy with the suffering and oppressed that was the cause of his mood."[29] Of the innumerable incidents of similar nature, I am tempted to mention one touching incident that took place at Belur Math. Swami Vijnanananda — a brother disciple of Swamiji — once saw Swamiji at 2 A.M. pacing in the veranda with an anguished mind. When asked, Swamiji told: "See, brother, I was sleeping well but suddenly I got a jerk and my sleep was gone. I have a premonition that somewhere many people are suffering due to a sudden disaster." This explanation of Swamiji's sleeplessness, obviously did not satisfy the enquirer, who, of course, remained silent. The next day newspapers reported a great volcanic eruption causing the death of many people near Fiji Islands exactly about the same time. Swami Vijnanananda was very much astonished to note that Swamiji's nervous system was more delicate than a seismograph. Swamiji's nervous system was found more responsive to human miseries.

Swamiji went to Amarnath in Kashmir in November, 1898, along with Nivedita. There "a profound mystical experience came to him, of which he never spoke beyond saying that Shiva Himself had appeared before him, and that he (the Swami) had been granted the grace of Amarnath, the Lord of Immortality, namely not to die until he himself should choose to do so."[30] Nivedita reported, ". . . so saturated had he (Swami) become with the Presence of the Great God that for days after he could speak of nothing else. Shiva was all in all: Shiva, the Eternal One, the Great Monk, rapt in meditation, aloof from the world."[31] At Belur Math in November 1898, when asked by his disciple, Sarat Chandra Chakravarty, Swamiji said, "Since visiting Amarnath, I feel as though Shiva were sitting on my head for twenty-four hours a day and will not come down."[32] After Amarnath and before Kshir Bhavani, Swamiji was intoxicated with the thought of the Divine Mother. This concentrated devotion to the Mother found expression in the worship of the four-year-old daughter of his Muslim boatman. He reported to his disciples thus: ". . .that during these days, wherever he turned, he was conscious of the presence of the Mother, as if she were a person in the room."[33] He felt that it was she, or his own Master, "whose hands are clasped upon my own and who leads me as though I were a child." In another context we get a little more elaboration of this experience. "Again, in the last winter of his life, he told his disciple Swarupananda that for some months continuously, he had been conscious of two hands, holding his own in their grasp. Going on a pilgrimage, one would catch him telling his beads."[34] "And now, through his intensity of devotion, everything in the life of his companions became associated with the Mother, as it had been before with Shiva."[35] It was not as if this was the first time Vivekananda had been held by the Mother. Reminiscing of his youth, Vivekananda described that experience thus: "I had great misfortunes at that time you know. My father died, and so on. And She [the Mother Kali] saw Her opportunity to make a slave of me. They were Her very words, — 'To make a slave of you'."[36] "At that time Kali took hold of his wrists. For the next seventeen years Swamiji always felt two hands holding his wrists; six months before he died they had stopped."[37] The spell of Mother-devotion became so concentrated that he bitterly "complained of the malady of thought, which would consume a man, leaving him no time for sleep or rest, and would often become insistent as a human voice." In the second week of September, one evening he had an experience similar to that in the Kali temple at Dakshineshwar. With this dominant mood, he retired to a solitary place. The Swami's mind was wholly absorbed with the thought of Mother. He meditated deeply on Mother Kali and had a vision of Her. In the excitement of his experience, he wrote one of his magnificent poems, *Kali the Mother*. In that poem he depicted the terrific as well as the compassionate aspect of Mother Kali. We may have a glimpse of his state of mind of that period. "His mind was at a pitch. In that tense state Revelation must come, or the mind burst. One evening it came . . . It was vision, tremendous vision, commingled with luminous knowledge, a world of poetic feeling and the ecstasy of a saint."[38] All these experiences, visions and revelations found eloquent expression in that poem and after finishing it, "he fell down on the ground absorbed in *bhava-samadhi*."

Next, Swamiji went to Kshir Bhavani on September 30, 1898, and stayed there until the sixth of October. He rigorously led a very austere life and worshiped mother with great fervour. He offered every day "*kheer* (thickened milk) made from one mound of milk, rice, and almond."[39] He, like any ordinary devotee, did his daily *japam* with his rosary, and worshiped every morning a little girl as the Divine Virgin. After returning from Kshir Bhavani, he told his disciples about one of his experiences. He was very sad while dwelling gloomily on the ruined and desecrated temple of the Mother, which apparently occurred without any resistance. He thought: "How could the people have permitted such sacrilege without offering strenuous resistance! If I were here then, I would never have allowed such things. I would have laid down my life to protect the Mother."[40] He heard the voice of the Mother saying, "'What, even if unbelievers should enter my temples, and defile My images! What is that to you? Do you protect Me? Or do I protect you?' So there is no more patriotism. I am only a little child."[41] As he related to a disciple the above incident, the disciple asked, "Sir, you used to say that Divine voices are the echo of our inner thoughts and feelings." Swamiji "gravely replied, 'Whether it be internal or external, if you actually hear with your ears such a disembodied voice, as I have done, can you deny it and call it false? Divine voices are actually heard, just as you and I are talking'."[42] Reading from his poem, *Kali the Mother*, he said: "It all came true, every word of it; and I have proved it, for I have hugged the Form of Death." Other visions of an extraordinary nature he confided to one or two brother disciples.

While in the West, Swamiji, on more than one occasion experienced the beatitude of Divine Consciousness. On June 6, 1895, Swamiji, along with a party of five went to Camp Percy, New Hampshire. He was greatly fascinated by the quietude of the beautiful place and expressed his desire to spend more time in meditation and the reading of the *Gita* in this solitary forest. As told in *New Discoveries*: "One morning before breakfast Swamiji came out from his room with a Sanskrit *Gita* in his hand. I (Josephine Macleod) was behind him. Seeing me, he said, 'Joe, I am going to sit under that pine (pointing to a nearby pine) and read the *Bhagavad Gita*. See that the breakfast is sumptuous today.' Half an hour later I went over to the pine tree and saw Swamiji sitting there motionless. The *Gita* had fallen from his hand and the front of his robe was wet with tears. I went nearer and saw that his breathing had stopped altogether. I trembled in fear — Swamiji must be dead. I did not shout, but ran to Francis Leggett and told him, 'Come quick, Swami Vivekananda has left us.' My sister ran to the spot with loud cries and my [future] brother-in-law also came with tears in his eyes. By now seven or eight minutes had passed. Swamiji was still in the same position. But my brother-in-law said, 'He is in a trance; I will shake him out of it.' I stopped him, shouting, 'Never do that!' I remembered that Swamiji had said once that when he would be in deep meditation one should not touch him. Another five minutes or so passed, then we saw the signs of breathing. His eyes had been half closed; now slowly they opened. And then Swamiji, as if soliloquizing, said, 'Who am I, where am I?' Thrice he spoke like that, and then, wide awake, he saw us, was very much embarrassed, stood up, and said, 'I am sorry to have frightened you all. But I have this state of consciousness now and then. I shall not leave my body in your country. Betty, I am hungry, let's hurry'."[43] According to *New Discoveries*, "On the shore of Lake Michigan he had also entered into *samadhi*, but on that occasion it was Shri Ramakrishna who, appearing to him, drew him back 'to the work for which he had come to the world'."[44] While at Thousand Island Park, Sister Christine speaks of his deep meditative moods thus: "There was nothing set or formed about these nights on the upper veranda. He sat in his large chair at the end, near his door. Sometimes he went into a deep meditation. At such times we too meditated or sat in profound silence. Often it lasted for hours and one after the other slipped away."[45]

And here too, at Thousand Island Park, he experienced *nirvikalpa samadhi*. "Swamiji left Thousand Island Park on August 7, 1895. It was possibly on the same day that he had an experience of *nirvikalpa samadhi*, that is referred to in *The Life*. Possibly also this had happened as has been described by Mrs. Funke when she and Sister Christine were out for a walk with Swamiji as desired by him. The place where he possibly entered into *nirvikalpa samadhi* has now been tentatively identified. It was beneath a big oak tree about half a mile from the cottage, and Swamiji may have sat on a big, flat, boulder there. The incident is described by Mrs. Funke as follows; "This morning there was no class. He asked C. and me to take a walk, as he wished to be alone with us. (The others had been with him all summer, and he felt we should have a talk.) We went up a hill about half a mile away. All was woods and solitude. Finally, he selected a low-branched tree, and we sat under the low-spreading branches. Instead of the expected talk, he suddenly said, 'Now we shall meditate. We shall be like Buddha under the Bo-tree'. He seemed to turn to bronze, so still was he. Then a thundershower came up, and it poured. He never noticed it. I raised my umbrella and protected him as much as possible. Completely absorbed in his meditation, he was oblivious of everything. Soon we heard shouts in the distance. The others had come out after us with raincoats and umbrellas. Swamiji looked around regretfully, for we had to go, and said, 'Once more I am in Calcutta in the rains.' So far as the Teacher himself was concerned, that was the crowning moment of his days at Thousand Island Park. The pupils felt blessed at the sight."[46]

In the foregoing pages, we have given a profile of Swamiji's numerous mystical experiences. We never pretend to know his spiritual eminence through such humble study. A spiritual iceberg like him will ever remain unknown to us. Shri Ramakrishna who alone knew him once remarked, "Let no one judge Naren. No one will be able to understand him fully."[47] At another occasion, Ramakrishna said, ". . . He loses normal consciousness in meditation for whole nights . . . he is a true knower of Brahman. He sees light when he sits for meditation."[48] . . . ."Narendra belongs to a very high plane — the realm of the Absolute."[49] Swamiji's normal mind was God-conscious. With little effort under the impulsion of intense desire, his mind drifted to *nirvikalpa samadhi*. It was really hard for him to keep his mind in the world.

The modern mind is rationalistic and practical — merely on the sense plane, while the mystic is more inclined to a meditative life. His spiritual insight makes him extremely useful, dynamic and unselfish. The mystic feels, enjoys, becomes illumined, and gives us saving truths. He insists on the rectitude of life geared to spiritual enlightenment. He advocates a strenuous life devoted to the real welfare of the people. He is a real genius, exhibiting a high quality of life devoid of the human weakness. He represents the eternal ideal of human excellences. The whole world looks upon him as a lighthouse of hope and clear guidance. Faith in spiritual values is the very essence of higher life of the spirit as envisioned by a mystic. Modern man is groping for a living Faith, a sound and rational philosophy and the shining example of an illumined mystic who is the most persuasive testimony of God's existence. Swamiji's life may help him to fullfill all the demands of a modern mind. In the words of Sister Nivedita, "He was an apostle making an appeal to man. . . . calling on the world to enter into the kingdom of God."[50] His blazing life, strength of character and all-encompassing love for humanity authenticates the presence of an all-pervading Truth in which we live, move and have our being.

15

SWAMIJI AND MADAME CALVÉ

Madame Calvé, the celebrated singer, was in Chicago in 1894. The world was at her feet. Calvé, the toast of two continents, was seen by her flamboyant admirers as well as by the celebrities composing the cream of the society, as a bright new star sailing forth to conquer the world. One evening in the opera, she had her worst attack of stage fright. She felt nervous going on the stage after the interval, although the first act was a tremendous success. She felt terribly depressed and thought of giving up the performance that night. She could hardly stagger from her dressing room to the wings. She stood stock-still as though paralysed, and had to be persuaded by the stage manager. But she sang magnificently. After her second act, returning to her dressing room, she virtually collapsed and asked the manager to announce her inability to appear due to illness. She had breathing trouble and was terribly depressed. The manager and the people around her almost carried her to the stage for the last act and she made the greatest effort of her life to finish the performance, which proved to be one of the most glorious of her entire career. The public gave her a tremendous applause. After a rousing exit she ran to her room only to see several long faces. Her mind was filled with foreboding of some impending grave peril. The tragic news awaited her — that her only beloved daughter was dead, burnt to death during her performance. Calvé fainted.

Calvé had showered every mark of tender affection on her daughter. How she could live now? Her unprecedented success lost its charm. She resolved to put an end to her agonizing suffering by committing suicide: she would throw herself in the lake. Notwithstanding all the pious entreaties of her well-wishers, she was helplessly borne, like a straw on the stream, upon the current of emotion. Swami Vivekananda was at that time in Chicago, and news of his great and saving spiritual power was in the air. Many were seeking interviews, for his help and guidance. This was well-known to her, but she had a misconception about spiritual power. She didn't visit the Swami.

Three times she left her house to drown herself, and went towards the lake, and each time destiny brought her unconsciously to the road leading to Swamiji's house. Each time she refused to see the Swami and went back to her house. Finally, the fourth or fifth time, she unintentionally came, as though in a trance, to the Swami's house and sat down in a chair. She was in a dreamy state, when she heard a consoling voice coming from the next room saying, "Come, my child. Don't be afraid." She got up and went to Swamiji as though hypnotized. It would be interesting to give here the reminiscences of Madame Calvé, of her first meeting with Swami Vivekananda — and of the profound impact the Swami's teaching produced in her life:

> It has been my good fortune and my joy to know a man who truly 'walked with God,' a noble being, a saint, a philosopher and a true friend. His influence upon my spiritual life was profound. He opened up new horizons before me, enlarging and unifying my religious ideas and ideals; teaching me a broader understanding of truth. My soul will bear him eternal gratitude.
>
> . . . . He was lecturing in Chicago one year when I was there; and as I was at that time greatly depressed in mind and body, I decided to go to him, having seen how he had helped some of my friends. When I entered the room, I stood before him in silence for a moment. He was seated in a noble attitude of meditation, his eyes on the ground. After a pause he spoke without looking up.
>
> 'My child,' he said, 'what a troubled atmosphere you have about you: Be calm: It is essential.'
>
> Then in a quiet voice, untroubled and aloof, this man who did not even know my name talked to me of my secret problems and anxieties. He spoke of things that I thought were unknown even to my nearest friends. It seemed miraculous, supernatural.
>
> 'How do you know all this? I asked at last. 'Who has talked of me to you?'
>
> He looked at me with his quiet smile as though I were a child who had asked a foolish question.

'No one has talked to me,' he answered gently. 'Do you think that it is necessary? I read in you as in an open book.'

Finally it was time for me to leave.

'You must forget,' he said as I rose. 'Become gay and happy again. Build up your health. Do not dwell in silence upon your sorrows. Transmute your emotions into some form of eternal expression. Your spiritual health requires it. Your art demands it.'

I left him, deeply impressed by his words and his personality. He seemed to have emptied my brain of all its feverish complexities and placed there instead his clean calming thoughts. I became once again vivacious and cheerful, thanks to the effect of his powerful will. He did not use any of the hypnotic or mesmeric influences. It was the strength of his character, the purity and intensity of his purpose that carried conviction. It seemed to me, when I came to know him better, that he lulled one's chaotic thoughts into a state of peaceful acquiescence, so that one could give complete and undivided attention to his words.

A great spiritual personality who is perfectly established in higher realizations can transmit this knowledge to a disciple even if the disciple has not undergone vigorous spiritual practices. Swami Vivekananda himself experienced it and says in his lecture, "I began to go to that man (Shri Ramakrishna), day after day, and I actually saw that religion can be given. One touch, one glance, can change a whole life. I have read about Buddha and Christ, about all those different luminaries of ancient times, how they would stand up and say, "Be thou whole," and the man became whole. I now found it to be true, and when I myself saw this man, all scepticism was brushed aside. It could be done, and my Master used to say, "Religion can be given and taken more tangibly, more really than anything else in the world."[1]

Dr. Hans Jacobs, an eminent Western psychiatrist, has written a wonderful book, — *Western Psychotherapy and Hindu Sadhana*. He says, "There can be no greater inspiration for strength and power than the idea of the Indian Vedanta that the soul is essentially divine . . . . Actually the more we can think of our divine heritage the more divine we become. Error brings about sorrow and is ultimately the result of weakness. Consequently remedy is seen in strength and strength is conveyed by basing oneself not on the individual but on the universal." Dr. Jacobs believes that the repetition of *mantras* under the guidance of a spiritual preceptor is of great help to the seekers after truth. "If well selected," he says, "the *mantra* is of such a nature that by the vibrations it produces it counteracts psychological drawbacks of the *sadhaka,* providing those elements which, in his subtle body, are lacking, counteracting those which are in excess. . . . We want healers of souls rather than of bodies. A pure heart is the most essential requisite for mental and physical health." St. Paul has beautifully expressed the truth: "Be Ye transformed by the renewal of your mind." Great spiritual souls or their messages or the holy *mantras* given by them only arouse the latent divinity in the *sadhaka* and thereby help him to know his inner potentiality. This brings success in his life.

Psychosis is generated by the conflicts, confusion, and frustration of the mind and by uncontrolled emotions. Those tendencies can hardly be removed unless higher values are absorbed by the person and then practically applied in his life. When a man has the religious ideal and regulates all his activities by it, he has a satisfactory way of life. Hence we are to associate ourselves with spiritual souls or their messages. Their snow-white peaks of sanctity, purity and holiness in life will act as a lighthouse of inspiration to drooping souls. This is the value of having an exalted ideal, a strong love for a noble person, a lofty purpose which translates itself into service, and an absorbing devotion to a holy cause.

16

SWAMI VIVEKANANDA
AN INCARNATION OF MANLINESS

The essential nature of Swami Vivekananda's complex personality may very well be presented in a capsule form by depicting him as an *avatara* of *shakti*. He was, really speaking, a veritable embodiment of Divine energy. The dynamic personality of Swamiji did create a different impact on different minds. He was known, even to the common person, as the "Cyclonic-Monk," "Hindu-Napoleon," "Warrior-Monk," etc. Everyone was impressed by one aspect of his blazing personality. Swamiji was indeed, a living dynamo, radiating an aura of power and fearlessness. His spiritual dimension, robust optimism and absolute fearlessness and above all, his message, are the eternal source of a living philosophy of life, "a tonic of the soul." Mary C. Funke, a close friend of Swamiji, writes, "After thirty-one years Swamiji stands out in my consciousness a colossal figure — a cleaver of bondage, knowing when and where not to spare. With his two-edged sword came this Man "out of the East" — this Man of Fire and Flame and some were there who received him, and to those who received him he gave Power." In India Sister Christine saw Swamiji in 1902 and wrote: "Here I saw the lion in his natural surroundings."[1]

Gurudas Maharaj — a Dutch immigrant in the U.S.A. — who later became Swami Atulananda, gave his first impression thus: "But when I saw him for a few minutes standing on a platform surrounded by others, it flashed into my mind: What a giant, What strength, What manliness, What a personality! Everyone near him looks so insignificant in comparision."[2] He was an embodiment of Energism, Individuality and Freedom. This spokesman of Divine Logos gave his message of fearlessness to everyone by addressing man as Divine. Marie Louise Burke, the celebrated researcher on Swamiji says, "As I see it, his gigantic mission in America (and also, of course, in England) was to alter at its deepest source the whole thought-current of the western people . . . . His reiterated definition of man as not body or mind, but pure, infinite Spirit rang through his lectures like a gong — sometimes as a steady background note, sometimes — more often — as dominant thunder. One cannot but feel that this was the crux of his message."[3]

There is beauty and power in his words that certainly cast their spell on the reader. Referring to this, Romain Rolland says in his *Life of Vivekananda*: "His words are great music, phrases in the style of Beethoven, stirring rhythms like the march of Handel choruses. I cannot touch these sayings of his, scattered as they are through the pages of books at thirty years' distance, without receiving a thrill through my body like an electric shock. And what a shock, what transports must have been produced when in burning words they issued from the lips of the hero."[4] Swami Virajananda records his first impression about Swamiji thus: "His eyes were captivating . . . . Light appeared to emanate from his entire body. What a charming figure — combining beauty and power, a nonchalant air and a dazzling personality! My first reaction was love, devotion and a sense of fear."[5] In a speech on Swami Vivekananda, Pandit Nehru said that if he were to name a single individual as an ideal for children and young men to follow, he would name Swami Vivekananda. Also he said, "He was the very picture of vigour and strength. . . . He came as a tonic to a depressed and demoralized Hindu mind and gave self-reliance and some roots in the past."

The vital question that looms large in our mind is an inquisitiveness about the secret source of his dynamism. The Upanishads are dominated by one supreme conception, that of the essential non-duality of the individual and God. God is the source of infinite courage, strength, virility, energy, power and fortitude. By realizing God within through discipline, man obtains real strength and through knowledge, immortality. Manliness is the outcome of man's Self-knowledge. Those who are in possession of even a little knowledge are capable of controlling ordinary men and oppress them. But an illumined soul, having experienced divine consciousness becomes absolutely fearless, as there is nothing else apart from God. Fear stems from the sense of duality. Hence Self-knowledge or divine consciousness alone can make man fearless. Divinity is the supreme source of all beatitudes and spiritual excellences. Its manifestation is experienced through exacting discipline. Man achieves a great strength of character when the dormant divine energy is harnessed. This is the greatest asset in man's life as outer possessions, which are the external, cannot give us that strength and courage. The character of an illumined soul alone is the greatest source of virility. God being the source of infinite virility, this illumined life — life lost in the source of Life — becomes transfigured and consequently attains immortality. The spiritual dimension was discovered by the Indian mystic, with the help of intuitive knowledge.

The faculty of "intuition" which is far superior to rational intellect can alone pierce the veil of mystery which is otherwise inaccessible. Speculative philosophy cannot determine it convincingly and can decipher it far less. Intuition, although super-rational, is never irrational. Human mind is capable of developing this "intuition" through spiritual struggle. To Swamiji's enlightened vision, divine potentiality encased in a human being is struggling to get Itself manifested through pure character. The breadth of the vision and constructive genius exhibited by Swamiji in his clarion call for human development is unique in character. He was essentially an illumined soul of high stature preaching the life-giving ideas of Vedanta philosophy.

His sole ambition was to take advantage of this great philosophy to make religion the life force of the nation, the instrument for galvanizing the entire aspect of human life. He was never tired of preaching the lofty ideal of dynamic life bent upon searching for the unity of life in divinity. He gave everyone the tremendous courage that comes from this unity of life. One Supreme Reality is behind manifoldness and this ideal of oneness of all is to be realized by all. Hence Swamiji "was more concerned with providing the intellectual and emotional fuel for social and economic change than in providing a blueprint for a new society. . . . He chose his interpretation of Vedanta to be the means of providing this fuel."

In a trumpet voice he preached this gospel of dynamic life ceaselessly to rouse the people from lethargy, moral stupor and depression. This gospel of strength, valour, hope and self-confidence breathed life into the almost dead bones of the Indians. He assured all that there is infinite capacity in each one of us waiting to be harnessed by a strong character. This monistic ideal of Vedanta, if cultivated properly in life, will certainly make people prosperous in every walk of life. In his lecture, *The Mission of the Vedanta,* he said: "I am no preacher of any momentary social reform. I am not trying to remedy evils. I only ask you to go forward to complete the practical realization of the scheme of human progress that has been laid out by our ancestors. I only ask you to work to realize more and more the Vedantic ideal of the solidarity of man and his inborn divine nature."[6] Again in the same lecture he said: "What our country now wants are muscles of iron and nerves of steel, gigantic wills which nothing can resist, which can penetrate into the mysteries and the secrets of the universe, and will accomplish their purpose in any fashion even if it meant going down to the bottom of the ocean and meeting death face to face. That is what we want, and that can only be created, established, and strengthened by understanding and realizing the ideal of the Advaita, that ideal of the oneness of all. Faith, faith, faith in ourselves, faith, faith in God — this is the secret of greatness. If you have faith in all the three hundred and thirty millions of your mythological gods, and in all the gods which foreigners have now and again introduced into your midst, and still have no faith in yourselves, there is no salvation for you. Have faith in yourselves, and stand up on that faith and be strong; that is what we need."[7]

This cultivation of a daring attitude, this passionate urge of a strong, virile person braving the fury of death are not the normal requisite of a seeker for spiritual truth. Its great impact for social regeneration is implicit. Swamiji gave the people a great *mantra*, a key to unlock the great mystery of life, his recipe for sucess. He exhorted constantly in his stentorian voice, "Feel that you are great and you become great." What we earnestly think, we become. Swamiji hit the nail on the head over and over, simply because he was true to himself and because he saw with such clearness divinity in all human beings. He said, "No books, no scripture, no science can ever imagine the glory of the Self that appears as man, the most glorious God that ever was, the only God that ever existed, exists, or ever will exist. . . ."[8]

In his lecture, *Man the Maker of His Destiny*, Swamiji shared his own experience with the audience, to inspire them. "I was once travelling in the Himalayas and the long road stretched before us. We poor monks cannot get anyone to carry us, so we had to make all the way on foot. There was an old man with us. The way goes up and down for hundreds of miles, and when that old monk saw what was before him, he said, 'Oh, sir, how to cross it; I cannot walk any more; my chest will break.' I said to him, 'Look down at your feet.' He did so, and I said, 'The road that is under your feet is the road that you have passed over and is the same road that you see before you; it will soon be under your feet'."[9]

Virility enables us to tackle the baffling problems of life and if not solved, to endure the situation with the help of our character efficiency. Swamiji gave another account of his chequered life and thereby he made a deep impact on us. "Once when I was in Varanasi, I was passing through a place where (there) was a large tank of water on one side and a high wall on the other. It was in the grounds where there were many monkeys. The monkeys of Varanasi are huge brutes and are sometimes surly. They now took it into their heads not to allow me to pass through their streets, so they howled and shrieked and clutched at my feet as I passed. As they pressed closer, I began to run, but the faster I ran, the faster came the monkeys and they began to bite at me. It seemed impossible to escape, but just then I met a stranger who called out to me, "Face the brutes." I turned and faced the monkeys, and they fell back and finally fled. That is a lesson for all life — face the terrible, face it boldly."[10] Like the brutes, the problems of life fall back or get themselves solved when we squarely face them with tremendous self-confidence.

"Calmness of mind," Swamiji exhorted always, to manifest our dormant energy to fight against depression and ignorance, to score victory over them. The very first "commandment," if we want to use this word, of Swamiji was his dynamic message of strength. He commanded us to give up this nauseating, soul-killing weakness. He admonished everyone even for feeling weak. To him, "Weakness is sin; weakness is death; strength is life." He, therefore, laid down the programme of character transformation through the right type of education. Education to him, was the master-key in the development of human personality. This will impart the sense of self-respect and self-confidence. He gave a definition of ideal education. — "Education is the manifestation of the perfection already in man."[11] "The training by which the current expression of will is brought under control and becomes fruitful is called education."[12] Elaborating this point he said: "Education is not the amount of information that is put into your brain and runs riot there, undigested, all your life. We must have life-building, man-making, character-making assimilation of ideas. If you have assimilated five ideas and made them your life and character, you have more education than any man who has got by heart a whole library."[13]

He advised his real followers to preach the message of the divinity of the soul to one and all. The mission of Vedanta, according to Swamiji, is to inspire everyone with this life-giving message of the Upanishads — Arise, Awake, and Stop Not till the goal is reached. The goal he intended to mean here is all-comprehensive and brings all-round development to the human life.

Hence, deep abiding faith in our innate divinity is the surest way to make our life dynamic. "All the scholastic scaffolding," says Napoleon, "falls as a ruined edifice before one single word, 'faith'." Deep experience and wide observation have taught us that the fundamental need of the world is far deeper than the so-called progress in material life, and is a spiritual re-awakening, and a recovery of the faith in our divine heritage. Arnold Toynbee in his *Civilization on Trial* anticipates this spiritual vision of life which alone can give us the opportunity to live a life with dignity and freedom. We suffer terribly from a deep sense of insecurity. This alienation from divine ground, this development of fissure or a cleavage in our life, has caused in us restlessness and confusion. Consciousness of divinity, constant meditation on its infinite unselfish work, alone can create a hope in our life. We can remould ourselves to attain glory in our life if we regain our spiritual consciousness. That is why the role of faith in life is immense. "Faith celestial, faith consoling, you do more than lift up the mountains, you lift the oppressive burden that weighs on the mind." Swamiji repeatedly dinned into our ears his soul-stirring message, "The history of the world is the history of a few men who had faith in themselves. That faith calls out the divinity within. You can do anything. You fail only when you do not strive sufficiently to manifest infinite power. As soon as a man or a nation loses faith, death comes."[14] And again he said, "Faith, faith, faith in ourselves, faith, faith in God — this is the secret of greatness. If you have faith in all three hundred and thirty millions of your mythological gods, and in all the gods which foreigners have now and again introduced into your midst, and still have no faith in yourselves, there is no salvation for you."[15]

Faith remoulds our life and in that awakened life the great significance of Swamiji's comprehensive scheme of life is understood. Therefore, he spent his entire energy in bringing that awakening of the human spirit from its forgetfulness of divine heritage and its consequent illness. To this gigantic task of recreating human life Swamiji dedicated his own life. His concepts of "man-making religion," "man-making education," is very vital in the scheme of human development. Manliness can never be achieved without moral regeneration. Through such physical, mental and spiritual strength he wanted to make our civilization vigorous, energetic and fresh. This new surge of life, this optimism, this zest for living will emancipate us from the parochial mould in which the people of this world are cast. His lectures *From Colombo to Almora* and *Letters* are the greatest source for inspiration. These two books are the Bible of modern healthy living.

Manliness is required to call forth our hidden potentialities. Manliness means virile life, taking courage in both hands to achieve fulfillment in life. Once this awakening comes, human beings will create new history.

"Great convictions are the mothers of great deeds," said Swamiji. Without this deep faith in our infinite potentiality human life fails to exhibit divine dynamism. This is a saving "knowledge" which alone overcomes the limitation and weakness of the finite and the fragmentary character of human life. It impels him to serve God in man. Swamiji's scheme of moral and spiritual regeneration found powerful articulation in his exhortation theme: "A hundred thousand men and women, fired with the zeal of holiness, fortified with eternal faith in the Lord, and nerved to lion's courage by their sympathy for the poor and fallen and the downtrodden, will go over the length and breadth of the land, preaching the gospel of salvation, the gospel of help, the gospel of social raising-up — the gospel of equality."[16]

Swami Vivekananda exhorted us to study the Upanishads for this purpose. "The Upanishads are the great mine of strength. Therein lies strength enough to invigorate the whole world; the whole world can be vivified, made strong, energized through them. They will call with trumpet voice upon the weak, the miserable, and the downtrodden of all races, all creeds, and sects to stand on their feet and be free. Freedom, physical freedom, mental freedom, and spiritual freedom are the watchwords of the Upanishads."[17] Swamiji's *Complete Works*, if assimilated properly and intelligently, gives one idea and one idea alone — the divine image of man. Himself a living apostle of manliness and the secret of his strength being his deep faith in God within, he wanted us all to cultivate that eternal tower of strength lying dormant in us.

Prophets and illumined souls like Swamiji can save us by creating conviction in us by their exemplary life, their strong faith, by the force of their high character and above all by their infinite sympathy for all of us. Swamiji brought back the pristine glory of moral power associated with true spirituality from conventional attitudes towards religion. "Religion is the manifestation of the Divinity already in man." The real force —

not words or an intellectual concept — comes to us by accurate or methodical spiritual practice. That power stems from our spiritually awakened life. Sleeping divinity in us is not only the source of life but also the very source of power. Swamiji wanted to reawaken man from the moral stupor and its consequent weakness by drawing his attention to the inner divinity — a veritable magazine of power.

The whole history of mankind is replete with the shining examples where great illumined souls brought new life to a worry-bound and confused society. Arnold Toynbee, in his *Civilization on Trial*, says: "Now who are the individuals who are the greatest benefactors of the living generation of mankind? I should say Confucius, Lao-Tse, the Buddha, the prophets of Israel and Judah; Zoroaster, Jesus, the Mohammed, and Socrates."[18] They infused moral power in the people and thereby helped them to solve the problems of life through their reawakened moral power.

We know the mystery of the atom but the mystery of our life still remains unknown to us. But in the dim past, in the age of the Upanishads, the Indian mystics gave articulation to their intense experience that the essence of life is divine. The world is a manifestation of divine power of God.

In his lecture in Madras in 1897, Swamiji pointed out how this Vedantic idea is capable of bringing moral and spiritual reawakening. He said: "These conceptions of Vedanta must come out, must remain not only in the forest, not only in the cave, but they must come out to work at the bar and the bench, in the pulpit, and in the cottage of the poor man, with the fishermen that are catching fish, and with the students that are studying. They call to every man, woman, and child whatever be their occupation, wherever they may be. . . . If the fisherman thinks that he is the Spirit, he will be a better fisherman; if the student thinks he is the Spirit, he will be a better student. If the lawyer thinks that he is the Spirit, he will be a better lawyer."[19]

Therefore, to be profited by this doctrine one need not change one's life or work environment, it is sufficient if this "man-making" idea is followed with deep conviction. This is Swamiji's message of comprehensive spirituality which came out of his famous utterances: "Teach yourselves, teach everyone his real nature, call upon the sleeping soul and see how it awakes. Power will come, glory will come, goodness will come, purity will come, and everything that is excellent will come, when this sleeping soul is roused to self-conscious activity."[20]

Swamiji represented the modern spirit of freedom and equality, manliness and energy of action and also he demonstrated the basic unity of godliness and manliness. Swamiji saw with his naked eyes the sleeping God in man. This profound reverential attitude bordering on his worshipful mood found eloquent expression in one of his moving talks in the West: ". . . We should look upon man in the most charitable light. It is not so easy to be good. What are you but mere machines until you are free? Should you be proud because you are good? Certainly not. You are good because you cannot help it. If you were in his position, who knows what you would have been? The woman in the street, or the thief in the jail, is the Christ that is being sacrificed that you may be a good man. Such is the law of balance. All the thieves and the murderers, all the unjust, the weakest, the wickedest, the devils, they all are my Christ! I owe a worship to the God Christ and to the demon Christ! That is my doctrine, I cannot help it. My salutation goes to the feet of the good, the saintly, and to the feet of the wicked and the devilish! They are all of my teachers, all are my spiritual fathers, all are my Saviours. I may curse one and yet benefit by his failings; I may bless another and benefit by his good deeds. This is as true as that I stand here. I have to sneer at the woman walking in the street because society wants it! She, my Savior, she, whose street-walking is the cause of the chastity of other women! Think of that. Think, men and women, of this question in your mind. It is a truth — a bare bold truth! As I see more of the world, see more of men and women, this conviction grows stronger. Whom shall I blame? Whom shall I praise? Both sides of the shield must be seen."[21]

To the cynical humanist and also to the self-righteous hypocrites this verbal bomb did send waves of shocks. A real well-wisher and lover of humanity has to lay the foundation of solid philosophy to usher in a radical change of attitude. The Vedantic view of soul, as self-luminous, eternal and divine, if accepted, will certainly become an adequate philosophy capable of spiritualizing all cultures. Since divinity is fearlessness and courage, and life is divine, Swamiji's gospel of manliness finds its rationale. Courage in the real sense of the term is never equated with a momentary display of extraordinary feats. It certainly means to bear the yoke of life with fortitude and courage. If this "positive, strong and helpful thought" is allowed to fashion our character, it will certainly lead us to divine life through gradual unfoldment of our real nature.

Swamiji was not a Utopian. He was a die-hard realist. His life will unmistakably attest to our statement. He gave us Atman-centric philosophy of life calculated to bring us immense practical help in our everyday life.

Again, as courage is imperative in human development, Swamiji wanted us to cultivate manliness as a basic virtue of other excellences of life. In this respect Swamiji rendered a great service to humanity by laying the foundation of the existential philosophy of courage. He said: "It is weakness, says the Vedanta, which is the cause of all misery in this world. Weakness is the one cause of suffering. We become miserable because we are weak. We lie, steal, kill, and commit other crimes, because we are weak. We suffer because we are weak. We die because we are weak. Where there is nothing to weaken us, there is no death nor sorrow."[22] Being an authentic messenger of the Upanishadic spirit he spelled out his philosophy of manliness in tune with Vedantic ideas. He exhorted: "Strength, strength is what the Upanishads speak to me, from every page. This is the one great thing to remember, it has been the one great lesson I have been taught in my life; strength, it says, strength, O man, be not weak. Are there no human weaknesses? — says man. There are, say the Upanishads, but will more weakness heal them, would you try to wash dirt with dirt? Will sin cure sin, weakness cure weakness? Strength, O man, strength, say the Upanishads, stand up and be strong. Ay, it is the only literature in the world where you find the word *abhih*, "fearless," used again and again . . . . The

Upanishads are the great mine of strength. Therein lies strength enough to invigorate the whole world; the whole world can be vivified, made strong, energized through them. They will call with trumpet voice upon the weak, the miserable, and the downtrodden of all races, all creeds, and all sects to stand on their feet and be free. Freedom, physical freedom, mental freedom, and spiritual freedom are the watchwords of the Upanishads."[23]

Swamiji, being an embodiment of courage, recommended this fundamental virtue as the panacea for all troubles. According to Swamiji, the central message of the *Gita* is the art of cultivation of strength through spiritual disciplines. "The *Gita* is 'the audio-visual exposition' of the Vedanta philosophy." The message of the *Gita* is topical to the people prone to depression. Faith in our divine nature and strength harnessed out of this conviction is the only antidote to spiritual sickness.

Swamiji very much appreciated the great lesson imparted to the drooping mind of Arjuna: the calling forth of his attention to his immortal, omnipotent soul which is the sole source of all divine excellencs and spiritual beatitude. We quote Swamiji: "Here, in Arjuna, the mighty warrior, it (*tamas*) has come under the guise of *daya* (pity).

"In order to remove this delusion which had overtaken Arjuna, what did the *Bhagavan* say? As I always preach that you should not decry a man by calling him a sinner, but that you should draw his attention to the omnipotent power that is in him, in the same way does the *Bhagavan* speak to Arjuna. 'It doth not befit thee!' 'Thou art Atman imperishable, beyond all evil. Having forgotten thy real nature, thou hast, by thinking thyself a sinner, as one afflicted with bodily evils and mental grief, thou hast made thyself so — this doth not befit thee!' — so says the *Bhagavan*: 'Yield not to unmanliness, O son of Pritha. There is in the world neither sin nor misery, neither disease nor grief; if there is anything in the world which can be called sin, it is this — 'fear'; know that any work which brings out the latent power in thee is *punya* (virtue); and that which makes thy body and mind weak is, verily, sin. Shake off this weakness, this faint-heartedness! Thou art a hero, a *vira*; this is unbecoming of thee.'

"If you, my sons, can proclaim this message to the world, then all this disease, grief, sin, and sorrow will vanish from the face of the earth in three days. All these ideas of weakness will be nowhere. Now it is everywhere — this current of the vibration of fear. Reverse the current; bring in the opposite vibration, and behold the magic transformation! Thou art omnipotent — go, go to the mouth of the cannon, fear not.

"Hate not the most abject sinner, look not to his exterior. Turn thy gaze inward, where resides the *Paramatman*. Proclaim to the whole world with trumpet voice, 'There is no sin in thee, there is no misery in thee; thou art the reservoir of omnipotent power. Arise, awake, and manifest the Divinity within!'

"If one reads this one *shloka*, one gets all the merits of reading the entire *Gita*; for in this one *shloka* lies imbedded the whole Message of the *Gita*."[24]

The illumined soul is the real teacher of humanity. When he is heard with love, sympathy and devotion, the ignorant and depressed become intelligent and energetic and the wavering become steady.

Mrs. Ella Wheeler Wilcox, one of the foremost poetesses and writers of America, gave her impression of Swamiji thus: "Twelve years ago I chanced one evening to hear that a certain teacher of philosophy from India, a man named Vivekananda, was to lecture a block from my home in New York.

"We went out of curiosity (the man whose name I bear and I), and before we had been ten minutes in the audience, we felt ourselves lifted up into an atmosphere so rarefied, so vital, so wonderful, that we sat spell-bound and almost breathless, to the end of the lecture.

"When it was over we went out with new courage, new hope, new strength, new faith, to meet life's daily vicissitudes; 'This is the Philosophy, this is the idea of God, the religion, which I have been seeking,' said the man. And for months afterwards he went with me to hear Swami Vivekananda explain the old religion and to gather from his wonderful mind jewels of truth and thoughts of helpfulness and strength. It was that terrible winter of financial disasters, when banks failed and stocks went down like broken baloons and business men walked through the dark valleys of despair and the whole world seemed topsy-turvy — just such an era as we are again approaching. Sometimes after sleepless nights of worry and anxiety, the man would go with me to hear the Swami lecture, and then he would come out into the winter gloom and walk down the street smiling and say: 'It is all right. There is nothing to worry over.' And I would go back to my own duties and pleasures with the same uplifted sense of soul and enlarged vision.

"When any philosophy, any religion, can do this for human beings in this age of stress and strain, and when, added to that, it intensifies their faith in God and increases their sympathies for their kind and gives them a confident joy in the thought of other lives to come, it is a good and great religion . . . ."[25]

Swamiji exerted much influence on his audience and his books continue to supply that power in ever increasing measure to the world. Being an illumined soul of high stature he will ever inspire us to develop character-efficiency and manliness. The strength of his character comes from his realization of eternal and imperishable truth in his own life. His greatness is not in time, it is eternal. Rooted in divinity and nourished therefrom, his magnetic personality, breadth of outlook, loving heart and purity of character will compel humanity to accept him as an eternal teacher. To quote Sri Aurobindo: "Swami Vivekananda was a soul of puissance, if ever there was one, a very lion among men. . . . We perceive his influence still working gigantically, we know not well how, we know not well where, in something that is not yet formed, something leonine, grand, intuitive, upheaving — that has entered the soul of India, and we say, 'Behold! Vivekananda still lives in the soul of his Mother, and in the soul of her children'."

17

SWAMI VIVEKANANDA AN APOSTLE OF STRENGTH

Swami Vivekananda touched human life at many points and always in a redeeming manner. But undoubtedly his greatest service has been in the sphere of religion, which, of course, covers life in its entirety. He made religion multidimensional. He brought it out from the grooves of seclusion, from the caves of the Himalayas, to the place of everyday life. He clarified the concept of religion by teaching us to see the ocean of one basic religion behind the waves of many religions. He made religion attractive by explaining the strength-giving ideas and ideals of religion. He combated the prevalent idea that religion was anaemic, dull, insipid and substance-less and hence useless and even degrading. He vitalized religion by calling for a scientific scrutiny of all religious phenomena. He made religion life-giving and life-sustaining. The true spirit of religion, as pointed out by him, exhorts us to galvanize our souls with a force that will change our entire outlook and vision of life. The way to develop physical and mental strength is ceaseless effort, constant *tapasya.* At every step we must fight against nature. Constant vigilance is the price of strength. "Yield not to weakness" — this is the essence of the *Gita*, according to Swami Vivekananda.[1] Spiritual life is not at all passive indolence, but is all-fullness and intrepid activity. Weakness — physical, mental and moral — is the source of all evils. Cowardice is tantamount to death. Swamiji amplified and ennobled the idea of religion by pointing out how all the activities of life could be made a sacrifice at the altar of God. The dividing wall between secularism and spirituality has to be broken. Life is a preparation, a journey, a struggle for inner illumination. From this point of view life itself is *tapasya*, an active and sincere endeavour by means of all our activities to bring about the inflow of the divine urge, a constant equipping of the will and mind for the advent of the light and life of God.

To the question, "Is it any particular creed you mean by religion?" the Swamiji answered: "The essence of my religion is strength. The religion that does not infuse strength into the heart is no religion to me, be it of the Upanishads, the *Gita* or the *Bhagavata*." Vedanta may be professed even by a coward, but it could be translated into action only by the most stouthearted. It is a strong dish for weak stomachs. The quintessence of the Vedas and Vedanta lies in that one word — strength. "Strength is the only thing needful," the Swamiji used to say, "Strength is the medicine for the world's disease. Strength is the medicine, which the poor must have when tyrannized over by the rich. Strength is the medicine, which the ignorant must have when oppressed by the learned. And it is the medicine, that the sinners must have when tyrannized over by other sinners." We must not forget that Swamiji was a soul of might, encased in an energetic, though short-lived body. He worked all his life with the divine strength which Mother gave him through Shri Ramakrishna. Soul-force is quite different from the brute-force of man which believes that might is right. The Swamiji reasserted the Upanishadic dictum: *nayamatma balahinena labhyah.* "This Self is not attainable by the weak." With some people religion comes to be identified with sentimental and infantile devotion, which, if practised on a wide scale will weaken society. In preaching the gospel of strength Swamiji warned people against developing this tendency, which he called "sentimental nonsense." The real followers of the *bhakti* cult have to be men of solid character. Purity, unselfishness and dispassionate love are the only things that transform the ordinary man into a man of character. Nonattachment brings in its wake fearlessness and strength and the power to concentrate. It thus improves the mettle of men. It must be understood well that spiritual life on the one hand and vigour and strength on the other are not contradictory, but complementary.

Swami Vivekananda called for "sappers and miners in the army of religion," in order to regenerate the world through religion. In him we find the age-old confict — between spiritual life in retirement in quest of happiness in the beyond, and the active life on earth — being resolved in an atmosphere of workable idealism, which he expressively called "Practical Vedanta." His life's mission was to inculcate strength — to bring about all-round progress in life and in society. He realized that on the strength of individuals lay the strength of the nation. The weak and the cowardly cannot achieve anything. He asked for iron wills and stout hearts that did not know how to quake. He repeatedly said: "Be strong and manly." He had respect even for one who was wicked, provided the vicious person was manly and strong. The strong man can change his life with an exercise of his will, but it is impossible to inject that willpower from without into a weak man. Willpower must be a growth from within. Physical weakness is the cause of at least one-third of our miseries, he used to say, for, *sariramadyam khalu dharmasadhanam* — "with the help of the body alone can righteousness be practised."

Swamiji attributed the maladies of our country to the miserable lack in us of self-confidence. He preached with all the spiritual force at his command that self-confidence was the greatest asset. He realized that one must help oneself and never look to others for help. "We have lost faith" said he, "we have less faith than the Englishmen and women, a thousand times less faith. Why is it that we, three hundred and thirty millions of people have been ruled for the last one thousand years by any and every handful of foreigners who chose to walk over our prostrate bodies? Because they had faith in themselves, and we had not." So the recurring theme of his message was: Arise, awake, stop not till the goal is reached: *uttisthata, jagrata, prapya varan nibodhata, abhih, abhih* — "Be fearless, fearless." These ideas Swamiji dinned into the languid ears of his confounded countrymen, for he knew that all our sins and sufferings, crimes and cruelties, exploitations and oppressions in life originated from fear which was born of the ignorance about the glory of the Atman. Swamiji, by preaching this bold religion of Vedanta, tried to wake up the sleeping soul in the Indians. "Arise, Awake, Awake from this hypnotism of weakness. None is really weak, the soul is infinitely omnipotent and omniscient. O, ye, modern Hindus, dehypnotize yourselves, teach yourselves, teach everyone his real nature, call upon the sleeping soul, and see how it awakens. Power will come, glory will come, and everything that is excellent will come, when the sleeping soul is roused to self-conscious activity."

Swamiji used to speak in appreciative terms of the Irish colonists who came to settle in America. At the outset of their life in America they were haunted by the spectre of inferiority. For they were then conditioned by a very depressing and fatalistic attitude to life. But in a short while they became a different people. The same men walked upright, their attire had changed, their look had become bold and fearless. Why so much of change? . . . because in Ireland everyone of them had been kept surrounded by contempt and had always been told, "Pat, you have no more hopes, you are born a slave and will remain a slave"; believing this he had hypnotized himself, but, as soon as he came to America, he was told, "Pat, you are a man, as we are men . . . . a man like you and me can do everything, have courage." Pat raised his head and saw that it was so — and so the transformation. This change in the Irish settlers had impressed Swamiji much and so he used to refer to it as an example of what environment can do.

Swamiji himself had many times experienced the thrill of that spiritual strength which comes by asserting one's divine heritage in the midst of despondency and gloom. The Swami said in one of his letters: "Many times I have been in the jaws of death, starving, foot-sore and weary; for days and days I had had no food, and often could walk no farther; I would sink down under a tree, and life would seem to be ebbing away. I could not speak, I could scarcely think, but at last the mind reverted to the idea, 'I have no fear, nor death . . . the whole nature cannot crush me, it is my servant. . . .' And I would rise up reinvigorated, and here I am living today."

The single word — 'Strength' was the core and the kernel of Swamiji's exhilarating philosophy of life.

Swamiji's every word, every action, every writing was a lofty, spiritual flame that illumined the environment. He did not want us to float meekly and passively on the raft of social conventions, without trying to understand the real significance of spiritual life.

He exhorted us to grow inwardly, manifesting sublime spiritual strength. This inner strength has been appropriately described by the Swamiji as "the strength that comes from touching the feet of God." What the Swamiji really wanted was the glow of soul combined with the vigour of the body, *brahmateja* plus *kshatravirya*. As we are born in a custom-ridden, tradition dominated society, we have to make heroic efforts to cultivate manliness and character. Custom is inherited, but character has to be created. Character is something that is essentially individual, independent of social control, and refreshingly free as well as firm. In the words of Nivedita, Swamiji wanted to see Hinduism no longer as the preserver of Hindu custom, but as the creator of Hindu character.

The most significant feature of the Swamiji's gospel of strength is that he did not make a fetish of nonviolence. Nonviolence, to the Swami, was not a doctrine of weakness; he conceived it as a dynamic doctrine. He expressly enjoined, "To his enemies the householder must be a hero. Them he must resist." He interpreted Buddha's doctrine of nonviolence and noninjury as a message of true spiritual strength. It was the expression of that "Reverence for Life" that is realized in the understanding of the unity of existence. He termed this as "a better way of teaching the same thing, strength." For "it is weakness that conceives the idea of resistance." The path of the monk was not for the householder. Even forgiveness, if weak and passive, was not true; fight was better. Such were the convictions of the Swami. In the right spirit of Hinduism he freely advocated the cultivation of power and the use of it against the enemy unreservedly and for rooting out the evil from spreading further. For, the development of our physical strength and the renewed and incessant study of the Upanishads and the application of the greatest Vedantic truths to the facts and problems of life will lead to a new resurgent spirit in us, the spirit that will transform a moribund society groaning under stagnation. Recent history shows us how far Swami Vivekananda's message of strength has been responsible for India's awakening.

People may well ask: "Swamiji might have roused the people of India from stupor by his thundering voice, but what about his impact on the people beyond the borders of India?" His enlightened interpretation of religion, his spiritual conviction, his manliness, his wide catholicity, his reverence for all ways of life sanctified by age — these certainly created an impact on his audience all over the world. His exposition of religion ushered in quite a revolution in the religious thinking of men of culture, kindling in them the rational spirit of enquiry in regard to matters relating to the spirit. Men had grown to be sceptical of myths, dogmas, narrow notions and theological interpretations which condemned man to the wrath of an angry God. Swamiji's broad based view of man (man is divine and not a sinner) made a deep impression on the minds of the earnest seekers of truth. The effect on them was immediate and almost magical. They were drawn out of intellectual and spiritual inanity towards something sublime, something positive, something significant and full of value, something leading to the spirit of understanding and toleration against a felt background of unity. They understood that the spirit of religion was ever ready to show hospitality to all sincere endeavours to know the Reality. The Swami ushered in a renaissance in man's approach to the Reality. This gave the people new hope, courage and strength. He gave men what they sadly lacked, the bread of life. The message of Swamiji brought solace where dejection once held sway. His call was not made of empty words. His words were pulsating with life, and if cut would bleed, they were vascular and alive, they walked and ran, laughed and smiled — because they were uttered by a mighty soul, and his description of life burst upon people like a blaze of reddish gold, which seemed to have caught the concentrated sun's rays. Like a cloud pouring soothing showers, he sent forth his message of divinity and hope. The Bible, the Koran and all other sacred books were but so many pages, according to him, and other pages remained yet to be unfolded. So he could chant, "Salutations to all the prophets of the past, to all the great ones of the present and to those that are to come in the future." Swamiji said:

"Children of immortal bliss! — what a sweet name — heirs of immortal bliss! Yea, the Hindu refuses to call you sinners; you are the children of God; the sharers of immortal bliss, holy and perfect beings." As life kindles life, so the life of Swamiji brought a new lease of life to lacerated hearts. His words were charged with a fire whose heat was actually felt by his auditors. Even today they carry that fire and they will do it throughout the ages, as long as men expose themselves to them. "His words are great music, phrases in the style of Beethoven, stirring rhythms like the march of Handel choruses. I cannot touch these sayings of his, scattered as they are through the pages of the books at thirty years' distance, without receiving a thrill through my body like an electric shock. And what shocks, what transports must have been produced when in burning words they issued from the lips of the hero!"

18

SWAMI VIVEKANANDA AN INCARNATION OF *SHAKTI*

In a speech on Swami Vivekananda, Pandit Nehru said that if he were to name a single individual as an ideal for children and young men to follow, he would name Swami Vivekananda. "He was the very picture of vigour and strength . . . He came as a tonic to a depressed and demoralized Hindu mind and gave self-reliance and some roots in the past," he said. Swamiji and his teachings are inseparable. What he taught flowed directly from his entire being. His flaming words were the very vibrations of his immortal soul. We may say about the teachings of Swamiji that they are but God become words. And what words are they! There is no end to the power-reserve of his words. Romain Rolland used to feel a thrill like an electric shock while going through his works. To use Mahatma Gandhi's own words, "the love that I had for my country has become a thousandfold after reading his works thoroughly." To Sri Aurobindo, "Swamiji was a soul of puissance if ever there was one. . . ." Swamiji was the personification of dynamism, fearlessness and strength that came from the experience of the immortality of the soul.

Physically of an athletic build, healthy and strong, he knew no fear. He maintained the heroic attitude in all concerns. The fierce was not fierce to him, the terrible not terrible. His massive intellect was duly matched by his burning enthusiasm for the welfare of the poor. He also had a luminous and passionate urge to see God face-to-face. This quest for God brought him to Shri Ramakrishna at Dakshineswar. It was here that the spiritual breakthrough happened which made him finally, a great monk. There he got into the forge of God wherein he was mercilessly hammered into what he became in his later stage. Shri Ramakrishna fashioned the model of his chief disciple with the "finger of fire." This disciple was charged by his *guru* with a noble mission of awakening his people by preaching the life-giving message of Neo-Vedanta. Swamiji found a "mine of strength" in Vedanta. It was tantalizingly fascinating to him. The quintessence of Vedanta lies in that one word — "Strength." He combated the prevalent idea that religion was anaemic, dull, insipid, substance-less, and hence useless and degrading. In him we find a happy synthesis of *kshatravirya* of the heroes of *Mahabharata* and *brahmateja*, characteristic of the ancient sages.

Inclined to an itinerant life, he travelled all over India on foot. He saw with his prophetic eye the predominance of *tamas* that had settled over the race like a miasmal fog. Weakness was mistaken by the people to be a *sattvic* quality. Ignorance, like a mantle, covered the race; superstition ran riot with human imaginations, and credulity occupied the throne of reason. Fear — pervasive, oppressing, strangling fear — gripped the people. Worst of all was the paralysis of resignation. Tears rolled down his cheeks. With a bleeding heart he went to the U.S.A. to get aid for his hungry people.

In the World's Parliament of Religions held at Chicago, Swami Vivekananda, thirty years old, was an intellectual giant and when he rose to speak, the essence of *Bharata-dharma* flowed from his lips. The profundity of the message he delivered, and the impact it created in the world, was staggering. By making a unique juxtaposition of a mere five words he created spiritual history. "Ye divinities on earth, — sinners!" The first four words thundered into being the new gospel of joy, fearlessness, strength, love and service, and freedom for the races of men. And with the last word he struck the mightiest blow to the whole structure of "Soul-degenerating, Cowardice-producing," negative and pessimistic thought and set in motion a new wheel of *dharma*: virility, energy and mastery over nature — inner and outer.

Swamiji was a veritable embodiment of Energy. He was known as "Cyclonic-Monk," "Hindu Napoleon," "Warrior-Monk," etc., for his dynamism. The cry of his soul, the song of his life was the regeneration of India. Indication of his propulsive energy has been noted thus: "As soon as the Swami found clear as noon-day which way the path lay before him for a fructification of his ideas, he was seized with such a paroxysm of intense *rajas*, such a tremendous force surging within him and struggling for an outlet, that he felt as if he would burst. It was this mighty force that fell upon the world in its flood-tides of spirituality, destined to sweep away all that was weak and debasing, and bear in its contents all that was ennobling and life-giving."[1]

The triumphant march of Swamiji all over the country demonstrated to the people that Hinduism had regained its vitality. He breathed life into our moribund religion by forcefully explaining the strength-giving ideas and ideals. The true spirit of religion, as pointed out by him, exhorts us to galvanize our souls with a force that will change the entire outlook and vision of life. All power is within us. Purity, unselfishness, and sincere love for a holy cause will bring out that power. In the right spirit of Hinduism he freely advocated the cultivation of power and its unreserved use against the enemy to root out evil and keep it from spreading further. He repeatedly said: "Physical weakness is the cause of at least one third of human miseries. This is not the time for us to weep, . . . we have had weeping enough; no more is this the time to be soft. What our country now wants are muscles of iron and nerves of steel, gigantic wills, which nothing can resist. . . . Have faith in yourselves and stand up on that faith. Strength is the medicine for the world's disease. Strength is the medicine which the ignorant must have when oppressed by the learned. And it is the medicine that the sinners must have when tyrannized over by other sinners." So the recurring theme of his message was: *Arise, awake and stop not till the goal is reached.* Fearlessness, fearlessness. The single word "Strength" — physical, mental and moral — was the core and the kernel of his exhilarating philosophy of life. His fiery lectures *From Colombo to Almora* are being read as a modern *Gita.*

It was indeed a stupendous task and daring adventure — to bring solidarity in the hopelessly divided Hindu fold. So much emphasis was laid, for at least half a millennium, on the grand futility of secular life, that the general concept of a strong, respectable, spiritual personality united with action was sadly lacking. It was a matter of first blasting away the boulders of ignorance, with the sheer force of his dynamic personality. Sluggish, befuddled and deluded people came out of a centuries-old cocoon of *tamasic* sleep. His lectures had the force of a tornado in their intensity. His fire and blasts fell on the hypocrites and on the traders in religion, too. Every single word emanated from the magazine of his spiritual experiences. He symbolised India's aspirations and vindicated our manhood in the eyes of the world. Pride and self-confidence swelled in the breast of the people and enthusiasm swept the nation like a forest fire. The mental shackles were broken and India was spiritually free. This is a part of our history.

19

SWAMI VIVEKANANDA ON INDIAN WOMEN

A nation lives by the idealism that shapes its destiny. The dominant feature of Hinduism is her emphasis on the development of spiritual life, which finds fulfillment in seeking God within and without. Civilization is sustained by its ability to transmit the spiritual elements of its culture to posterity. The essential feature of the Indian outlook on life is to glorify the spirit over matter, light over darkness, eternal freedom over temporal enjoyments. The philosophy of material self-sufficiency is dangerous as it keeps us bound to the objective world. The real fulfillment in human life is found in the realization of Truth which makes us absolutely free. The one doctrine by which Indian culture is best interpreted by her ablest exponents is that of *tat tvam asi* — That thou art. The divine which is within us, and which is behind everything, is the essence of our soul.

The Indian attitude accepts the spirit in man as immortal. It is eternal, all-pervading, unchanging, immovable. By realizing this great truth, we become free and divine. The Indian mind is coloured by this vision of truth. This eternal longing for the realm of spirit, its deep and abiding faith in the divinity of man, of which all beings and things are the manifestation, the indispensable necessity of having spiritual experience in life are the distinguishing features of Indian culture.

The Indian mind does not create division between nature and spirit, between worldly life and spiritual quest. It seeks to create harmony in life by its ability to accept the unity behind diversity. The goal of religion is the opening of a new dimension in life. With the deepening of our spiritual consciousness, we see this reflection of divinity within and without. From the emphasis on this immanence of the Divine in life, it follows that each individual is potentially divine. This renewal of consciousness is the second birth. To have this spiritual awakening leading to communion with God is the goal of Indian culture. This brings out the distinction between intellectual recognition and spiritual realization.

Ideas and ideals are not dead things. They are living and charged with immense vitality. They impel us to think that life is not merely a physical phenomenon or a biological process. Life is divine. The goal of life is communion with the divinity which pervades and upholds this world. He is the life of our lives, the ground of existence. He is the source of strength, purity, peace and illumination. India in every age has produced great souls who radiated that great culture through their illumined character. They remained unknown but their spiritual glow inspired millions of men and women of all persuasions to highlight this sacred trust, to make an attempt to make life spiritually oriented, to encourage others to civilize the race through self-sacrifice.

In the modern period India gave births to innumerable great women who dedicated themselves to realize truth in their natural habitat, who exemplified the idealism of discharging one's natural obligations in life to be of higher importance than outside engagements. Their unselfish character, abiding loyalty, loving heart, and the capacity to undergo suffering for idealism have enabled us to remember our divine heritage. Women are everywhere the custodians of cultures. The position of women in any society is a true index of its spiritual and cultural growth. Through their loving sacrifice, other members of the family remain sober, gentle, and civilized. If each woman dedicates her life in creating harmony and peace by taming the brutish nature of man, this world will certainly be a better place to live in. "The refinement of man by woman is said to be the essence of civilization." The impulsive and harsh nature of man is changed in the presence of a pure and loving woman. By creating a healthy and peaceful family life, we will be entitled to live in a "global village." No wonder that the ancient lawgiver, Manu, said: "One Vedic teacher excels ten ordinary teachers in glory; a father excels a hundred Vedic teachers in glory; but a mother excels even a thousand fathers in glory." Mothers are the greatest custodians of Hindu culture. The noble character of parents does evoke the reverential attitude of the children. The home and its healthy atmosphere is a great source of spiritual training in India. It has been well said, "centuries of life make a little history and centuries of history make a little tradition." A culture may be compared to "a torch that is passed on from hand to hand down the generations."

Indian culture deteriorated in course of time and the women lost their prestige in the social fabric. Swami Vivekananda wrote to Sister Nivedita on July 29, 1897: "Let me tell you frankly that I am now convinced that you have a great future in the work for India. What was wanted was not a man, but a woman; a real lioness, to work for the Indians, women specially. India cannot yet produce great women, she must borrow them from other nations. Your education, sincerity, purity, immense love, determination, and above all, the Celtic blood make you just the woman wanted."

Backwardness of the women and the people in general made Swamiji restless and he drained out every ounce of his energy in exhorting us to give our sympathetic cooperation to find solutions to the problem. Sister Nivedita writes in *The Master as I Saw Him*: "Our Master, at any rate, regarded the Order to which he belonged, as one whose lot was cast for all time with the cause of Woman and the people. This was the cry that rose to his lips instinctively, when he dictated to the phonograph in America, the message he would send to the Raja of Khetri. It was the one thought, too, with which he would turn to the disciple at his side, whenever he felt himself nearer than usual to death, in a foreign country, alone. 'Never forget!' he would then say, 'the word is, woman and the people'."[1]

Swamiji's own spiritual experience, backed by his deep and penetrating knowledge of Vedanta, enabled him to see God behind man and woman. Therefore he was convinced of their innate capacity to elevate their own position by harnessing this divine energy lying deeply embedded in every self. Hence, Swamiji said: "The uplift of the women, the awakening of the masses, must come first, and then only can any real good come about for the country, for India."[2] His emphatic opinion on the subject: "In India, there are two great evils: trampling on the women, and grinding the poor through caste restrictions."[3] Swamiji had a great hope about the potentiality of our women. He said: "Women must be put in a position to solve their own problems in their own way. No one can or ought to do this for them. And our Indian women are as capable of doing it as any in the world."[4] To Swamiji "education" is the real key that will open the door for all-round advancement. According to Swamiji, education is "the manifestation of perfection already in man," and religion is the innermost core of education. The human being is endowed with infinite power and potentiality. The role of a comprehensive education is to bring forth hidden power to enable the student to have "life-building, man-making, character-making, assimilation of ideas." Swamiji spelled out his scheme for national regeneration: "My idea is first of all to bring out the gems of spirituality that are stored up in our books and in the possession of a few only, hidden, as it were, in monasteries and in forests — to bring them out; to bring the knowledge out of them, not only from the hands where it is hidden, but from the still more inaccessible chest, the language in which is preserved, the encrustation of centuries of Sanskrit words. In one word, I want to make them popular."[5] History has paid eloquent tribute to Swamiji for being the apostle of Practical Vedanta.

Swamiji looked upon women as *shakti* incarnate, as living embodiments of the Universal Supreme Mother of the universe. Therefore, he never accepted the inequality between the sexes. As he wrote: "It is very difficult to understand why in this country (India) so much difference is made between men and women, whereas the Vedanta declares that one and the same conscious Self is present in all beings."[6] One should not think that Swamiji was unaware of the psychological and physiological differences between male and female. That is fundamental. Swamiji knew very well that men and women need not compete with each other, for each is great in his or her open place as assigned by nature. Their roles are complementary, "the perfect balance" and harmony in nature can be achieved for the real well-being of the society through their mutual cooperation based on cordiality and respect. Swamiji said: "Woman is as courageous as man. Each is equally good in his or her own way. What man can bring up a child with such patience, endurance, and love as the woman can? The one has developed the power of doing, the other, the power of suffering. If woman cannot act, neither can man suffer. The whole universe is one of perfect balance. I do not know, but some day we may wake up and find that the mere worm has something which balances our manhood. The most wicked person may have some good qualities that I entirely lack. I see that every day of my life. Look at the savage! I wish I had such a splendid physique. He eats, he drinks, to his heart's content, without knowing perhaps what sickness is, while I am suffering every minute. How many times would I have been glad to have changed my brain for his body! The whole universe is only a wave and a hollow; there can be no wave without a hollow. Balance everywhere. You have one thing great, your neighbour has another thing great. When you are judging man and woman, judge them by the standard of their respective greatness. One cannot be in others' shoes."[7]

Swamiji always advocated equal rights and opportunities for all women. Woman's life is fulfilled in motherhood. In motherhood we see the perfect manifestation of divine qualities — self-forgetfulness and self-negating love that knows no limitations. So Indians see every woman on earth — irrespective of her social status and age — as an emblem of sweetness, ungrudging love, patience, forbearance, modesty, faithfulness and all other divine qualities. She is a true replica of the Divine Mother eternally engaged in the welfare of her children. Speaking about Shri Ramakrishna, his spiritual preceptor, Swamiji said: "This man (Shri Ramakrishna) meant by worshiping woman, that to him every woman's face was that of the Blissful Mother, and nothing but that. I myself have seen this man standing before those women whom society would not touch, and falling at their feet bathed in tears, saying, "Mother, in one form Thou art in the street, and in another form the universe. I salute thee, Mother, I salute Thee."[8]

Following the great teachings of Shri Ramakrishna, Swamiji regarded all women, high or low, ascetic or householder, married or unmarried, child or adult, as the living and visible embodiment of the Divine Mother and therefore he exhorted us to worship them in a pure way, as Mothers. They are *shakti* or Powers of God. Says Swamiji: "Do you know who is the real '*Shakti* Worshiper'? It is he who knows that God is the omnipresent force in the universe and sees in women the manifestation of that force. Many men here look upon their women in this light. Manu, again, has said that gods bless those families where women are happy and well treated. Here men treat their women as well as can be desired, and hence they are so prosperous, so learned, so free, and so energetic. But why is it that we are slavish, miserable, and dead? The answer is obvious."[9] Now, the ideal of women in India is Mother, the mother first, and the mother last. The word woman calls up to the mind of the Hindu, motherhood; and God is called Mother."[10] Swamiji says further: "In India, the Mother is the center of the family and our highest ideal. She is to us the representative of God, as God is the Mother of the Universe. Our God is both Personal and Absolute; the Absolute is male, the Personal female. And thus, it comes that we now say: 'The first manifestation of God is the hand that rocks the cradle'."[11] Swamiji wanted to make every woman conscious of her inner divinity and to behave accordingly. This great cultural heritage, if allowed to orient our mind, will enhance the dignity of national life.

Without the ability to create this spiritual consciousness, it is not possible to teach ethics. Swamiji wanted us to cultivate a sympathetic attitude so that "we should look upon man (and woman) in the most charitable light." Even the public women received sympathy from him. "I have to sneer at the woman walking in the street, because society wants it! She, my saviour, she, whose, street-walking is the cause of the chastity of other women! Think of that. Think, men and women, of this question in your mind."[12]

Having deep conviction in the fundamental Indian doctrine of the motherhood of God, Swamiji, unlike other great reformers like Rammohan and Swami Dayananda, found justification in the ideal of Mother-worship of the *Tantras* — of course in its ideal form. He definitely condemned from the depth of his heart the diabolical practices of degenerated *Tantric* rites. Here again due to Shri Ramakrishna's teaching. Swamiji did appreciate the real spirit behind such practices. "I never objected to the worship of women who are the living embodiments of the Divine Mother . . . a knower of Brahman." Hindu scriptures declare that mother is superior to father, because of her painstaking vocation of motherhood. She cheerfully and courageously undertakes the responsibility of nurturing the child and thereby commands our respect. Hence, the mother is more worthy of veneration than father or anyone else. Building on the natural self-sacrifice inherent in motherhood, their cultural training encourages them to honor the ideals of chastity, unselfishness, patience, and forbearance with the hope of raising the spiritual consciousness of the people.

The modern materialistic attitude of life keeps us riveted to gross enjoyment and consequently, we lose our soul in the game of life. To the Hindu mind the marriage is sacramental, and family life, imbued with this sublime attitude, affords each member the unique scope to manifest his or her native divine qualities through mutual service and self-sacrifice. Conjugal love is to be sublimated into devotion to the spiritual welfare of the entire family, helping all to widen and deepen their character and to perform their domestic and social duties as a means to spiritual growth and enlightenment. That great idealism is thwarted by the encroachment of rampant sensualism. "Ay! The Hindu mind fears all those ideals which say that the flesh must cling unto the flesh. No, no! Woman! thou shalt not be coupled with anything connected with the flesh. The name has been called holy once and forever, for what name is there which no lust can ever approach, no carnality ever come near, than the one word mother? That is the ideal in India."[13]

Motherhood is the natural outcome of wifehood. Hindu woman enters into family life to prepare herself through austerity, penances, fasts and prayers, to become a good mother. Their physical contact takes place with "the greatest prayer between man and wife, the prayer that is going to bring into the world another soul fraught with a tremendous power for good or for evil. Is it a joke? Is it a simple nervous satisfaction? Is it a brute enjoyment of the body? Says the Hindu: No, a thousand times, no!"[14] Prenatal influence is of momentous importance in the life of a child and therefore, Hindu tradition enjoins certain rigorous disciplines on the couple. An *Aryan* (noble) child is born through prayer. "The child must be prayed for." Romantic love, frivolous attitudes, and sensuous enjoyment do not help to bring forth good children. "Those children that come with curses, that slip into this world, just in a moment of inadvertence, because that could not be prevented — what can we expect of such progeny?"[15] These children "may be veritable demons — burning, murdering, robbing, stealing, drinking, hideous, vile."[16]

The ideal woman of India as envisioned by Swamiji was the one who could emulate the greatness of Sita, Savitri, Gargi and Lakshmi Bai. Swamiji paid eloquent tribute to the immortal character of Sita — "This glorious Sita, purer than purity itself, all-patience and all suffering." At the same time, he wanted Indian women to imitate the intellectual brilliance of Gargi, the spiritual resources and fearlessness of Savitri, and physical prowess of Lakshmi Bai. Indian woman should make herself a model of high idealism based on spiritual excellence and practical efficiency and dynamism. He definitely urged Indians to be self-reliant, courageous, and active without losing the eternal feminine qualities which add grace to life. Swami Vivekananda, "the modern prophet of the Motherhood of God and the divinity of all women," gave us a blueprint for a social regeneration on the firm basis of equality of the sexes and the divinity of all persons. Body-consciousness keeps us down to the earth. Unless spiritual evolution takes place in a substantial manner, unless spiritual consciousness takes deep root in our mind, healthy relationships between the sexes can never be established and consequently, a real welfare society cannot be enjoyed. Swamiji was a great lover of freedom but the idea of having total emancipation from the weakness of the body-mind complex was the dearest to his heart. His idea was expressed by Nivedita in her work, *The Master as I Saw Him*: "He would never tolerate any scheme of life and policy that tended to bind tighter on mind and soul the fetter of the body. The greater the individual, the more could she transcend the limitations of femininity in mind and character, and the more was such transcendence to be expected and admired."[17]

Having known the great privileges enjoyed by the western women to manifest their personalities and having spoken on many occasions eulogistically, Swamiji never lost sight of his main point — the goal of human life is to seek total freedom — *moksha*. He was very explicit on it. "Hinduism indicates one duty, only one, for the human soul. It is to seek to realize the permanent amidst the evanescent. No one presumes to point out any one way in which this may be done. Marriage or non-marriage, good or evil, learning or ignorance, any of these is justified, if it leads to that goal."[18] Nivedita writes: "He could not foresee a Hindu woman of the future entirely without the old power of meditation. Modern science, women must learn; but not at the cost of the ancient spirituality."[19] "The frivolous, the luxurious, and the de-nationalized, however splendid in appearance, was to his thinking not educated, but rather degraded. A modernized Indian woman on the other hand, in whom he saw the old-time intensity of trustful and devoted companionship to the husband, with the old-time loyalty to the wedded kindred, was still to him, 'the ideal Hindu wife'."[20] His idea was to have a synthesis, an ideal where the ideas of the East and the West will be happily combined.

We should never forget that he was a great champion of absolute equality and liberty for all. Yet he never approved of freedom for cheap popularity and public approval. Everybody is expected to follow the guidelines of the eternal core of truth embodied in our Upanishads. Swamiji was a prophet of strength, "strength that comes of touching the feet of God" and he wanted us all to cultivate this strength through our spiritual evolution. Hence all the problems of human life have to be solved by each one of us through the cultivation of spiritual strength. No society is ever lost. Evolution and involution go together. "Society is like the earth that patiently bears incessant molestation; but she wakes up one day, however long that may be in coming, and the force of the shaking tremors of that awakening hurls off to a distance the accumulated dirt of self-seeking meanness piled up during millions of patient and silent years."[21]

Therefore, men and women of vision and strength of character will be the "creative minority," ushering in a new change in society. Swamiji thus had tremendous faith in the glorious future of Indian women who will be inspired to seek after the excellence of modern living without ever losing the excellences of their ancient Indian heritage. In short, he exhorted Indian women to have a comprehensive philosophy of life, a life of expanded spiritual consciousness.

All our ills will be tackled by using that single word "Education." "Of course, they have many and grave problems, but none that are not to be solved by that magic word 'education'."[22] Said Swamiji, "With such an education, women will solve their own problems. They have all the time been trained in helplessness, servile dependence on others, and so they are good only to weep their eyes out at the slightest approach of a mishap or danger. Along with other things they should acquire the spirit of valor and heroism. In the present day, it has become necessary for them also to learn self-defence. See how grand was the queen of Jhansi!"[23]

20

SWAMIJI'S DEVOTION TO HIS MOTHER BHUVANESHWARI DEVI

The study of the cultural history of the world gives us an insight about the deep impact of religion affecting human development. Deep religious ideas, unflinching faith in divinity and holy living, permeate the thoughts of our daily life. Without a sympathetic understanding of the religious values of life, we cannot understand any culture.

As Dawson puts it: ". . . throughout the greater part of mankind's history, in all ages and states of society, religion has been the great unifying force in our culture. It has been the guardian of tradition, the preserver of the moral law, the educator and the teacher of wisdom. In all ages, the first creative works of a culture are due to a religious inspiration and dedicated to a religious end."[1]

It is really amazing how, throughout the ages, notwithstanding the social and political upheavals, successive generations of the Indian people, by virtue of their deep religious culture, have transmitted the eternal values of healthy living for the sole purpose of preserving and presenting old traditional values to posterity. Writes Dr. Radhakrishnan: "The civilization which is inspired by the spiritual insight of our sages is marked by a certain moral integrity, a fundamental loyalty, a fine balance of individual desires and social demands and it is these that are responsible for its validity and continuity. To a departure from the ideals can be traced the present weakness and disorder of the Hindu civilization."[2] This great heritage is still alive in Hindu consciousness. "The sages who meditated in the jungles of the Ganges Valley 600 years B.C. are still forces in the world."[3]

"The reason that we Indians are still living," said Swami Vivekananda, "in spite of so much misery, distress, poverty, or oppression from within and without, is that we have a national ideal, which is yet necessary for the preservation of the world!" What is that national ideal? Spiritual quest — attaining perfection through Self-discovery, Self-knowledge and Self-fulfilment — has been the one single dominating impulse of the individual and collective life in India. Religion forms the backbone, the life-current of the nation. Hence, the ideals of "Renunciation and Service" have permeated our outlook of life.

Throughout the world, the great writers have paid their highest tributes to the selfless love of the mothers. "Women have more heart and imagination than men. Enthusiasm arises from imagination, self-sacrifice springs from the heart. They are, therefore, by nature more heroic than heroes."

India is a peculiar country. She has always placed spiritual values higher than others. The timeless values of spiritual growth are still honoured as an ideal mode of living in spite of all the changes. National ideals of India are "Renunciation and Service" — as much for woman as for man; woman is looked upon as "mother." This is the purest and noblest conception of woman in India. Woman is a replica of Divine Mother, she is held in high esteem as the *shakti*, but woman as mother is regarded as the living example of a loving and living God. This motherhood ideal symbolizing self-effacing love is known to the Hindu as divine love. God is the Mother of all creation. National life, conditioned by that great idea, looks upon woman with the utmost tenderness and reverence. This ideal has entered into our blood. The mother is more respected than the father or the teacher, according to our Scriptures. "From the point of view of reverence due, a teacher is tenfold superior to a mere lecturer, a father a hundredfold to a teacher, and a mother a thousandfold to a father."[4] That is the secret behind her social status. Woman preserves the culture through her regard for it. She is the main person, the cementing force in the family. The peace and happiness of the family depend on her quality of life. As Sister Nivedita points out, "There is thus a point of view from which the lives of Indian women may be considered as a vast co-operation of the race to perform necessary labour, dignifying it meanwhile by every association of refinement, tenderness and self-respect. And it might also be claimed that the orthodox Hindu household is the only one in the world which combines a high degree of civilization with the complete elimination of any form of domestic slavery."

The spiritual and ethical culture of any race can preserve its qualities. "It is a change of the Soul itself for the better . . ." Swamiji highlighted the role of real culture: "It is culture that withstands shocks, not a simple mass of knowledge . . . There must come culture into the blood . . . Until you give them that, there can be no permanence in the raised condition."[5]

In India, mothers are the custodians of the cultural training of their children. Therefore, the entire future of the country is completely in the hands of mothers. Swamiji said, "We must not forget that all over the globe the general effort is to express love and tenderness and uprightness, and that national customs are only the nearest vehicles of this expression. With regard to the domestic virtues I have no hesitation in saying that our Indian methods have in many ways the advantage over all others."

Keeping this idea before us, it will be easier for us to study the great character of Bhuvaneshwari Devi (1841-1911). She was the only child of her parents who were very well-known in North Calcutta. She was very beautiful, short in stature and had a regal gait which Narendranath inherited from her. A disciple of Swamiji who saw her in her old age has given this account about her: "Her very appearance commanded respect. She was a strongly built lady with large fine eyes and long eyelashes. She had a remarkably strong personality that commanded respect without any questioning. No wonder that Swamiji had inherited these qualities from her."[6] She was married to Vishwanath Datta (1835-1884) when she was only ten years old. The Datta family of Simla, in North Calcutta, was very well-known for its wealth, education and charity. Vishwanath's father, Durgaprasad, having a strong desire to become a monk, renounced the world in 1835 after a son was born. He paid only a brief visit to Simla after twelve years of spiritual practices and that, too, in obedience to scriptural injunctions. An interesting anecdote in connection with his visit to his birthplace reveals the mettle of the monk. He took shelter in a friend's house with the assurance of being incognito. Unable to conceal his joy, the friend informed the family of the monk, who was whisked away immediately, to his embarrassment. The monk did not lose his mental equipoise, and sat in the corner of the room given to him, the door of which had been locked. For three days he did not touch any food. Apprehending his death, the door was opened and the monk disappeared. Vishwanath Datta later went to Varanasi in search of his father, but in vain. Vishwanath's mother showed her mettle by accepting the great responsibility of bringing up the child with utmost difficulty as she was deprived of her share of property. She died suddenly when Vishwanath was about twelve years old. Now an orphan, Vishwanath grew up in the family of his uncle, Kaliprasad.

In spite of the unsympathetic behaviour of his uncle, who usurped much of the property of his orphan nephew, Vishwanath "reverenced and generously helped the uncle, though he was well aware that he had been cheated by him at every step." Vishwanath was a man with a modern outlook. He was proficient in many native languages. He learned English well. He was a great lover of music and learned it under a teacher. He enrolled himself as an attorney-at-law in the High Court of Calcutta. Due to his high reputation in legal practice, he had to travel to many places in northern India. He was at home with his Muslim and English friends. A man of liberal temperament, he enjoyed the good cultures, literature and the companionship of people belonging to other religions. He once presented a copy of the Bible to his son, Narendranath, with the comment, "All of religion is to be found in this one book." He also read the poems of Hafiz and Hindu religious books. He was free from superstitions. One time, while he was in Lahore, he worshipped the Divine Mother Durga in a picture, and enjoyed the festival in the company of many people by offering them consecrated food. "But to earn money, live amply, and make others happy by practising charity as far as possible — these constituted the highest purpose of his life," according to Swami Saradananda. Vishwanath's huge earnings in the legal profession were extravagantly spent in maintaining a large retinue of dependents. One of his sons later wrote of him: "Extending charity to the poor and the distressed was like a disease with him." Vishwanath was very fortunate in having Bhuvaneshwari as his wife, who was his good companion in every respect. She shared the joys and sorrows of the large joint family with her husband, faithfully following the traditional pattern of life. She showed her exceptional capacity in the management of large and complicated household affairs. In the midst of her extremely busy life, she learned English and read daily from the *Ramayana* and the *Mahabharata.*

She had a prodigious memory and Narendranath learned many stories of the Epics and the Puranas at his mother's knee. Narendranath inherited his melodious voice, musical taste and extraordinary memory from his mother. "Above all, Bhuvaneshwari Devi was deeply religious in temperament, and used daily to perform herself the worship of Shiva. She was not given to much talking. Calm resignation to the will of God in all circumstances, power, and reserve characterized this noble Hindu woman. The poor and helpless were the special objects of her solicitude. Like Vishwanath, Bhuvaneshwari Devi had a very sweet voice and could sing beautifully songs on Sri Krishna, as heard in religious dramas. When beggars singing religious songs came to the house to beg, she could learn their songs by listening only once. She was, indeed, noted for her unusual memory and knew by heart long passages from the *Ramayana* and the *Mahabharata*. More importantly, she had absorbed the essence of these timeless epics, and that essence, together with the culture to which it was the key, she passed on to her children as their great heritage."

"It was, then, to these two, Vishwanath and Bhuvaneshwari Devi, that the boy who was to become the greatest man of his age, whose influence was to shake the world, and who was to lay the foundation of a new order of things, was born."[7]

This couple had four sons and six daughters. Their first child, a son, and their second, a daughter, died in childhood. Their next three children were all daughters. The birth of a son, according to ancient tradition, is always welcome in a Hindu family. Bhuvaneshwari Devi naturally had a longing for a son. Down the ages, Hindu women would invoke the grace of God to tide over the difficulties of life. Their wants and grievances were made known to God, and they practised various austerities and read scripture to invoke His grace. Bhuvaneshwari Devi observed the *somvara vrata* (fasting and praying on Mondays) and prayed to Lord Shiva. One aged aunt of the family who was residing in Varanasi, was requested ". . . to make necessary offerings and prayers to Vireshwar Shiva that a son might be born to her."

Thus, Bhuvaneshwari Devi did observe all the injunctions meticulously, and her whole-souled devotion to Lord Shiva was fulfilled through the grace of Lord Shiva. One night she had a vivid dream. "She saw Lord Shiva rouse himself from His meditation and take the form of a male child who was to be her son." A son was born on Monday, January 12, 1863. The time of his birth was very auspicious. The newborn babe bore strong resemblance in features to his grandfather, Durgaprasad.

The highest and best law in motherhood is the law of sacrifice. That is the lifeblood of her existence. Her prayer-born child was raised by Bhuvaneshwari Devi with utmost care, infinite patience and constant prayer. The child became her whole being. As we read about the early life of this child, we are struck by the deep impact of her personality in the formation of the child's character. One anecdote will reveal a special trait of her personality.

On one occasion, the child — Narendra — was punished by his school teacher without any justification. When Bhuvaneshwari Devi heard it from Narendra, she consoled him and said, "If you are right, my boy, what does it matter? It may be unjust and unpleasant, but do what you think right, come what may."[8] She ever counselled all her children to be truthful, chaste, dignified and humane. She imprinted in their plastic minds the eternal values of healthy living. There is some truth in the familiar statement, "The hand that rocks the cradle rules the world."

Swamiji delivered a series of lectures at Mrs. Ole Bull's home in Cambridge in December 1894. One of them, *The Ideals of Indian Women*, made a particularly deep impact on the women. Highly impressed by his talk, American women sent a letter to his mother in India, together with a beautiful picture of the Child Jesus in the lap of the Virgin Mary. The full letter can be read in the *Life of Swami Vivekananda*: by his Eastern and Western Disciples. Referring to this lecture, Mrs. Bull had written: ". . . he (Swamiji) paid his filial homage to his own mother as having enabled him to do the best he had done, by her own life of unselfish love and purity, that caused him by his very inheritance to choose the life of a monk."[9]

"It was conspicuous in the Swami that wherever he went, he paid the highest tribute to his mother, whenever occasion arose. One of his friends, recalling the few happy weeks spent as a fellow guest in the house of a common friend, writes: 'He spoke often of his mother. I remember his saying that she had wonderful self-control, and that he had never known any woman who could fast so long.' 'She had once gone without food,' he said, 'for as many as fourteen days together.' And it was not uncommon for his followers to hear such words upon his lips, 'It was my mother who inspired me to this. Her character was a constant inspiration to my life and work'."[10] Swamiji as usual, glorified the motherhood of Indian women who are the embodiment of the most unselfish love: ". . . always suffering, always loving, and what love can represent the love of God more than the love which we see in the mother? . . . The love which my mother gave to me has made me what I am and I owe a debt to her that I can never repay . . . I believe whatever religious culture I have I owe to that. It was consciously that my mother brought me into the world to be what I am. Whatever little good impulse I have was given to me by my mother, and consciously, not unconsciously . . ."[11]

"At the end he saluted his own mother to whose unselfish love and purity he owed, he said, all that he had been able to accomplish in this world."[12]

Swamiji never tired of speaking highly about his mother. In a lecture in America, on January 18, 1900, entitled *Women of India*, he said, "My mother fasted and prayed for years so that I should be born. Says our great lawgiver Manu, giving the definition of an Aryan, 'He is the Aryan who is born through prayer . . . The child must be prayed for. Those children that come with curses, that slip into the world just in a moment of inadvertence, because that could not be prevented, what can you expect of such progeny'?"[13]

Bhuvaneshwari Devi lived almost all her long life in the Datta family from her marriage at ten till her death in 1911. How difficult was her life in a joint family headed by an unscrupulous uncle who cheated their legitimate claims at every step, can only be imagined. After the death of her husband in 1884, it was her resourcefulness that kept the family from disaster. "Fallen on bad days after her husband's death, she was put on her mettle and showed wonderful patience, calmness, frugality and adaptability to sudden changes of circumstance. She who spent 1,000 rupees monthly to manage her household affairs, had now only 30 rupees a month to maintain herself and her sons and daughters. But she was never for a day seen to be dejected. She managed every affair of her family with that meager income in such a way that those who saw it took her monthly expenditure to be much higher. One shudders indeed to think of the terrible condition into which Shri Bhuvaneshwari fell at the sudden death of her husband. There was no certain income with which to meet the needs of her family and yet she had to maintain her old mother, sons and daughters, who were brought up in opulence and to meet expenses for the education of her children. Her relatives, who had been enabled to earn a decent living by her husband's generosity and influence, now found an opportunity to their liking and were determined to deprive her even of her just possessions, let alone help her. Her eldest son, Narendranath, possessed of many good qualities, failed to find a job in spite of his best efforts in various ways, and, losing all attraction for the world, was making himself ready to renounce it forever. One naturally feels respect and reverence for Shri Bhuvaneshwari on thinking of the manner in which she performed her duties even in that terrible condition."[14]

Swamiji could never forget the pitiable condition of his mother and his two younger brothers — Mahendranath and Bhupendranath. Swamiji, anxious about his family due to their economic crisis, might have disclosed his troubled mind to Raja Ajit Singh, the Maharaja of Khetri, on the latter's enquiry about the situation of his family during his first visit to Khetri. Subsequently, it is known that the Raja took keen interest in Swamiji's family and also regularly sent Rs. 100/- every month to Swamiji's mother. This happy news removed "a terrible anxiety" from the mind of Swamiji and "made it possible for him to face the world and do some work." This monthly stipend was regularly sent to Swamiji's mother till her death in 1911.

When Swamiji was about to go to the West, his mind was completely upset as a result of a dream. Swamiji later said thus: "Once, while I was putting up at Manmatha Babu's place, I dreamt one night that my mother had died. My mind became much distracted. I used to send no letters in those days even to our Math. Not to speak of corresponding with anybody at home. The dream being disclosed to Manmatha, he sent a wire to Calcutta to ascertain the facts of the matter. For the dream had made my mind uneasy, on the one hand, and on the other, our Madras friends, with all arrangements ready, were insisting on my departing for America immediately. Yet, I felt rather unwilling to leave before getting any news of my mother. So Manmatha, who discerned this state of my mind, suggested our repairing to a man (named Govinda Chetti) living some distance from the town, who, having acquired mystic powers over spirits, could tell fortunes and read the past and future of a man's life. So at Manmatha's request, and to get rid of my mental suspense, I agreed to go to this man. Covering the distance partly by railway and partly on foot, we four of us — Manmatha, Alasinga, myself and another — managed to reach the place. There, what met our eyes was a man with a ghoulish, haggard, soot-black appearance, sitting close to a cremation ground. His attendants used some jargon of a South Indian dialect to explain to us that this was a man with perfect power over ghosts. At first the man took absolutely no notice of us; and then, when we were about to retire from the place, he requested us to wait. Our Alasinga was acting as interpreter and he explained the request to us. Next, the man commenced drawing some figures with a pencil, and presently I found him becoming perfectly still in mental concentration. Then he began to give out my name, my genealogy, the history of my long line of forefathers, my wanderings, intimating to me also good news about my mother. Furthermore, he foretold that I should have to go very soon to far-off lands to preach religion."[15]

We can have a glimpse of Swamiji's feelings for his mother in his letter of January 29, 1894, written from Chicago: "Dear Dewanji Saheb, Your last letter reached me a few days ago. You had been to see my poor mother and brothers. I am glad you did. But you have touched the only soft place in my heart. You ought to know, Dewanji, that I am no hard-hearted brute. If there is any being I love in the whole world, it is my mother. Yet, I believed and still believe that without my giving up the world, the great mission which Ramakrishna Paramahamsa, my great Master, came to preach would not see the light, and where would those young men be who have stood as bulwarks against the surging waves of materialism and luxury of the day? These have done a great amount of good to India, especially in Bengal, and this is only the beginning. With the Lord's help they will do things for which the whole world will bless them for ages. So on the one hand, my vision of the future of Indian religion and that of the whole world, my love for the millions of beings sinking down and down for ages with nobody to help them, nay, nobody with even a thought for them; on the other hand, making those who are nearest and dearest to me miserable; I choose the former. 'Lord will do the rest'."[16]

Swamiji's profound devotion to his mother, his constant anxieties to make her financially self-sufficient and his genuine respect for her great character are known to the students of Swamiji's life. After returning from the West in 1897, Swamiji, in spite of his very pressing engagement, saw his mother at the earliest opportunity and repeated his visits very frequently. A touching pen-picture of his first visit is given here: "After his glorious career in the West, he came and met his mother. With his head on her lap, with all the pranks and helplessness of a child, he cried, 'Mother, feed me with thine hands and make me grow'."[17] During his stay in America, Swamiji had to think about his mother and her problems of life. In his letter, dated January 17, 1900, Swamiji wrote to Mrs. Ole Bull: "It is becoming clearer to me that I lay down all concerns of the Math and for a time go back to my mother. She has suffered much through me. I must try to smooth her last days. Do you know, this was just exactly what the great Shankaracharya himself had to do!"

Swamiji's constant concern about his mother and his eagerness to make her a little happy can be glimpsed from this anecdote: Once Swamiji and Swami Brahmananda were staying at Balaram Bose's house. Swamiji, being a diabetic, could hardly sleep at night; he had to take a nap in the daytime. One day, his mother's maidservant casually asked Swami Brahmananda about "Naren" as she was passing through the area. Swami Brahmananda peeped into Swamiji's room and observing him asleep, reported him so and she left the place. On waking up, Swamiji got the news from Swami Brahmananda, who was severely scolded for not being informed about her. Thinking that the maidservant had come on some urgent business from his mother, Swamiji at once reached his mother's place in a hired carriage. On enquiry, Swamiji learned that his mother had not sent her; she had gone by herself. Swamiji regretted his harsh treatment and sent a carriage to bring Swami Brahmananda to his mother's place. On the latter's arrival, Swamiji, as was his wont, begged him to be forgiven.

This is but a minor event of his life-long devotion to his mother. From his letter to the Maharaja of Khetri on 22 November, 1898, one can get a glimpse of his agonized heart at not being able to do something for his mother's future support. After informing him about his deplorable condition of health, Swamiji said, "I have one great sin rankling in my mind and that is, to do a service to the world; I have sadly neglected my mother." It may be remembered that there were several causes for her suffering — illegal eviction from the family residence, deprivation of her legitimate share of property, the expensive law-suits for many years, the suicide of one of her daughters, Mahendra Nath's absolute silence about his whereabouts (he went to London to study law in 1896 and came back to his mother only after the demise of Swamiji) and acute financial difficulties. Swamiji's family got shelter at his grandmother's house at 7 Ramtanu Basu Lane, which was described by Swamiji in that letter as "a hovel." He wrote, "Now my last desire is to make *seva* and serve my mother for some years at least. I want to live with my mother . . . This will certainly smoothen my last days as well as that of my mother. She lives now in a hovel. I want to build a little decent home for her . . . Is it too much for a royal descendant of Ramchandra to do for one he loves and calls his friend? I do not know whom else to appeal to. The money I got from Europe was for the 'work' and every penny almost has been given over to that work. Nor can I go beg of others for help for my own self. About my own family affairs I have exposed myself to your Highness and none else shall know of it. I am heart-sick and dying — do, I pray, this last great work of kindness to me."[18]

This is one of his famous letters indicating every mark of tenderest affection for his mother. Love incarnate that he was, he seems to drip love in his every action, thought and feeling, in this letter. Here we find in him a rare blend of the strength of steel and the softness of dew.

The Maharaja, touched by the tone of this letter, immediately wrote to Swamiji. Swamiji wrote another letter to him on 1 December, 1898, giving him an idea of the cost for having a house for his mother. In that letter Swamiji again wrote, "One more thing will I beg of you — if possible the hundred rupees a month for my mother be made permanent. So that even after my death it may regularly reach her, or even if your Highness ever gets reasons to stop your love and kindness for me, my poor old mother may be provided, remembering the love you once had for a poor *sadhu*."[19]

The Maharaja at once sent Rs. 500/- to Swamiji, after having received the letter. For various reasons the idea was dropped. Some time later, Swamiji purchased a house from his aunt, taking a loan of Rs. 5,000/-. The aunt outrightly cheated him by refusing to hand over the title deed. Still later, Swamiji planned to build "a little cottage" on the Ganga for this purpose, but that ever remained a dream.

Swamiji, as a true follower of Indian tradition, always glorified the motherhood of Indian women. It was his strong conviction that no real greatness can ever be achieved by any child without being respectful to parents, particularly to mother. Swamiji did his best to make his mother happy in many ways. In obedience to her commandments, he paid a visit to the Kali Temple at Kalighat and performed *homa*, etc., there. Lastly, Swamiji made arrangements to take his mother and other relatives for pilgrimages to Dacca, Chandranath in East Bengal and Kamakhya in Assam, and he also accompanied them. Throughout his life, he caused pain to his family and this visit was arranged just to fulfill her desire. He had a desire to take his mother to Rameshwaram in South India but due to his failing health, it was cancelled.

We conclude our humble survey by giving one more fact of their sweet relationship. "She went up to the veranda of the first story and cried aloud 'Viloo-oo', and her child came out of the room at once. The Great Vivekananda was just like a teenaged son to his mother. He descended the stairs along with Bhuvaneshwari Devi, and then they walked on the garden path together and conversed softly on personal matters. During the last few years whenever Swamiji was at Calcutta he would go to his mother. While at Belur he would occasionally visit his mother at Calcutta, but if perchance he could not go to her for a week or two, she would herself come down to Belur to see him and also ask his advice on family matters."[20]

Swamiji was a "Condensed India." Eternal spiritual heritage of India found in him an inspired champion of Mother-worship in and through a human mother. Literature all over the world glorifies mother-love as the most sacred form of dedication. If we add to that the Indian ideal of Mother-worship, we get a perspective of his extraordinary devotion to his mother. Conditioned from birth by the spiritual idealism of the race, he represented an ideal and philosophy and he also became a model of that idealism. Bhuvaneshwari Devi and Swamiji are not born in a day. They are the product of Hindu culture. Swamiji, the living gospel of Practical Vedanta, has left this rich legacy of his exemplary devotion to his mother for the benefit of entire humanity.

21

SWAMI VIVEKANANDA ON THE FUNDAMENTALS OF EDUCATION

"Is there anything you know or care for?" asks Undershaft of Stephen in Shaw's *Major Barbara*. "Yes", replies Stephen. "I know the difference between right and wrong."

Undershaft: "You don't say so! What, no capacity for business, no knowledge of laws, no sympathy with art, no pretension to philosophy; only a simple knowledge of the secret that has puzzled all the philosophers, baffled all the lawyers, muddled all the men of business and ruined most of the artists; the secret of right and wrong. Why, man, you are a genius, a master of masters, a god!"

The supreme importance of this knowledge of right and wrong has been discussed by Plato thus: "It is not the life of knowledge, not even if it includes all the sciences, that creates happiness and well-being, but a single branch of knowledge — the science of Good and Evil. If you exclude this from other branches, medicine will be equally able to give us health; shoe-making, shoes; weaving, cloths; steamships will still save life at sea and strategy win battles. But without knowledge of Good and Evil, the use and the excellence of these sciences will be found to have failed us."[1]

In our time we find to our profound sorrow that with the steady increase of physical powers there is a corresponding decline of values. The tremendous explosion of knowledge has no counterpart in the increase of wisdom, and the colossal power is not matched by even a modicum of discrimination. This lamentable lack of ethical culture is a menace to our civilization. True religion as a self-preservational effort advocates a practice of restraint on its followers. Education without spiritual motivation simply produces a *rakshasa raj*, by starving the spirit.

How true is Swami Vivekananda's prophetic remark: "Excess of knowledge and power without holiness makes human beings devils." The reign of quantity has usurped our moral mores. The integrity of the "whole man" suffers violently in secularism by unduly inflating man's ego. Spiritual life thereby gets stultified.

Konrad Lorenz, in his book, *The Eight Capital Sins of Civilized Mankind* (1973), says: "The most terrible aspect of this apocalyptic procedure is that the highest and noblest qualities of man, exactly those nobilities which we feel specifically human, are apparently, the first to disappear."

Education is a great source of power, and as such that power is to be handled carefully and intelligently for creative purposes or else it will overpower us, and the misdirected power will spell disaster. Educational institutions have opened the doors but have failed to open the minds of those educated to higher purposes of life. The real problem of education has to be solved in the light of a true concept of man. Education wants to bring out the hidden potentialities of man without knowing him properly. Hence, the most important point is to have a proper concept of man. Man's outlook on life determines his way of life. The correct image of man is essential as it plays a vital role in deciding his pattern of life. It accounts for the strength and the weakness of each culture; a life devoid of meaning and purpose is regarded as of little value. The crowning glory of life is self-knowledge, as all troubles are due to ignorance, primarily ignorance of one's self. This kind of self-knowledge does not mean the superficial study of the objective person. It actually means probing into his essential being, the invisible and elusive aspect of life as it gives him his uniqueness in the world of nature. "In man," says Alexis Carrel in *Man the Unknown*, "things which are not measurable are more important than those which are measurable."

Man is the epitome of the cosmos, an immortal spirit with an effective will, and therefore, man occupies the most important position in Swami Vivekananda's life and teachings. This very vital feature can never be eliminated from his philosophy, as Swamiji's dominant interest in life was man. Naturally, then, in his scheme of education the spiritual concept of man and his glorious future loom large. His greatest contribution in education, hitherto unexclaimed, is his fascinating concept of man. Man is divine, and the entire purpose of effective education is to help unfold that inner divinity — the only great source of wisdom, peace, strength and all other excellences of life. It is here we discover, to our grand surprise, the beauty of Swamiji's educational psychology. Apart from body and mind, man has a soul; this soul — the divine essence, the Real Man — animates, integrates, sustains and directs his psychophysical organism. This inner essence is covered over with alien coverings of worldliness. "Under a golden brilliance the face of Truth lies hidden."[2] The supreme and sacred task of genuine education is to help remove these alien coverings so as to allow the divine spark to blaze forth. Hence, Swamiji says: "Knowledge is inherent in man; no knowledge comes from outside; it is all inside. . . . All knowledge that the world has ever received comes from the mind; the infinite library of the universe is in your own mind. The external world is simply the suggestion, the occasion, which sets you to study your own mind."[3] Heredity and environment are only helpful, but not of absolute importance.

If we are not mentally prejudiced, we are sure to discern from this grand concept of the divine heritage of man a new gospel of joy, hope, virility and emancipation to suffering humanity. This is the greatest discovery that outshines all other discoveries of all great scientists. Intellect, which can unravel the deepest secrets of nature, is unable to know the real essence of man. Only intuitive knowledge can comprehend that. The knowledge of the spiritual dimension of man is of supreme importance for his real well-being and right growth, more than secular knowledge. The spiritual side of man, if properly nurtured through appropriate education, will certainly solve all our crucial problems of life with its own inner strength. After having intellectual conviction of our own innate divinity, we must have a second birth, from sensuous being to spiritual being. This awakening will transform our life by enkindling our latent spiritual possibilities. Man must be educated in the knowledge of his own native divinity. There can never be a more hopeful message to him, especially in our present sick age. Effective education should give a proper direction, a proper perspective to channelize the emotions in higher directions. Power disciplined means power increased. Giving higher directions to this power will bring in its trail all sorts of blessings — purity, righteousness, honesty and integrity. But for this, accumulated power is apt to run riot in the lower plane of life, as the impure, unstable mind and the unrestrained senses are unfit to give higher direction. Value-oriented education must attach maximum importance to unfolding the inner man through spiritual disciplines of self-control and morality. Education is spiritual *sadhana* to manifest our latent divine possibilities. Moral life is closest to spiritual life. Unselfishness is the prime moral virtue. It is through the moral life that the real Self of man finds expression on other levels of life. As long as man is deluded by the body-mind idea, all human interest is bound to be subservient to sense life. He should be aware of his spiritual essence and its urges. Spirit sustains the body-mind complex. Its supremacy is to be recognized. Right understanding is necessary for right living. From moral virtues proceed happiness; from vice, misery. Vice undermines human life, whereas virtue stabilizes it at all levels — the physical, mental, intellectual, moral and spiritual. We suffer more from abuse of power and possessions than from lack of them. True education should help us to bring forth the latent divine excellences like holiness, truthfulness, heroism, patience, etc. The living manifestations of these qualities in our character will enable us to enjoy the glory and dignity of life. "Neither money pays, nor name nor fame, nor learning; it is character that can cleave through adamantine walls of difficulties."[4]

Man is essentially pure spirit ever shining. It is the radiance of the spiritual Self that illuminates the psychophysical system by giving the mind, the organs and the body a semblance of consciousness. They are entirely dependent on It. Spirit is the only source of energies. All other energies — physical, biological, psychical are simply diverse manifestations of the Spirit. By identifying ourselves with Spirit we inherit spiritual powers. Man has the choice of making decisions as well as choice of actions. He can overcome, control and direct the lower self by identifying himself with his wider, truer and higher self. This self-mastery constitutes the real nature of man. Man's spiritual progress is proportionate to the development of this spiritual energy. Man suffers much from his misconception of himself and also brings suffering unto others, thinking them separate from himself.

The doctrine of the "Divinity of Man" must be made the pivot from which all other types of education proceed. Our dismal failure in the things of the spirit, our failure to give a larger meaning and greater depth to life, has brought us nowhere near the true goal of life. It is a poor understanding that finds the true happiness of life in mere intellectual progress. Swamiji gave the greatest importance to the resurrection of man, the brute, into man, the God. This idea is no doubt found in ancient Hindu scriptures, but Swamiji was its most powerful exponent and its most indefatigable champion. His lucid exposition of the Vedantic view of man is rational and scientific. He is an experiencer of Truth also. So, in the gigantic task of education we have first to create a strong faith in the divinity of man and in the moral order of the universe. The dominance of the spiritual over the material must be the central plank in the educational programme of mankind, for there can be no ethos, no ethics without God. Secularism is paying a heavy price for its unspiritual pleasure-seeking goal of life. The animal forces in us can never be checked unless we are drawn to a higher life; proper development of higher values of life alone can check the lower impulses. Thus, the urgent necessity of having a vertical rather than horizontal progress. Education that does not take the initiative in arousing spiritual values of life is no education worth the name, as it gives knowledge but not wisdom. The new orientation is required to create a refreshing and constructive vision of education which is emotionally, intellectually and spiritually satisfying and inspiring. Swamiji's educational scheme based on Vedanta is such a grand philosophy as it is concerned with the development of the whole man.

There is another strong point in favour of self-knowledge. We cannot know ourselves by having knowledge of the world. "Man is thus his own greatest mystery. He does not understand the vast veiled universe into which he has been cast for the reason that he does not understand himself."[5] "Man is the most representative being," says Swamiji, "in the universe, the microcosm, a small universe in himself."[6] The objective world — animate and inanimate — is the projection of this spirit. The Supreme Reality sustains and permeates everything. God, man and subhuman beings live, move and have their being in it. The Spirit in man and the Spirit in the universe are not two, but one — identical in nature. That is the greatest discovery of Vedanta. Self-knowledge will, therefore, compel us to recognize the dignity of life, to develop a reverential attitude toward the cosmos.

To Swamiji, education is a sacred vocation and hence it is equated with spiritual struggle. "Education is the manifestation of the perfection already in man,"[7] says Swamiji. "Virtue is that which tends to our improvement, and vice to our degeneration. Man is made up of three qualities — brutal, human and godly. That which tends to increase the divinity in you is virtue, and that which tends to increase brutality in you is vice, you must kill the brutal nature and become human, that is, loving and charitable."[8] In this way, as explained by Swamiji, our mind and intellect will be purified, and in the pure mind Truth flashes. The sun is not reflected in stone or wood; it reflects in transparent glass or clear water. Hence, our mind has to be pure to be a good reflector, so that self-knowledge — the real nature of our being — may be realized.

Higher culture is the fruit of good education. Self-knowledge, self-discipline and the training to develop individuality form the keynotes in Swamiji's scheme of education. Like Socrates and Plato, Swamiji gave maximum importance to education in developing our all-round faculties. But modern education does not lay stress on the all-sided progress of life. Hence, we see only a broken image of human life all-round. We depend on the politicians who handle power without character and the scientists who are concerned with knowledge without purpose. Even in the spiritual quest, we find people having faith without Truth. Lopsided development of the brain has done far greater harm to society. "It is one of the evils of . . . civilization," exclaims Swamiji, "that you are after intellectual education alone, and take no care of the heart. It only makes men ten times more selfish, and that will be your destruction. . . . Intellect can never become inspired; only the heart when it is enlightened, becomes inspired. An intellectual, heartless man never becomes an inspired man."[9] Again, Swamiji declared that the "intellect has been cultured with the result that hundreds of sciences have been discovered, and their effect has been that the few have made slaves of the many — that is all the good that has been done. Artificial wants have been created; and every poor man, whether he has money or not, desires to have those wants satisfied, and when he cannot, he struggles and dies in the struggle. This is the result. It is not possible to solve the problem of misery through intellect, but through the heart. If all this vast amount of effort had been spent in making men purer, gentler, more forbearing, this world would have a thousandfold more happiness than it has today. Always cultivate the heart; through the heart the Lord speaks, and through the intellect you yourself speak."[10]

Good men — honest, broad-minded, well-integrated whole men with spiritual moorings — are the crying need of the day. They alone can change the society through their moral power. The crisis facing the world is not material poverty so much as the poverty of men — soulful men of vision taking their bold stand on spirit with faith in themselves. Down the ages, the contribution of such men to human welfare and world stability has been far greater than that of so-called educated people having no faith in themselves. So Swamiji always and everywhere searched for "real men." We do not find any moral values — the man-making and character building — in secular education. Modern man is alienated from nature, from God, from society and from himself. He has been increasingly mechanized, atomized and depersonalized. He is sick, embittered and weak. Hence, Swamiji tried to formulate an educational scheme based on spirituality which alone can give us strength, dignity and manliness. "Strength is the medicine for the world disease," says he.[11] Swamiji's life mission was to inculcate strength, to bring all-round progress in life and in society. He attributed the maladies of our education to the miserable lack of self-confidence in the educated man of modern times. Boldly, therefore, he tried to wake up the sleeping soul in man. "Teach everyone his real nature. Call upon the sleeping soul, and see how it awakens. Power will come. Glory will come, and everything that is excellent will come, when the sleeping soul is roused to self-conscious activity."[12] Such was Swamiji's method. His own life is a great testimony to this educational policy, and is a great source of inspiration to all students everywhere. If the tree is known by its fruit, then Swamiji's life is the most attractive as well as most nutritious fruit in the tree of his education.

Swamiji's luminous concept of man and his glorious future is most inspiring, interesting, enlightening and fascinating in contrast with the very depressing picture of man in contemporary history. Swamiji's concept of man and the universe is, in the words of Paul Deussen, "an inestimable value for the whole race of mankind." Says another commentator, "In the whole history of mankind, none has proclaimed the glory and grandeur of man — his absolute divinity, infinite greatness, immeasurable dignity — in such a vehement manner as Swamiji." The spiritual reservoir, a magazine of strength, is the panacea to cure our worst and fatal disease of self-hate which is so common today. This is the most poisonous fruit of secular education, which is completely bereft of the spiritual vision of life. Therefore, Swamiji has given so much importance to the role of the parent as well as the teachers who are responsible for awakening the latent spiritual dimension and qualities in children through the example and conviction of their life. The spirit of religion cannot be taught, but can be caught. Swamiji urged that utmost care be taken to impress upon the plastic minds of children the humane and moral values of life, even emphasizing the tremendous importance of such care during the prenatal stages of development. Modern scholars devoted to child welfare would do well to read Swamiji in this context.[13]

The very attitude of man in seeking happiness outside himself rather than within himself has landed man in a serious crisis. In the modern age, man has mercilessly exploited nature, made this century the bloodiest of all, and poisoned the biosphere; he has gone to the moon and to the depths of the ocean in search of knowledge, but he has not sought to explore the depths of his own infinite soul.

All the ills of secularism can be rectified by turning the mind to the majestic realm of the spirit. That education is real which teaches us to develop strong faith in our own divinity. There can be no grander conception, nor a more impressive lesson for all educationists than the supreme message and teachings of Swamiji. His method of education has given to mankind a stronger incentive for living a heightened glorious life, a far wiser tolerance towards fellowmen with love and sympathy, and a clearer outlook upon the universe, finding unity behind diversity. In Swamiji's divine concept of man, we have the unique chance to re-educate ourselves in the cultivation of self-knowledge which will grant us deeper satisfaction, greater joy and abiding peace.

22

EXISTENTIALISM AND SWAMI VIVEKANANDA

Existentialism is a movement, a predominant emotion, and not a precise system. It is one of the avenues through which the thinkers tried to respond to the challenge posed by the contemporary crisis. This crisis stems from the lack of knowledge about man. Man has forgotten his spiritual heritage and the dignity of life. He is considered as one of the things of the world. "There is something frightening about the last half century's description of modern man," says Karl Jaspers, a noted existentialist. "Burning the bridges to the past, he surrenders to the situation, to chance, to the mere instant. He still lives among stage-props left from other times, but they have ceased to set the stage of his life; they look like piles of rubbish. Man can see they are fictions. Man seems bound for the void, turning to it in despair or in a triumph of destruction."[1] From this depressive situation in man's life, existentialism aims at the freedom of man.

Existentialism has captured the mind of modern man, especially in Europe. Two great wars and their devastating effect, frustrations, and the scientific view of life gave birth to this philosophy. Existentialism is a revolt against naturalism, idealism, and over-intellectualism. Naturalism advocates a materialistic philosophy of life, and man loses his significance, being completely engulfed in matter. Idealism, though improving his self-image, still does not satisfy his innate craving. He feels helpless and sees no freedom ahead. He is goal-less. The overdose of intellectualism chokes life of passion and feeling with abstract thought. Existentialism raises its voice of protest against the rigour and discipline of reflective contemplation. It wants to give articulation to feelings through this philosophy as it was done through the ages of Romanticism, Nietzscheism, and Bergsonism in earlier periods. Ennui, emptiness, helplessness, and meaninglessness of life demand a new search for meaning, freedom, and peace in life. This philosophy poses the question: What is unique about man? Does man have anything unique in his character?

Existentialism urges nothing short of concrete reality. Can it pacify what is called the "metaphysical demand" of human nature? Man's individuality, freedom, and "responsibility" for being what he is, is emphasized in this philosophy. Man is not to be equated with things and beings. He is very unique.

There exist a number of different versions of existentialism. There is the nihilistic and atheistic existentialism of Sartre, the Protestant existentialism of Kierkegaard, the Catholic variety of Gabriel Marcel and varying shades of other opinions. It has no rigid or systematized philosophy. The schools vary in their principles and there is wide divergence in their philosophical outlook. There exist incoherent, loose ideas throughout their literary works. They seek to articulate their views more through novels and plays than through philosophical works. This is in substantial measure responsible for the popularity of their points of view. It is a developing philosophy with various ramifications extending into the various areas of art, literature, religion, psychotherapy, history, etc. It is also a highly controversial and much misunderstood system of thought. It has been interpreted in altogether contradictory ways. One group maintains that it has brought philosophy down to earth for the first time in the West. It is a new label for Christianity. Other groups denounce it for individual liberationism and its proneness to nihilism.

This school does not hold any fixed thought and therefore it does not come within the purview of any systematic philosophical discussion which is logically intelligible. Heidegger had political alliance with the Nazis. It is also difficult to say whether he was a theist or atheist. He, of course, in later life became a mystic, having deep faith in the ultimate mysterious nature of the Reality. Sartre in later life became a torrid Marxist and joined the French army to fight the Germans.

Soren Kierkegaard (1813-1855), a Danish thinker, who is regarded truly as the precursor of modern existentialism, raised his voice of protest against intellectualism, particularly in the form of Hegelian Absolutism which laid stress on the objectivity of truth. Hegel's objective idealism incorporates the truth of subjective idealism and realism. The world is the externalization of the Absolute. Kierkegaard asserted, "Subjectivity is truth or truth is subjectivity." He could never have thought that God was an object. Moreover, Hegel's system reduced man to an insignificant item in the universe and denied him any freedom. He laid stress upon simple truth, generally overlooked in traditional philosophy, that existence is primordial and irreducible. This concrete existence is unamenable to rational analysis and proof. It rather forms the very core of human reality in its inner subjective attitude. This philosophy tends to emphasize the importance of the individual's goals in life and the values he has discovered for himself. The fundamental strain of existentialism finds its explicit formulation in Sartre's statement: "Existence precedes essence. I am a man." The "I am" denotes existence and "man" signifies essence. "Essence is what a thing is, and existence that it is." Sartre makes it clear in his statement: "Man first is, and afterwards he is this or that." This point has been further clarified by Dr. S. N. L. Shrivastava as follows: "The existence which precedes essence is the cardinal principle of existentialism and the one which has been given the name of the movement. This principle, which is applicable to man is best understood when contrasted with its opposite principle viz., that essence precedes existence which is applicable to a material object, say, a paper knife: one cannot suppose that it has been brought into existence without essence, i.e., the manner in which it is made and the definite purpose for which it is made. In the case of man also, according to the theists, the individual before he is brought into existence, exists in the mind of God or his essence is there in the mind of God."[2] This idea is the pivot round which this philosophy moves. It has been criticized however by Dr. Ras Vehari Das in the following manner: ". . . the strength of the existentialist philosophers lies rather in their acute psychological or phenomenological analyses than in the logical coherence of their ideas. When they separate essence from human existence, I do not know how they can still make any significant assertion about human existence. If I am absolutely free, as Sartre points out, and if there is no God and no objective value, I do not see how and to whom I am still responsible, especially when there is no standing 'I' to bear the burden."[3]

Although existentialism has been stigmatized by several thinkers as the "philosophy of irrationalism," and "the philosophy of disillusionment," it has also been addressesd as "a philosophy of faith and crisis." Soren Kierkegaard was indeed a great genius, and the most daring and courageous exponent of the existentialist movement. His originality and serious thinking command our respect. He definitely inaugurated a new era of philosophical inquiry for the West by declaring the subjectivity of truth. He earnestly sought to shift the European speculative balance. Theodore Haecker described this dramatic reversal process of philosophical inquiry in the West thus: "He wishes to go from the person over the things to the person, and not from the things over the persons to the things." He extolled silence and detachment necessary for deep spiritual experiences. "God loves silence . . . . The moment I talk to another man about my highest concerns . . . in that very moment, God has less power over me." He says, ". . . God is a subject, and therefore exists only for subjectivity in inwardness." Human existence has to be understood subjectively as the real and intrinsic truth emerges out of one's inmost depth of existence. Actually he meant the kindling of inner light — the real source of wisdom.

European philosophers in general, excepting a few, take an objective attitude to comprehend the Self. They labour hard to explain the subjective in terms of the object, the inner in terms of the outer. This bias for objectivity is at the root of all the failures that spoil the Western theories of Self. Kierkegaard pinpointed, with all the emphasis at his command, the Western substitution of man for God is the root cause of all our maladies. He says, "Truth is naked . . . in order to explain the truth, one must . . . divest oneself of all one's inward clothes, of thoughts, conceptions, selfishness, etc. . . . ." The riddles of life stem from partial knowledge of life. The most fundamental problem of human experience — the relation of the one and many, changelessness and change, unity and plurality — can be solved only through the Vedantic approach of the Self. Swamiji says, "The background, the reality of everyone is that same Eternal, ... It is the Atman, the Soul in the saint and the sinner. . . ."[4] "All this universe was in Brahman, and it was, as it were, projected out of Him, and has been moving on to go back to the source from which it was projected, like the electricity which comes out of the dynamo, completes the circuit and returns to it. The same is the case with the soul. Projected from Brahman, it passed through all sorts of vegetable and animal forms, and at last it is in man, and man is the nearest approach to Brahman. To go back to Brahman from which we have been projected is the great struggle of life."[5]

This movement has rendered a signal service to us all by demanding our sincere attention upon the uniqueness of man inherent in all of us. This awareness of our own mystery and dignity of life is very important in view of our absolute helplessness in the midst of colossal organized structures threatening to reduce us to an object. This self-introspective mood, if sincerely pursued with greater acumen, finer insight and deep spiritual intuition, in due time, may evolve the concept of Atman as the true inner self of man, so dear to Swamiji. A speculative philosophy, based on reason and sense-experience cannot determine the immortal Self in us. As regards the incompetence of reason to unveil the supra-sensuous truth, Swamiji remarks, "The field of reason or of the conscious workings of the mind, is narrow and limited. There is a little circle within which human reason must move. It cannot go beyond. Every attempt to go beyond is impossible, yet it is beyond this circle of reason that there lies all that humanity holds most dear. All these questions, whether there is an immortal soul, whether there is God, whether there is any supreme intelligence guiding this universe or not, are beyond the field of reason. Reason can never answer these questions. What does reason say? It says, "I am agnostic; I do not know either yea or nay." Yet these questions are so important to us. Without a proper answer to them, human life will be purposeless. All our ethical theories, all our moral attitudes, all that is good and great in human nature, have been moulded upon answers that have come from beyond this circle."[6]

Gabriel Marcel, Karl Jaspers and others belonging to the rightist group (the group maintains a more or less milder attitude and accepts a theistic world-view while the leftist group is represented by Heidegger and Sartre who are spokesmen of atheism) resort to faith as an aid to having communion with God. They believe that life without communion with God is absolutely meaningless. This school puts much emphasis on mood, feeling, and other emotions as the means of knowing the problems of life and due to this dependence it has landed in great trouble. They have challenged the prevalent trend of intellectualism and its exclusive emphasis on the role of reason in philosophical discussion. However, this method of experience "is more like that of an artist than that of the scientist." Again, "by over-stressing the non-cognitive approach to reality, this school seems to be moving to the opposite pole — irrationalism. To prescribe the irrational at the cost of the principle of rationality may be inviting some sort of chaos in mental life, thought and conduct." That is why this school is "anti-intellectualist through and through."

In the modern age Swami Vivekananda is the best exponent and expounder of Vedanta, which postulates Pure Conciousness as the support and substance of the manifold. The central principle in all knowledge is consciousness, the light that reveals the object. Each and every act of cognition is but an expression of Pure Consciousness through a mental mode. In the Western thought a clear-cut demarcation between the mind and the cognizing Self is rarely seen. Mind, normally, is accepted in the West as characterized by consciousness. Self in Vedanta is not an "existent" but "existence" — not as in the sense of a category, but as identical with experience. The Self, thus, is pure being and plenary awareness. This is the real source of abiding happiness. Hence it is referred to as *ananda* (bliss).

Whatever be the labels of existentialism, there is a unanimity among them, which recognizes the primacy of man. They are not concerned about the existence as such, but with human existence. "Existential philosophy is a personal philosophy; the subject of inquiry is the human person." Man cannot know himself from the outside. Once the truth of his existence is known, the individual will give up the world and be contemplative in search of himself. They take man as a central theme of philosophy, and they accept man as a true, self-creating, self-transcending subject. The importance of existentialism consists in its turning the attention of man upon himself. It realizes the need of inwardness. But unfortunately they (philosophers) themselves never accepted this life of inwardness seriously. Moreover their method of self-analysis is defective in view of their mistake in accepting "the shadow of man for man." They accept the self as an existent, and separate man from himself and the objective world. This is not a satisfactory conception of man that we get from these philosophers. This is evident from the series of terms indicating "certain states or moods that they attribute to human existence." The students of this philosophy are constantly confronted by the negative terms such as: anguish, dread, frenzy, horror, despair, absurdity, nothingness, nausea and death. The man is surrounded by hostile forces without, and depressive forces within. Therefore his life is beset with problems which do not leave till death. This life of man "is a nucleus of nothingness," and man has been moving towards his destiny which is death. This constant threat of extinction causes nausea and its concomitant evils. Man leads a dull, drab, dreary and cheerless existence. "Man, thus, is an unwanted being; in the words of Sartre, he is a useless passion." Heidegger goes one step further and demands that man has to be aware of the inevitability of death every moment to enable him to meet the challenge of death. The greatest advantage of having a Vedantic view of man — divinity of man, man as a spiritual being — is here. The Self of man is eternal, immortal; hence it is beyond death. Weak man, through spiritual struggle can transcend the strong grip of cause-and-effect determinism and become completely free.

The existentialist conception of consciousness, as upheld by its atheistic school does not accept the Vedantic view. Sartre does not accept both Kant and Husserl for their belief in a Transcendental Ego. Jean Paul Sartre (1905-1980) who represented atheistic existentialism did not develop any clear unambiguous philosophy. Heinemann says about Sartre: "The French existentialist leader knows that most of his terms are ambiguous, but he needs them in this form in order to build up his system, which is in fact a philosophy of ambiguity." Swamiji's philosophy — essence of Vedanta — does not suffer from such defects. Vedanta is very helpful in solving the anomalies faced by Sartre. Vedanta admits a distinction between Real Self and individual self in the relative plane but this apparent duality vanishes in *samadhi.* Manifold being the reflection of the One underlying the many, gets completely eclipsed in super-conscious experience which is beyond all relativity. Following the spirit of Vedanta and testified by his personal experience, Swamiji accepts the unity of existence. There is only "One, eternal, unchanging, infinite" — the "One without a second."[7]

False knowledge divides us; true insight born of genuine mystical experience gives us the wisdom of Unity. Existentialists have deprived themselves of having the comprehensive vision of truth by giving undue stress upon choice, commitment, and action. Intense spiritual life may get the vision of truth through intuition. Vedanta accepts unity of existence, the latter is never divorced from the essence — the being of the manifold. Essence — being the source of ethics, values, and culture — has to be accepted in a comprehensive philosophy of life. Swamiji says, "The infinite oneness of the soul is the eternal sanction of all morality, that you and I are not only brothers — every literature voicing man's struggle towards freedom has preached that for you — but that you and I are really one. This is the dictate of Indian philosophy."[8] Swamiji's philosophy does give adequate importance to both — essence and existence. By experiencing the existence as the manifestation of the One, it does not create a false dualism that vitiates the existentialists. They dichotomize between essence and existence and thereby become an easy victim of dualism — the root of all anxieties. Swamiji is neither pessimistic nor optimistic. He is a die-hard realist who is sure of our great future in illumination.

The tragedy of human life stems squarely from our metaphysical ignorance — about our divinity. Rootlessness does create all problems of existential anguish. "A more serious source of resistance," says Rollo May, "is one that runs through the whole of modern western society — namely, the psychological need to avoid and, in some ways, repress, the whole concern with "being." In contrast to other cultures which may be very concerned with being — particularly Indian and Oriental — the characteristic of our period in the West, as Marcel rightly phrases it, is precisely that awareness of "the sense of the ontological — the sense of being — is lacking. Generally speaking, modern man is in this condition; if ontological demands worry him at all, it is only dully, as an obscure impulse."[9]

Swami Vivekananda's concept of man is a spiritual concept, Atman encased in a psychophysical organism. A thoroughly man-centered philosophy, in spite of the optimism of the philosophers, can never get any glimpse of Swamiji's Atman-centered man through logic. If, instead of the concept of a distant or extra-cosmic God giving His Grace to a devotee, life is looked upon as conceived and sustained in Divinity, revelation will be interpreted as the manifestation of the divinity in a pure heart. This experience of the supra-sensuous and the supra-mental does not depend on logical arguments, however brilliant. Direct insight into the depth of truth comes to those who are absolutely pure in thought, word, and deed. Vedanta is quite emphatic that impulses, weakness, and impurity undermine man's capacity to think clearly, perceive correctly, or reason rightly. "Blessed are the pure in heart, for they shall see God."

The difference between the two systems — existentialism and Vedanta — is radical. The Being of Vedanta, being spiritual in nature, can never be adequately conceived by any one system or by the numbers of systems depending on reason and sense experience. Although the existentialist movement has rightly upheld the glory and dignity of human life, yet it has failed to present any practical scheme of discipline leading to final emancipation from all bondage and consequent illumination. In Swamiji's philosophy *moksha* (illumination) is the bedrock on which his entire teaching is founded. Religion and life are not different poles apart, but they are one and the same. Indian genius discovered harmony in a higher synthesis where apparent contraries get dissolved. Vedanta sees One in many. The conflict between faith and reason is due to the dichotomizing tendency of the intellect. Moral life helps us to gain an insight into spiritual life. Morally pure persons with the help of their pure intellect can develop a supra-sensuous and supra-rational faculty of intuition which is far superior to intellect and does unravel truth hitherto not known.

Revelation introduces to us the aspect of life which is not otherwise accessible. Thus reason, in intense spiritual living, culminates in faith, and intellect to intuition, in due process of development. Therefore, they are not a leap "over seventy thousand fathoms of water." The thinkers of this school do not accept any divine plan behind the world. Vedanta accepts the presence of one self-effulgent reality which holds, penetrates, monitors and regulates worldly phenomena. The indwelling divinity within us enables us to have Self-knowledge. That is the sole purpose of creation. Man has been travelling always from lower truth to higher truth. This perception of the cosmic plan and the understanding that self-knowledge is attainable through the mastery of our weaknesses is a positive source of deep satisfaction and joy. Swamiji says, "Man's struggle is in the mental sphere. A man is greater in proportion as he can control his mind. When the mind's activities are perfectly at rest, the *atman* manifests Itself."[10]

Therefore in Vedanta the cause of evolution is much deeper. It is the innermost urge of life to experience the true nature of life. Our ego creates division and tension; therefore Vedanta exhorts us to transcend the finite ego to attain spiritual consummation. Kierkegaard's acceptance of the limitation of reason;

our sheer incapacity to know our real nature in our unregenerated state; real knowledge of ourselves as the saving truth in life, and not a mass of objective knowledge; all are accepted by Vedanta.

That truth is subjectivity, that the practice of detachment and the cultivation of true inwardness is a means of transcending one's weakness, and finally, that it is the individual's responsibility to attain Self-knowledge, receives hearty appreciation from the Vedantists. Vedanta wants to study the entire gamut of life in all its aspects; it is not interested in the superficial study of life. Existentialists lack both the breadth of vision and the comprehensiveness of understanding that Vedanta has. The mistake lies in the one-sided view of life they study. They are no doubt men of extraordinary insight and scholarship. But fundamental misconceptions about the timeless Truth underlying the manifold has caused their shortsightedness. Most of the high priests of this school of thought are definitely original thinkers with deep insight. However, they did not attain the beatific vision of that timeless Truth due to a materialistic concept of life. If thay had such an experience, as we find in the life of Swamiji, this philosophy would have been completely different. That certainly does not mean we are not aware of their singular achievement in giving a new philosophy of the dignity of life. Existentialism is a new name for an ancient Vedantic way of self-inquiry — *atmanam viddhi* or 'Know Thyself,' so beautifully delineated in the Upanishads. True existentialism gets full articulation in the *mahavakya* (the great saying): *Tat Tvam Asi,* "That Thou Art."[11] Swami Vivekananda became a great humanist in the real sense of the term by experiencing in his personal life the Absolute and visualizing the Divine in and through all. He realized that one Supreme Brahman who pervades the whole universe and is the sum total of all souls. Therefore, from a superficial point of view, we find many of his ideas in common with this School. Beyond that, agreement must stop.

23

SWAMI VIVEKANANDA AND THE MODERN INTELLECTUALS

Shri Ramakrishna's silent *tapasya* at Dakshineshwar was fanning the smouldering embers of latent spirituality in our religion into a roaring flame. He took a plunge into the invigorating ocean of spirituality and was enabled to present many a beautiful gem hitherto unknown to the agnostic world suffering from various maladies. Swami Vivekananda was trained by Shri Ramakrishna to preach the age-old message to suffering humanity according to the need of the age. Swami Vivekananda, in his historic speech at Chicago, dwelt on the spiritual heritage of man. He was a rare personality born with an aroma of divine fragrance. The bewildered man of the Western hemisphere was stupefied to find in him supramental light in its mellowed grandeur and soft lustre. His interpretation of Hinduism removed the much misconceived idea that it was a museum of beliefs and medley of rites. His life-giving message — man is not a bundle of flesh, he is a spirit encased in a body — ushered in a new hope in the minds of people steeped in materialism. His thunderous voice — "Ye divinities on earth" — brought the gospel of joy, hope, virility and emancipation to tormented humanity. We are still living within the mental reverberations of that historic event. He was neither a sky-blue idealist, nor an earth-bound philosopher, nor a mere reformer. He was a realist to the core and hence his message was immensely practical. He realized the Truth which adumbrates Divinity in all beings. He brought spiritual consciousness to men and assuaged the misery of the humble and the poor. He exhorted us to build a social structure rooted in the principles of truth, freedom and equality. His ideals are not mere words. They cannot be guillotined on the scaffold of practicality. He says in his *Karma Yoga*, "Love, truth and unselfishness are not merely moral figures of speech, they form our highest ideal; because in them lies such a manifestation of power."

The world was for the Swami a reality and not an illusion, since the mission of his life viz., service to humanity, had to be fulfilled in the world. He was eager to see the culmination of his ethical and spiritual endeavours. Spirituality was the breath of his life. He said, "Without the struggle towards the infinite, there can be no ideal." Again he says, "without supernatural sanction, as it is called or the perception of the superconscious, as I prefer to term it, there can be no ethics." Against the wide canvas of his absorbing public life, the wealth of imagination, the depth of emotion, the vigour and variety of intellect that are found in him are simply superhuman.

Divinity of the Soul, unity of existence and unity in diversity — these were the main themes of his teachings. The purpose of human life is to unfold the inner Divinity. If we are not entombed by our stupidity and selfishness, we are sure to discern from his message that we live in the cosmic process — its perpetual progression from matter to life, life to mind, mind to intelligence, intelligence to spirit, — which has an order and a purpose. We must have a second birth; from dry intellectuality to spirituality, from justice to charity, from law to love. This is the most significant discovery, the way to new dimensions of existence.

The clouds of confusion and agnosticism could not hide the sun of true religion. Human life acquired suddenly a new momentum and value. The promises of the high priests, scientists, materialists and diplomats, paled like a candle light at sunrise, and a new outlook of life based on spirituality ran like wildfire through the intellectual horizon of the world. People began to ignore worldly standards set by the hedonists and grounded themselves on the intuitions of prophets and commandments of God. His message of strength, faith, energy and solidarity injected new life in our moribund nation. His dynamism had an irresistible appeal to the Indians. In the words of Romain Rolland, "Swami Vivekananda was himself the conscience of India, its unity and its destiny. All of them incarnated in him." He did not want us to keep away the foreign culture. He was a great protagonist of synthesis. He said, "India has to learn from the West the conquest of external nature and the West has to learn from India the conquest of internal nature. . . . There will be neither Hindus nor Europeans. . . . there will be the ideal humanity which has conquered both the natures, the external and the internal. We have developed one phase of humanity and they, another. It is the union of the two that is wanted." To quote him again, "Can you become an occidental of occidentals in your spirit of equality, freedom, work and energy and at the same time a Hindu to the very back-bone in religious culture and instincts?"

The practical teaching of the Swami based on his realizations influenced all and sundry. To Romain Rolland, "He was energy personified and action was his message to men. But his pre-eminent characteristic was kingliness. He was a born king and nobody ever came near him either in India or America without paying homage to his majesty." Unfortunately, our educated people even today have shown their studied negligence to his words, which can be regarded as a beacon light in our dark age. The scholars of our country have not, as yet, outgrown a slavish mentality. Their misguided genius with pigeon-holed patterns of thought have landed us in a crisis. Bereft of the cultural moorings of our country as well as original thinking power, they are even today hewers of textbooks and drawers of book-learning. To their clouded intellect and oppressive narrowness, the glory of human life and the spiritual heritage of man are so nebulously distant and unreal. They are insularly modern and as such they are not going to be guided by anybody other than their guardians — Freud, Marx, Darwin and their henchmen who are largely dominated by the materialistic view of life. Although with the passage of time, they were proved to be ludicrously false, with the falsehood of sophisticated foolishness, their minds cling to these sinister dogmas steadfastly.

It is a matter of great regret that the brilliance which captivated most of the intellectual stalwarts of our country in the 19th century and which has powerfully provoked the imaginations of the scholars of the West including Russia, has miserably failed to win over the hearts of our educated people. To Mr. Nehru his message is still very fresh and capable of solving all our problems. To Romain Rolland, it cannot be read without receiving a thrill through the body like an electric shock. Still, our educated people do not care to read it; what a tragedy!

Swamiji entered upon a crusade against the materialistic civilization. "The whole of the Western world is on a volcano which may burst tomorrow, go to pieces tomorrow."[1] He was standing in the shadow of events still long in coming. The history has painfully witnessed the fulfilment of his prophetic utterances. When scholars like A. Toynbee, B. Russell, C. E. M. Joad, P. A. Sorokin, Lewis Mumford and a host of others are sincerely trying to come out of the death trap by resorting to his scheme of life and devoting their indefatigable energies for the propagation of the spiritual view of life, the ideal of our educated gentry, generally speaking, is still with the Faustian thirst for information and desire for material comforts. Their secular way of life and insatiable lust for material goods have forced them to live in a world of blasted hopes, despair, dejection and irreparable disillusionments. Empiricism and rationalism reign supreme in their mind and transworldly values are banished beyond its frontiers. Among the educated people, frustration looms large. The glaring drawback of our age is nihilism. We, in India especially, are habituated to bare bodies. It no longer shocks us. But the horror of the naked mind is more than we can bear. We do not find any Indian outlook among these people. They are westernized sans their efficiency and character. Faith is sabotaged by almighty reason. Religion is an "opiate for the people" or "regression to infantile primitivism" and, the "idea of God is merely a symptom of functional disorders in the brain," — these are the ideas they believe in. There is lack of vitality, a spiritual flagging. Scepticism in matters of belief and indifference with regard to spiritual values are the outstanding characteristics of the mood of most of the educated.

The consequences of a materialistic outlook of life have been beautifully depicted by Thomas Hardy, quoted by Radhakrishnan in his *Recovery of Faith*: "Whether owing to the barbarising of taste in the younger minds by the dark madness of the late war, the unabashed cultivation of selfishness in all classes, the plethoric growth of knowledge with the stunting of wisdom, a degrading thirst after outrageous stimulation or from any other cause, we seem threatened with a new Dark Age."[2] The baneful effect of Western education hardly helps us in our life's struggle. We come out without our mental dimensions expanded, attitudes oriented and crystallized, outlook broadened and knowledge increased. The restlessness, split personality and fear-obsession which growingly characterize the generations are on the anvil of contemporary thought. "Despite the marvels of scientific civilization, human personality," says Dr. Carrel, "tends to dissolve." In spite of the warnings of the coolheaded great men of this century we are letting each puff of wind from the West blow us whither it pleases. Long before the admonitions of Toynbee, Russel, Sorokin and others the great Swami challenged the attempt of the West, which builds its trust on "reeking tube and iron shard" and leaves out of its calculation the invincible soul of man. Our dismal failure in the things of the spirit, our failures to give a larger meaning and greater depth to life have brought us nowhere near our goal.

Intellectual stalwarts of our country, in the late 19th century, were the products of our culture. They had no vapourish misconceptions regarding the essence of our culture. They believed in the synthesis of culture and had the strength to clear the cobwebs of discouragement from brains and drive away fear, inferiority complex and disappointments. After the long, long winter of centuries we had the unique privilege to see before our eyes the real specimens of our culture. Their character was "an elemental creation of destiny." Their snow-white peaks of sanctity, purity and holiness in life are beyond our imagination. They were successful in projecting an image of their innate goodness in public as well as in private life. That glorious age was, indeed, characterized by a spacious intellectual expansion, noble endeavour and bright aspirations. The outflanking attempt of the West to indoctrinate was stemmed in no time under the avalanche of awakened Indian indignation. We were insulated against the internal and external disintegrating forces. From the intellectuals of that age to their modern compeers is only a few years in time, a few miles in space; but what a vast distance in terms of spirit. We are pygmies in the land of the giants. They moved like lions in the dependent India but we live like sheep in free India. Behind their manliness and strength we discern the strength of the spirit. They were mountains of self-confidence. The cause for the present state is the failure of the intellectuals to give the correct lead.

It is the bounden duty of all educated people of our country to declare war against the materialistic view of life that is eating into the vitals of the nation. "The world has need of a philosophy or a religion," says B. Russell, ". . . .If life is to be fully human, it must serve some end which seems, in some sense, outside human life, some end which is impersonal and above mankind, such as God or truth or beauty." Dr. Alexis Carrel wants the leadership of the spiritualists who possess the real knowledge of human nature, its aims and aspirations: "Perhaps religious order, whose members possessed a character, at once scientific and sacerdotal, should be founded for this very end."

We should do well if we give serious thought to the following message of Swamiji who has been hailed by Romain Rolland as "the pilot and guide of the needs of the present age." "Religion, and religion alone, is the life of India and when that goes India will die, in spite of politics, in spite of social reforms, in spite of Kubera's wealth poured upon the head of every one of her children."[3]

24

SWAMI VIVEKANANDA ON BUDDHA

Buddha represented an Everest-high ascent of human genius in the realm of life's supreme values. His forty-five years of unceasing spiritual ministration was indeed something unique in the history of religion. Down the scores of centuries his deep meditative posture has been standing before us as a model of humanity, as the polestar of our life. This dynamic character of Buddha, for centuries together, was out of the Indian mind, and His idealism and teaching had become archaic in the national consciousness. India is deeply indebted to western scholars for the revival of the Buddha spirit and its vast literature, through the research and writings in the last century. Swami Vivekananda was one of the few great thinkers of India to acknowledge the greatness of Buddha's flaming message. He paid many heartfelt tributes to Buddha. He once said: "I am the servant of the servants of the servants of Buddha. Who was there ever like Him? — the Lord — who never performed one action for Himself — with a heart that embraced the whole world! So full of pity that He — prince and monk — would give His life to save a little goat! So loving that He sacrificed Himself to the hunger of a tigress! — to the hospitality of a pariah and blessed Him! And He came into my room when I was a boy and I fell at His Feet! For I knew it was the Lord Himself!"[1] And again, "We cannot approach that strength. The world never saw anything compared to that strength."[2] Further he said, "The life of Buddha has an especial appeal. All my life I have been very fond of Buddha, but not of His doctrine. I have more veneration for that character than for any other — that boldness, that fearlessness, and that tremendous love! He was born for the good of men. Others may seek God, others may seek truth for themselves; He did not even care to know truth for Himself. He sought truth because people were in misery. How to help them, that was His only concern. How can we ignorant, selfish, narrow-minded human beings ever understand the greatness of this man?"[3]

Buddha was the foremost existential philosopher of the world. He did His best to help mankind enjoy its freedom from bondage.

The root of man's suffering is his own mind. His endless desires make him bound. None is responsible for his suffering. Hence Buddha's message to His dear disciples was, "Be ye lamps unto yourselves. Be ye a refuge to yourselves."

Buddha never declared Himself as the Saviour. He never wanted to be looked upon as anybody's master. Swamiji said, "None of his adulators could draw from him one remark that he was anything different from any other man."[4] He only pointed out certain basic facts of life causing us troubles, which can be rationally traced by any intelligent person. On his deathbed he said, "Work out diligently your salvation. Each one of you is just what I am. I am nothing but one of you. What I am today is what I made myself. Do your struggle and make yourselves what I am."[5] He also said: "Believe not because other people like you believe it. Test everything, try everything, and then believe it, and if you find it for the good of many, give it to all."[6]

Swamiji admired Buddha for his rational temper tinged with a compassionate heart. Swamiji said about him, "(He was) the sanest philosopher the world ever saw. Its best and its sanest teacher. And never that man bent before even the power of the tyrannical Brahmins. Never that man bent. Direct and everywhere the same: weeping with the miserable, helping the miserable, singing with the singing, strong with the strong, and everywhere the same and able man."[7]

In the Parliament of Religions, Swamiji gave a talk on September 26, 1893, *Buddhism, The Fulfilment of Hinduism*. In that talk he said: "You have just now heard that I am going to criticize Buddhism, but by that I wish you to understand only this. Far be it from me to criticize him whom I worship as God incarnate on earth. But our views about Buddha are that he was not understood properly by his disciples. The relation between Hinduism (by Hinduism, I mean the religion of the Vedas) and what is called Buddhism at the present day is nearly the same as between Judaism and Christianity. Jesus Christ was a Jew, and Shakya Muni was a Hindu. The Jews rejected Jesus Christ, nay, crucified him, and the Hindus have accepted Shakya Muni as God and worship him.

But the real difference that we Hindus want to show between modern Buddhism and what we should understand as the teachings of Lord Buddha lies principally in this: Shakya Muni came to preach nothing new. He also, like Jesus, came to fulfill and not to destroy. Only, in the case of Jesus, it was the old people, the Jews, who did not understand him, while in the case of Buddha, it was his own followers who did not realize the import of his teachings. As the Jew did not understand the fulfillment of the Old Testament, so the Buddhist did not understand the fulfillment of the truths of the Hindu religion. Again, I repeat, Shakya Muni came not to destroy, but he was the fulfillment, the logical conclusion, the logical development of the religion of the Hindus."[8]

The spirit of Hindu scriptures — practice of being good and doing good — was fulfilled by Buddhism which was nothing but Practical Vedanta. Vedic truths could not be available to the masses due to the prevalence of priest craft. Swamiji admired Buddha because "he had the large-heartedness to bring out the truths from hidden Vedas and through them broadcast all over the world."[9]

Buddha also preached his sermons in Pali instead of Sanskrit, the language of the elites. He said: "I am for the poor, for the people; let me speak in the tongue of the people."[10] For this reason, Buddha's sermons were available to the masses. In due course, Buddhism lost its original vigour, freshness of outlook and strength of character that affected Hinduism also. The loss was in terms of "that reforming zeal, the wonderful sympathy and charity for everybody, that wonderful leaven which Buddhism had brought to the masses. . ." as indicated by Swamiji in his talk.[11]

Buddha was a supreme *karma yogi* to carry this message of love. Swami Vivekananda highlighted the great character of the *Tathagata* as an exemplar of *karma yoga* in this fitting testimony: "Let me tell you in conclusion a few words about one man who actually carried this teaching of *karma yoga* into practice. That man is Buddha. He is the one man who ever carried this into perfect practice. All the prophets of the world, except Buddha, had external motives to move them to unselfish action. The prophets of the world, with this single exception, may be divided into two sets, one set holding that they are incarnations of God come down on earth, and the other holding that they are only messengers from God; and both draw their impetus for work from outside and expect reward from outside, however highly spiritual may be the language they use. But Buddha is the only prophet who said, 'I do not care to know your various theories about God. What is the use of discussing all the subtle doctrines about the soul? Do good and be good. And this will take you to freedom and to whatever truth there is.' He was, in the conduct of his life, absolutely without personal motives; and what man worked more than he? Show me in history one character who has soared so high above all. The whole human race has produced but one such character, such high philosophy, such wide sympathy. This great philosopher, preaching the highest philosophy, yet had the deepest sympathy for the lowest of animals, and never put forth any claims for himself. He is the ideal *karma yogi*, acting entirely without motive, and the history of humanity shows him to have been the greatest man ever born; beyond compare the greatest combination of heart and brain that ever existed, the greatest soul power that has ever been manifested. He is the first great reformer the world has seen. He was the first who dared to say, 'Believe not because some old manuscripts are produced, believe not because it is your national belief, because you have been made to believe it from your childhood; but reason it all out, and after you have analyzed it, then, if you find that it will do good to one and all, believe it, live up to it, and help others to live up to it'."[12] He works best who works without any motive, neither for money, nor for fame, nor for anything else; and when a man can do that, he will be a Buddha, and out of him will come the power to work in such a manner as will transform the world. This man represents the very highest ideal of *karma yoga*.

India does not profess to be a Buddhistic country. Still, she adores Buddha; nay, Buddha is accepted by the Hindus as one of the incarnations of God. Buddhism has been absorbed by Hinduism, the former has lost its separate entity in India. Swamiji's strong conviction was that "Hinduism cannot live without Buddhism". For the all-round growth of human society or individuals, we require the intellectual acumen of the Hindus, their philosophy of the Self as well as the wonderful heart of Buddha, his all-compassionate love.

Buddha gave his love to the weak and the lowly. His life, from his early days of spiritual ministration to his very last days, taught this grand message of purity, renunciation and love for one and all. His religion was widespread, according to Swami Vivekananda, "because of the marvellous love which, for the first time in the history of humanity overflowed a large heart and devoted itself to the service not only of all men but of all living things — a love which did not care for anything except to find a way of release from suffering for all beings.[13]

His all-encompassing love for all beings, even to animals, was emulated by every sect from that time in India. "This kindness," says Swamiji Vivekananda, "this mercy, this charity — greater than any doctrine — are what Buddhism left to us."[14]

"If he was great in life, he was also great in death."[15] Buddha's vision of equality and compassion for the downtrodden was so profound that he ate the unwholesome food offered by Chanda, a man of humble origin, lest the latter be hurt by his refusal. Chanda's food was the cause of his death. He told his followers, "Do not eat this food, but I cannot refuse it. Go to the man and tell him, he has done me one of the greatest services of my life — he has released me from the body."[16] To him this food was equally valuable to that of Sujata, whose rice pudding had once saved his life. Religious-minded people down the ages had been worshiping God. "This was the first time they turned to the other God — man. It is man that is to be loved. It was the first wave of intense love for all men — the first wave of true unadulterated wisdom — that, starting from India, gradually inundated country after country, north, south, east, west."[17] Buddha's greatness lies in "his unrivalled sympathy" and not in *nirvana*. Swami Vivekananda says, "Those last dying words of his always thrilled through my heart."

25

JOSIAH JOHN GOODWIN, THE FAITHFUL DISCIPLE

History periodically shows the influence of the manifestation of the Divine in man. The Supreme Being manifests Itself in a special way from age to age through those individuals known as "the makers of history". Through a multitude of His agents, in an unbroken succession of geniuses, God disseminates spiritual teachings to the world. When our dormant spiritual life is awakened through such messengers of Truth, we struggle to experience our innate divinity. Thus, God reveals Himself through great lives which act as transmitters of spiritual idealism among people. The timely emergence of these high souls in every epoch, and their various activities bring forth a new awakening and a new dimension to life. We distinctly perceive that a series of events is not a sport of chance, but well calculated and timely actions of an ever watchful God.

The advent of Swami Vivekananda in the world's history was the result of a deep irrepressible moral necessity of the age. In him, we witness a brilliant manifestation of divine splendour, creating in our minds a conviction of its authenticity. Swamiji exhorted people to value the spiritual in life and he incorporated in his own personality the manliness of the West and the saintliness of the East. He appeared in the history of humanity to fulfill God's spiritual mission. A most important phenomenon in the history of the last century was the meeting of the East and the West through Swamiji, who inaugurated this rapprochement during and after the Parliament of Religions held in Chicago in 1893. He was a great champion of universal cooperation and understanding. So the New World looked upon him as a pilot and guide of humanity.

Swami Vivekananda's illuminating and universal teachings are available to us mainly due to the loving and untiring services of Mr. J. J. Goodwin (1870-1898), a brilliant stenographer. His contribution to the Vedanta movement is well-known. Swamiji had been in the U.S.A. since 1893. The year 1896 was a remarkable one because of the invaluable services of Mr. Goodwin, who did his best in every possible way to preserve the lectures and class notes of Swamiji. He came to Swamiji at the right time when Swamiji wanted to publish his lectures in a book form. Swamiji's main message to the world can be found in his speeches delivered in the U.S.A., London and India. Feeling the necessity of having a qualified stenographer to take notes of his lectures and classes, Swamiji's friends placed an advertisement, only once (December 13, 1895), in both *The New York Herald* and *The New York World* newspapers. Its text reads as follows:

WANTED — A RAPID SHORTHAND WRITER
TO TAKE DOWN
LECTURES FOR SEVERAL HOURS A WEEK.
APPLY AT 228 WEST 39TH STREET.

Mr. Goodwin responded promptly and was immediately hired.

From Swamiji's biography it appears that, before the appointment of Mr. Goodwin, two other stenographers had applied and were tested. One seems to have been Kripananda who, in spite of his hard labour in acquiring expertise in stenography, was not suitable for the task. The second applicant, though efficient, was found unsatisfactory due to his lack of comprehension of Swamiji's ideas. So, Mr. Goodwin was literally a "God-sent" man who "at once took over as Secretary and right-hand man." He was very useful in many other works as well. Not only was he exceptionally gifted as a stenographer, but also he had the capacity to understand Swamiji's ideas and thoughts. His spiritual sensitivity was accentuated by his loving association with Swamiji:

> From the beginning, 'he would work day and night over the lectures, the *Life* (by his Eastern and Western Disciples) tells us, 'taking them down stenographically and then typewriting them, all in the same day.' Even if he took down only the advanced morning class, this was in itself a feat for, as Kripananda wrote in reference to Swamiji's *karma yoga* class, 'These lectures are very long if taken down verbatim.' To keep pace with Swamiji was to have little time to spare, and if there had been an unoccupied room in the same lodging

house, Goodwin most probably would have taken it. As it was, he took a room almost directly across the street at 247 West Thirty-ninth, and it was undoubtedly there that he did his typing, going from the morning class to his typewriter and back again to the evening class, or first perhaps to dinner at Swamiji's table.[1]

In no time Goodwin's entire outlook was radically transformed from within and he blossomed into one of Swamiji's fruitful devotees. His sparkling sincerity, unflagging patience, and sacrifice for the propagation of Vedanta, was a gift of incalculable magnitude. These sterling virtues along with his professional efficiency, made him the only "ideal person" available at the time. He could transcribe Swamiji's thoughts almost as they were uttered, to everyone's joy and satisfaction. Any serious scholar of Swamiji's works can easily find the difference between his earlier lectures as reported in newspapers and the later transcriptions that came to us through Goodwin. The research work of M. L. Burke has thrown much light on this point:

> We are forced to recognize that much of the originality and subtlety of his ideas and many of the fresh and shining insights that must have flashed through his lectures, illuminating whole fields of knowledge, were lost upon the general run of reporters — and thus lost to us. The newspaper reports, moreover, are for the most part short. While we are often told by the reporters of Swamiji's clarity and strength of thought, of his genius for imparting new ideas, we are seldom given a verbatim account of those ideas. Lectures that took him two hours to deliver were summarized (often incompletely) in one or two columns, and ideas which must have poured forth in torrents were reduced to a trickle.[2]

Swamiji was well aware of his divine mission and was, therefore, confident of securing someone fit for the task. In that vein, he said earlier that year, "I have intense faith in Truth, . . . the Lord will send help and hands to work with me."[3]

It will be very interesting to know about Goodwin's background and the circumstances under which he joined Swamiji. M. L. Burke, in her above mentioned book, unearthed certain facts about his past. Goodwin's paternal grandfather, the Rev. Josiah Goodwin, was a minister connected to the Wesleyan Church of Scarborough, Yorkshire, in England. His son, Josiah the younger, was born in 1817 and became a well-reputed journalist, having proficiency in shorthand writing. He lived permanently in Bath-Easton, a suburb of Bath. He was very talented and a celebrity in social life. He died in 1890.

Josiah John Goodwin was born in September, 1870. He inherited his father's talents and received a good training in his early life. He grew "restless" in spirit, though, and, after having some unsuccessful attempts at newspaper publication in Bath in 1893, he moved, first to Australia and thereafter to the United States, in search of a more promising future. He made his living in different ways, mostly "editing things here and there." This instability of life and uncertainty of a steady income, made him prone to mental depression and agnosticism. The grace of God brought him in December, 1895 to 228 West 39th Street. The magnetic influence of Swamiji's luminous personality moved him deeply from the very first instance. "'The Swami told him many incidents of his past life, and this created such a moral revolution in him,' the *Life* narrates, 'that henceforth his whole life was changed'."[4] The spiritual eminence of Swamiji coupled with his loving nature and sympathetic understanding conquered Goodwin's heart. "'He was as simple as a child,' Swami Sadananda reports, 'and wonderfully responsive to the slightest show of kindness'."[5] No wonder Goodwin accepted Swamiji as Christ and prostrated before him like a Hindu. In the spring of 1896, prior to his arrival in London in order to join Swamiji, he wrote to Miss Macleod, "Shall I shock you very much if I tell you that the Swami takes the place of Christ to me? I think not, for you will understand what I mean."[6] Goodwin received *brahmacharya* from Swamiji in New York, in February, 1896.

After acquiring this new view, Goodwin dedicated his life entirely to the spread of Vedanta. As he wrote in a letter of August, 1896 to Mrs. Ole Bull, he had to accept a very nominal salary, due to the lack of other resources: "If I am to work for the Vedanta — and my wishes are all that way: I think I may say my heart is thoroughly in the work — I am afraid I shall have to accept bare living, but beyond that, I would not consent to any arrangement."[7] Goodwin also worked with Swami Saradananda for some time in the United Kingdom, as well as in the United States. At this time, he articulated his feelings about Swamiji to Swami Saradananda: "Being poor from childhood, I have gone many places trying to make a living. I have hobnobbed with all kinds of people: they gave me work and a salary, but no one gave me his heart's love. Then in America I met Swami Vivekananda; then alone could I understand what love was. So, income or no income, I am caught! Never have I found such a noble being as Swami Vivekananda. One is drawn to him as if to one's very own."[8]

Swamiji, along with his English disciples, Mr. and Mrs. Sevier, left London on December 16, 1896. Goodwin followed a short while after. They reached Ceylon (Sri Lanka) on January 15, 1897. Goodwin travelled with Swamiji from Colombo to Almora, from one end of India to the other. He was present at every single lecture Swamiji gave, at every single interview granted to reporters. Further, he did not miss "one single report of any utterance of his in any paper."[9] This life of dedication elicited admiration from everyone. Swami Virajananda, one of Swamiji's disciples, informs us: "Goodwin used to serve the Swami day and night. Oh, what a wonderful spirit of service he had!"[10] He was a vegetarian and lived like a monk.

About Goodwin's complete identification with the spirit of monastic life, Swami Akhandananda wrote: "Goodwin mostly stayed at the Math. . . . Goodwin. . . . used to eat with us. Goodwin would dance and sing like a small child. It was very sweet to hear him sing '*Shankara Shiva Vyom Vyom Bhola...*'"[11] In July, 1897, at the request of Swamiji, Goodwin went to Madras to start a newspaper and he gave his services to the *Brahmavadin*, a religious periodical started by some of Swamiji's followers. He then took a job on the staff of *The Madras Mail*. Unfortunately, he did not live long thereafter. He died of enteric fever on June

2, 1898, at Ootacamund, where he was buried at the St. Thomas Cemetery.

The sad news reached Swamiji at Almora. He maintained his poise in spite of this severe shock and wrote about his "Faithful Goodwin" as follows:

> The debt of gratitude I owe him can never be repaid and those who think they have been helped by any thought of mine ought to know that almost every word of it was published through the untiring and most unselfish exertions of Mr. Goodwin. In him I have lost a friend true as steel, a disciple of never-failing devotion, a worker who knew not what tiring was, and the world is less rich by one of those few who are born, as it were, to live only for others.[12]

The Swami also sent the following poem to Goodwin's mother in England, for her consolation:

REQUIESCAT IN PACE

Speed forth, O Soul! upon thy star-strewn path;
Speed, blissful one! where thought is ever free,
Where time and space no longer mist the view,
Eternal peace and blessings be with thee!
Thy service true, complete thy sacrifice,
Thy home the heart of love transcendent find;
Remembrance sweet, that kills all space and time,
Like altar roses fill thy place behind!
Thy bonds are broke, thy quest in bliss is found,
And one with That which comes as Death and Life;
Thou helpful one! unselfish e'er on earth,
Ahead! still help with love this world of strife![13]

On April 23rd, 1967, a 10-foot high granite marble memorial was erected on his burial place at the initiative of the Ramakrishna Math at Ootacamund.

Thus, Goodwin has become immortal in the history of the Ramakrishna movement through his life of absolute dedication and purity of character. Swami Premananda, a direct disciple of Shri Ramakrishna, used to place flowers in remembrance of Goodwin, while worshipping Shri Ramakrishna in the shrine:

> Our 'mother' — I mean Mrs. Sevier — is an example of superb renunciation. Her husband, too, was of the same type. I remember Goodwin — Swamiji's Ganesha[14] — and Nivedita. What an exquisite ideal of self-sacrifice they showed! To tell you the truth, the day when I have to perform worship in the shrine, I offer flowers in their memory... I am a humble servant of these disciples of Swamiji.[15]

In the history of the world, a bare handful of individuals are known to have developed such a strong character as did Mr. Goodwin. Only these great characters are able to project such a balanced unity of moral courage and integrity, with creative idealism. We pay our reverential homage to this great hero of the Spirit.

REFERENCES

Chapter 1

THE INDIVIDUAL AND THE SUPREME

1. *Katha Upanishad,* 1.3.3.
2. *Brihadaranyaka Upanishad,* 1.4.7.
3. *Kena Upanishad,* 2.4.
4. Ibid., 2.4.
5. Ibid., 2.4.
6. *Brihadaranyaka Upanishad,* 3.4.1.
7. Ibid., 1.4.8.
8. Ibid., 2.4.5.
9. Ibid., 1.4.7.
10. *Taittiriya Upanishad,* 11.1.
11. *Brihadaranyaka Upanishad,* 3.9.28.7.
12. *The Gospel of Sri Ramakrishna*, Sri Ramakrishna Math, Madras, p. 102.
13. *The Complete Works of Swami Vivekananda,* Advaita Ashrama, Calcutta, Vol. VIII, p. 255.
14. *Brahma Sutras,* 1.1.2.
15. *Taittiriya Upanishad,* 111.1.
16. *Brihadaranyaka Upanishad,* 11.5.19.
17. Ibid., 1.4.10.
18. *Aitareya Upanishad,* 111.1.3.
19. *Brihadaranyaka Upanishad,* 1.4.10.
20. *Rig Veda,* 1.164.24; *Mundaka Upanishad,* 3.1.1; *Svetasvatara Upanishad,* 4.6; *Mundaka Upanishad,* 3.1.2.
21. *The Complete Works of Swami Vivekananda,* Advaita Ashrama, Calcutta, Vol. VIII, p. 5.
22. *Chandogya Upanishad,* 8.14.1.
23. Ibid., 8.1.2.
24. *Mandukya Upanishad,* 11.
25. *Chandogya Upanishad,* 6.8.1-2; *Brihadaranyaka Upanishad* 4.3.11.
26. *Brihadaranyaka Upanishad,* 4.3.35.
27. *Bhagavad Gita,* 8.6.
28. *Mundaka Upanishad,* 111.2.2.
29. *Rig-Veda,* 10.90, 121-129.
30. Paul Deussen, *Philosophy of the Upanishads,* p. 86.

31. *The Complete Works of Swami Vivekananda,* Advaita Ashrama, Calcutta, Vol. II, p. 250.
32. *The Gospel of Sri Ramakrishna,* Sri Ramakrishna Math, Madras, p. 345.
33. Ibid., p. 419.
34. *Chandogya Upanishad,* 6.8.7.

Chapter 2

THE CONCEPT OF GOD IN HINDU RELIGION

1. *Rig-Veda,* 1.64.46; *Chandogya Upanishad,* 6.2.1.
2. *Rig-Veda,* 10.129.4.
3. *Brihadaranyaka Upanishad,* 1.4.23.
4. *The Complete Works of Swami Vivekananda,* Advaita Ashrama, Calcutta, Vol. VII, p. 53.
5. Shankara, *Mandukya Karika,* 11.33.
6. *Aitareya Upanishad,* 111.1.3.
7. *Katha Upanishad,* 11.2.15.
8. *Svetasvatara Upanishad,* 6.2.
9. *Taittiriya Upanishad,* 2.7.1.
10. Ibid., 2.9.
11. *Svetasvatara Upanishad,* 1.3.
12. *The Complete Works of Swami Vivekananda,* Advaita Ashrama, Calcutta, Vol. II, "Maya".
13. *The Complete Works of Swami Vivekananda,* Advaita Ashrama, Calcutta, Vol. I, p. 378.
14. *The Gospel of Sri Ramakrishna,* Sri Ramakrishna Math, Madras, pp. 134-35.
15. *The Complete Works of Swami Vivekananda,* Advaita Ashrama, Calcutta, Vol. III, p. 37.
16. *The Gospel of Sri Ramakrishna,* Sri Ramakrishna Math, Madras, p. 282.
17. *Rig-Veda,* 10.90.3; *Brihadaranyaka Upanishad,* 111.9.26; *Bhagavad Gita,* 10.42.
18. *Chandogya Upanishad,* 6.11.
19. *Rig-Veda,* 10.121.2.
20. *Bhagavad Gita,* 9.18.
21. *Svetasvatara Upanishad,* 4.3.
22. *The Complete Works of Swami Vivekananda,* Advaita Ashrama, Calcutta, Vol. I, p.11.

23. *Brihadaranyaka Upanishad,* 3.7.3-23; *Bhagavad Gita,* 15.5, 18.61.
24. *The Complete Works of Swami Vivekananda,* Advaita Ashrama, Calcutta, Vol. II, p. 228.
25. *Brahma Sutra Bhashya,* 1.1.5.
26. *Bhagavad Gita,* 4.6-8.
27. *Taittiriya Upanishad,* 111.6.
28. *Mundaka Upanishad,* 1.1.7.
29. *Brihadaranyaka Upanishad,* 2.4.5.
30. Ibid., 4.4.5.
31. Ibid., 4.4.22.

Chapter 3

THE FUNDAMENTAL TEACHINGS OF VEDANTA

1. H. Stutfield, *Mysticism and Catholicism,* p. 31.
2. *The Complete Works of Swami Vivekananda,* Advaita Ashrama, Calcutta, Vol. III, p. 106.
3. Ibid., Vol. III, p. 274.
4. Will Durant, *The Story of Civilization,* Vol. I, "Our Oriental Heritage," Simon & Schuster, New York, 1935, p. 33.
5. *Taittiriya Upanishad,* 1:6.
6. *Brihadaranyaka Upanishad,* 1-3.27.
7. *The Complete Works of Swami Vivekananda,* Advaita Ashrama, Calcutta, Vol. I, pp. 2-4.
8. Ibid., Vol. IV, p. 216.
9. Dr. Radhakrishnan, *Eastern Religion and Western Thought,* George Allen and Unwin, London, p. 322.
10. *The Complete Works of Swami Vivekananda,* Advaita Ashrama, Calcutta, Vol. I, p. 15.
11. Ibid., Vol. II, p. 336.
12. *The Sayings of Sri Ramakrishna,* Sri Ramakrishna Math, Madras, p. 207.
13. *The Complete Works of Swami Vivekananda,* Advaita Ashrama, Calcutta, Vol. I, p. 124.
14. *Rig-Veda,* 1.1.8.
15. *Brihadaranyaka Upanishad,* 3.2.13.
16. *The Complete Works of Swami Vivekananda,* Advaita Ashrama, Calcutta, Vol. I, p. 98.
17. Mathew, 22:39; Mark, 12:31.
18. *The Complete Works of Swami Vivekananda,* Advaita Ashrama, Calcutta, Vol. III, p. 193.

19. R.E. Hume, *The Thirteen Principal Upanishads,* p. 36.
20. *The Complete Works of Swami Vivekananda,* Advaita Ashrama, Calcutta, Vol. II, p. 250.
21. Arnold J. Toynbee, "Foreword", Swami Ghanananda, *Sri Ramakrishna and His Unique Message*, Ramakrishna Vedanta Centre, London, 1970, 3rd ed., pp. viii-ix.

Chapter 4

VEDANTA AND SWAMI VIVEKANANDA

1. *The Complete Works of Swami Vivekananda,* Advaita Ashrama, Calcutta, Vol. III, p. 238.
2. Ibid., Vol. III, p. 193.
3. Ibid., Vol. I, p. xv.
4. Ibid., Vol. II, p. 201.
5. Ibid., Vol. II, p. 146.
6. *Chandogya Upanishad,* 3.14.1.
7. *Brihadaranyaka Upanishad,* 4.4.5.
8. *The Complete Works of Swami Vivekananda,* Advaita Ashrama, Calcutta, Vol. III, p. 225.

Chapter 5

SWAMIJI'S PRACTICAL VEDANTA - I

1. Will Durant, *Our Oriental Heritage,* p. 463.
2. Romain Rolland, *The Life of Vivekananda,* p. 316.
3. K. M. Panikar, *The Determining Periods of Indian History,* p. 53.

Chapter 6

SWAMIJI'S PRACTICAL VEDANTA - II

1. Romain Rolland, *The Life of Ramakrishna,* p. 155.
2. *The Complete Works of Swami Vivekananda,* Advaita Ashrama, Calcutta, Vol. V, p. 53.
3. Ibid., Vol. V, p. 37.
4. Ibid., Vol. IV, p. 187.
5. *The Gospel of Sri Ramakrishna,* Sri Ramakrishna Math, Madras.
6. Swami Saradananda, *Sri Ramakrishna: The Great Master,* Sri Ramakrishna Math, Madras, p. 871.

7. *Vivekananda Centenary Memorial Volume,* p. 264.
8. Romain Rolland, *The Life of Vivekananda,* p. 219.
9. *The Complete Works of Swami Vivekananda,* Advaita Ashrama, Calcutta, Vol. V, p. 104.
10. Ibid., Vol. VII, p. 498.
11. Romain Rolland, *The Life of Vivekananda,* pp. 316-18.
12. *The Complete Works of Swami Vivekananda,* Advaita Ashrama, Calcutta, Vol. I, Intro., p. xv.
13. *Bhagavad Gita,* 18.46.
14. Romain Rolland, *The Life of Vivekananda,* p. 131.
15. *Brihadaranyaka Upanishad,* 4.4.25
16. *The Complete Works of Swami Vivekananda,* Advaita Ashrama, Calcutta, Vol. II, p. 198.
17. Ibid., Vol. III, p. 160.
18. *Bhagavad Gita,* 2.3.
19. Sister Nivedita, *The Master as I Saw Him,* Udbodhan Office, Calcutta, p. 170.
20. *Panchadasi,* 1.8.
21. *The Complete Works of Swami Vivekananda,* Advaita Ashrama, Calcutta, Vol. III, p. 194.
22. Ibid., Vol II, p. 143.
23. Ibid, Vol. II, p. 97.
24. R. Zaehner, *Hinduism,* p. 168.

Chapter 7

SWAMIJI AND THE EMANCIPATION OF RELIGION

1. *The Complete Works of Swami Vivekananda,* Advaita Ashrama, Calcutta, Vol. III, p. 271.
2. Ibid., Vol. I, p. 389.
3. Ibid., Vol. I, p.17.
4. Ibid., Vol. II, p. 374.
5. Ibid., Vol. II, pp. 67-68.
6. Ibid., Vol. II, pp. 363-66.
7. Ibid., Vol. II, p. 383.
8. Ibid., Vol. IV, p. 187.
9. Ibid., Vol. I, p. 4.
10. Ibid., Vol. II, p. 358.
11. Ibid., Vol. II, p. 396.

Chapter 8

UNIVERSAL RELIGION AND SWAMI VIVEKANANDA

1. *The Complete Works of Swami Vivekananda,* Advaita Ashrama, Calcutta, Vol. III, p. 1.
2. Ibid., Vol. III, pp. 187-88.
3. Ibid., Vol. II, p. 67.
4. Ibid., Vol. II, p. 67.
5. Ibid., Vol. II, p. 68.
6. Ibid., Vol. II, pp. 153-54.
7. Arnold J. Toynbee, *An Historian's Approach to Religion,* 1956, p. 296.
8. M. L. Burke, *Swami Vivekananda, Prophet of the Modern Age,* pp. 13, 16.
9. *The Complete Works of Swami Vivekananda,* Advaita Ashrama, Calcutta, Vol. I, p. 22.
10. Ibid., Vol. I, p. 19.
11. Ibid., Vol. III, p. 1.
12. Ibid., Vol. IV, p. 180.
13. Ibid., Vol. II, p. 371.
14. Romain Rolland, *The Life of Vivekananda,* Advaita Ashrama, Calcutta, p. 45.
15. *The Complete Works of Swami Vivekananda,* Advaita Ashrama, Calcutta, Vol. VI, pp. 415-16.
16. Ibid., Vol. IV, p. 301.
17. Ibid., Vol. II, p. 367.
18. Ibid., Vol. II, p. 365.
19. Ibid., Vol. III, p. 108.
20. Sister Nivedita, *The Master as I Saw Him,* Udbodhan Office, Calcutta, p. 228.
21. *The Complete Works of Swami Vivekananda,* Advaita Ashrama, Calcutta, Vol. I, p. 4.
22. Ibid., Vol. II, pp. 373-74.

Chapter 9

HARMONY OF RELIGIONS AND SWAMI VIVEKANANDA

1. *The Complete Works of Swami Vivekananda,* Advaita Ashrama, Calcutta, Vol. II, p. 357.

2. Ibid., Vol. II, p. 425.
3. Ibid., Vol. I, p. 416.
4. Ibid., Vol. I, p. 375.
5. Ibid., Vol. II, p. 252.
6. Ibid., Vol. II, p. 396.
7. Ibid., Vol. VII, p. 361.
8. Ibid., Vol. VI, p. 81.
9. Ibid., Vol. IV, p. 180.
10. Ibid., Vol. II, p. 62.
11. Ibid., Vol. III, p. 189.
12. Ibid., Vol. II, pp. 414-15.
13. Ibid., Vol. II, p. 72.
14. Ibid., Vol. II, p. 125.
15. Ibid., Vol. II, p. 125.
16. Ibid., Vol. II, p. 42.
17. Ibid., Vol. VI, p. 46.
18. Ibid., Vol. II, p. 377.
19. Ibid., Vol. I, p. 41.
20. Ibid., Vol. I, p. 41.
21. Ibid., Vol. II, pp. 153-54.
22. Romain Rolland, *The Life of Vivekananda,* Advaita Ashrama, Calcutta, p. 150, footnote.
23. *The Complete Works of Swami Vivekananda,* Advaita Ashrama, Calcutta, Vol. III, p. 269.
24. Ibid., Vol. II, p. 140.
25. Ibid., Vol. VI, pp. 462-63.
26. Ibid., Vol. III, pp. 187-88.
27. Ibid., Vol. II, pp. 67-68.
28. Swami Nirvedananda, *Sri Ramakrishna and Spiritual Renaissance,* The R.K. Mission Institute of Culture, Calcutta, 1940, pp. 169-70.
29. *The Complete Works of Swami Vivekananda,* Advaita Ashrama, Calcutta, Vol. II, pp. 363-64.
30. Ibid., Vol. II, pp. 382-83.
31. Ibid., Vol. II, p. 383.
32. Ibid., Vol. III, p. 1.
33. Ibid., Vol. VII, p. 20.
34. Ibid., Vol. II, p. 374.

Chapter 10

SWAMI VIVEKANANDA'S IMPACT ON THE WORLD'S PARLIAMENT OF RELIGIONS - I

1. M. L. Burke, *Swami Vivekananda: His Second Visit to the West,* p. 602.
2. Swami Nikhilananda, *Vivekananda: A Biography,* p. 139.
3. *The Complete Works of Swami Vivekananda,* Advaita Ashrama, Calcutta, Vol. V, p. 135.
4. Ramakrishna Vedanta Center, London, *Swami Vivekananda in the East and West,* p. 215.
5. M. L. Burke, *Swami Vivekananda in America: New Discoveries,* p. 565.
6. Ibid., p. 566.
7. S. Kapoor, *Swami Vivekananda in the West,* pp. 350-51.
8. *Life of Swami Vivekananda,* by his Eastern and Western Disciples, p. 387.
9. Christopher Isherwood, *Vedanta for Modern Man,* p. xii.
10. Romain Rolland, *The Life of Vivekananda,* p. 150.
11. *Letters of Swami Vivekananda,* p. 136.
12. *Prabuddha Bharata,* January, 1983, p. 16.
13. Ibid., May, 1963, p. 260.
14. *Teachings of Swami Vivekananda,* Advaita Ashrama, Calcutta, 1963, p. 236.
15. Romain Rolland, *The Life of Ramakrishna,* pp. 13-14.
16. M. L. Burke, *Swami Vivekananda in America: New Discoveries,* p. 134.
17. *Vedanta for East and West,* viii, 5.
18. O. S. Guinness, *The East, No Exit,* p. 7.
19. *Prabuddha Bharata,* Vol. 89, p. 55.
20. Ibid., February 1969, p. 42.
21. M. L. Burke, *Swami Vivekananda: Prophet of the Modern Age,* 1974, p. 14.
22. Ibid., p. 3.

Chapter 11

SWAMI VIVEKANANDA'S IMPACT ON THE WORLD'S PARLIAMENT OF RELIGIONS - II

1. *The Complete Works of Swami Vivekananda,* Advaita Ashrama, Calcutta, Vol. VI, p. 134.
2. Ibid., Vol. II, p. 209.
3. *Prabuddha Bharata,* May 1963, p. 259.

4. M. L. Burke, *Prabuddha Bharata,* March 1979, p. 95.
5. *Prabuddha Bharata,* May 1983, p. 229.
6. A. D. White, *A History of the Warfares of Science with Theology in Christendom,* Vol. II, p. 366.
7. S. E. Ahlstrom, *A Religious History of the American People,* p. 773.
8. W. S. Hudson, *Religion in America,* p. 226.
9. M. E. Murthy, *Modern American Religion,* Vol. I, (1893-1919), p. 22.
10. Ella Wilcox, *Neeley's History of the Parliament of Religions,* p. 991.
11. Ibid., p. 827.
12. Dr. J. H. Barrows, *The World's Parliament of Religions.*
13. *Bhagavad Gita,* 4.5-7.
14. M. L. Burke, *Prabuddha Bharata,* March, 1979, p. 97.
15. Advaita Ashrama, Calcutta, *Spiritual Talks,* p. 254.
16. M. L. Burke, *Swami Vivekananda in America: New Discoveries,* p. 58.
17. Christopher Isherwood, *Vedanta for the Western World,* p. 23.
18. M. L. Burke, *Swami Vivekananda in America: New Discoveries,* p. 60.
19. *Vivekananda Centenary Memorial Volume,* p. 86.
20. M. L. Burke, *Swami Vivekananda in America: New Discoveries,* p. 76.
21. *Vivekananda Centenary Memorial Volume,* pp. 86-88.
22. S. Kapoor, *Swami Vivekananda and the West,* (1893-1896), p. 363.
23. M. L. Burke, *Swami Vivekananda in America: New Discoveries,* p. 63.
24. Ibid., p. 83.

Chapter 12

HUMAN DEVELOPMENT THROUGH WORK

1. *The Complete Works of Swami Vivekananda,* Advaita Ashrama, Calcutta, 1976, Vol. I, p. 30.
2. *Brihadaranyaka Upanishad,* 3.2.13.
3. *The Complete Works of Swami Vivekananda,* Advaita Ashrama, Calcutta, Vol. I, p. 27.
4. Ibid., Vol. II, p. 34.
5. Ibid., Vol. I, p. 262.
6. Ibid., Vol. VII, p. 14.
7. *Bhagavad Gita,* 2.50.
8. Galatians, 6.5.
9. *The Complete Works of Swami Vivekananda,* Advaita Ashrama, Calcutta, Vol. I, p. 81.
10. Ibid., Vol. I, pp. 81-82.
11. Ibid., Vol. I, p. 75.
12. Ibid., Vol. III, p. 125.

13. Ibid., Vol. I, pp. 29-30.
14. Ibid., Vol. I, p. 27.
15. Ibid., Vol. I, pp. 53-54.
16. Ibid., Vol. I, pp. 54-55.
17. Ibid., Vol. I, p. 54.
18. Ibid., Vol. I, pp. 207-208.
19. Ibid., Vol. I, pp. 32-33.
20. Ibid., Vol. I, pp. 28-29.
21. Ibid., Vol. I, p. 55.
22. Ibid., Vol. I, p. 111.
23. Ibid., Vol. II, p. 357.

Chapter 13

SWAMI VIVEKANANDA ON BHAKTI YOGA

1. *The Gospel of Sri Ramakrishna, tr.* Swami Nikhilananda, Ramakrishna-Vivekananda Center, New York, p. 936.
2. Ibid., p. 939.
3. Ibid., p. 939.
4. *Prabuddha Bharata,* May 1963, p. 234.
5. *The Complete Works of Swami Vivekananda,* Advaita Ashrama, Calcutta, Vol. III, p. 36.
6. Ibid., Vol. II, p. 146.
7. Ibid., Vol. IV, p. 3.
8. Ibid., Vol. V, pp. 300-301.
9. Ibid., Vol. III, p. 37.
10. Ibid., Vol. II, p. 142.
11. *Bhagavad Gita*, 12.13-20.
12. *The Complete Works of Swami Vivekananda*, Advaita Ashrama, Calcutta, Vol. III, p. 32.
13. Ibid., Vol. VIII, p. 383.
14. *Life of Swami Vivekananda,* by his Eastern and Western Disciples, p.126
15. *The Complete Works of Swami Vivekananda,* Advaita Ashrama, Calcutta, Vol. III, p. 33.
16. Ibid., Vol. III, pp. 72-73.
17. Ibid., Vol. IV, pp. 15-16.
18. Ibid., Vol. III, p. 32.
19. Ibid., Vol. VII, p. 62.
20. Ibid., Vol. III, p. 53.
21. Ibid., Vol. III, p. 63.
22. Ibid., Vol. III, p. 100.

Chapter 14

SWAMI VIVEKANANDA, A MYSTIC

1. Bertrand Russell, *Mysticism and Logic,* pp. 56-57.
2. Arnold J. Toynbee, *Civilization on Trial,* p. 156.
3. Evelyn Underhill, *Practical Mysticism,* p. 3.
4. *Mysticism and Logic,* p. 3.
5. *The Complete Works of Swami Vivekananda,* Advaita Ashrama, Calcutta, Vol. VI, p. 81.
6. Ibid., Vol. II, pp. 146-47.
7. Ibid., Vol. III, p. 376.
8. Sister Nivedita, *The Master as I Saw Him,* Udhodhan Office, Calcutta, p. 385.
9. Ibid., p. 165.
10. *The Complete Works of Swami Vivekananda,* Advaita Ashrama, Calcutta, Vol. II, p. 22.
11. S. N. Dhar, *A Comprehensive Biography of Swami Vivekananda,* Part I, p. 44.
12. *The Complete Works of Swami Vivekananda,* Advaita Ashrama, Calcutta, Vol. VII, p. 123.
13. Ibid.
14. *Life of Swami Vivekananda,* by his Eastern and Western Disciples, p. 40.
15. Ibid., p. 78.
16. Ibid., pp. 96-97.
17. Ibid., p. 26.
18. Ibid., p. 128.
19. Ibid., p. 250.
20. Ibid.
21. *The Complete Works of Swami Vivekananda,* Advaita Ashrama, Calcutta, Vol. VII, pp. 242-43.
22. Ibid., Vol. VII, p. 124.
23. *Life of Swami Vivekananda,* by his Eastern and Western Disciples, p. 302.
24. Ibid., p. 343-44.
25. Ibid., p. 353.
26. *The Complete Works of Swami Vivekananda,* Advaita Ashrama, Calcutta, Vol. VII, p. 137.
27. Ibid., Vol. VII, p. 389.

28. Ibid., Vol. VII, pp. 388-89.
29. *Life of Swami Vivekananda,* by his Eastern and Western Disciples, Vol. II, p. 373.
30. Ibid., p. 374.
31. Ibid., p. 390.
32. Sister Nivedita, *The Master As I Saw Him,* Udbodhan Office, Calcutta, p. 130.
33. Ibid., p. 385.
34. *Life of Swami Vivekananda,* by his Eastern and Western Disicples, p. 379.
35. S. P. Basu, ed., *Letters of Sister Nivedita,* Vol. I, p. 157.
36. Ibid., p. 157.
37. S. N. Dhar, *A Comprehensive Biography of Swami Vivekananda,* Part II, pp. 1098-1099.
38. *Life of Swami Vivekananda,* by his Eastern and Western Disciples, p. 381.
39. Ibid., p. 382.
40. Ibid.
41. *The Complete Works of Swami Vivekananda,* Advaita Ashrama, Calcutta, Vol. IV, p. 4.
42. M. L. Burke, *Swami Vivekananda in America: New Discoveries,* Vol. III, p. 107.
43. Ibid., p. 108.
44. *Reminiscences of Swami Vivekananda,* p. 153.
45. S. N. Dhar, *A Comprehensive Biography of Swami Vivekananda,* Part I, p. 748.
46. *Life of Swami Vivekananda,* by his Eastern and Western Disciples, Vol. I, p. 87.
47. Ibid., p. 91.
48. Ibid., p. 91.
49. Sister Nivedita, *The Master as I Saw Him,* Udbodhan Office, Calcutta, p. 18.

Chapter 15

SWAMIJI AND MADAME CALVE

1. *The Complete Works of Swami Vivekananda,* Advaita Ashrama, Calcutta, Vol. IV, p. 179, "My Master."

Chapter 16

SWAMI VIVEKANANDA, AN INCARNATION OF MANLINESS

1. *Reminiscences of Swami Vivekananda,* p. 257.
2. *With Swamis in America,* pp. 59-60.
3. *Swami Vivekananda, Prophet of the Modern Age,* pp. 14-15.
4. Romain Rolland, *The Life of Vivekananda,* p. 62.
5. Swami Shraddhananda, *The Story of an Epoch,* p. 62.
6. *The Complete Works of Swami Vivekananda,* Advaita Ashrama, Calcutta, Vol. III, p. 196.
7. Ibid., Vol. III, p. 190.
8. Ibid., Vol. II, p. 250.
9. Ibid., Vol. VIII, p. 187.
10. Ibid., Vol. I, p. 338.
11. Ibid., Vol. IV, p. 358.
12. Ibid., Vol. IV, p. 490.
13. Ibid., Vol. III, p. 302.
14. Ibid., Vol. VIII, p. 228.
15. Ibid., Vol. III, p. 190.
16. Ibid., Vol. V, p. 15.
17. Ibid., Vol. III, p. 238.
18. Arnold J. Toynbee, *Civilization on Trial,* 1948, p. 156.
19. *The Complete Works of Swami Vivekananda,* Advaita Ashrama, Calcutta, Vol. III, p. 245.
20. Ibid., Vol. III, p. 193.
21. Ibid., Vol. II, p. 34.
22. Ibid., Vol. II, p. 198.
23. Ibid., Vol. III, pp. 237-38.
24. Ibid., Vol. IV, pp. 109-10.
25. *Life of Swami Vivekananda,* by his Eastern and Western Disciples, pp. 394-95.

Chapter 17

SWAMI VIVEKANANDA, AN APOSTLE OF STRENGTH

1. *The Complete Works of Swami Vivekananda,* Advaita Ashrama, Calcutta, Vol. IV, p. 109.

Chapter 18

SWAMI VIVEKANANDA, AN INCARNATION OF *SHAKTI*

1. *Life of Swami Vivekananda,* by his Eastern and Western Disciples 1912, Vol. IV, p. 170.

Chapter 19

SWAMI VIVEKANANDA ON INDIAN WOMEN

1. Sister Nivedita, *The Master As I Saw Him,* Udbodhan Office, Calcutta, pp. 356-57.
2. *The Complete Works of Swami Vivekananda,* Advaita Ashrama, Calcutta, Vol. VI, p. 445.
3. *Our Women,* p. 49.
4. *The Complete Works of Swami Vivekananda,* Advaita Ashrama, Calcutta, Vol. V, pp. 229-30.
5. Ibid., Vol. III, p. 290.
6. Ibid., Vol. VII, p. 214.
7. Ibid., Vol. II, p. 26.
8. Ibid., Vol. IV, p. 176.
9. Ibid., Vol. V, p. 26.
10. Ibid., Vol. VIII, p. 57.
11. *Prabuddha Bharata,* October 1992, p. 433.
12. *The Complete Works of Swami Vivekananda,* Advaita Ashrama, Calcutta, Vol. II, p. 34.
13. Ibid., Vol. VIII, p. 58.
14. Ibid., Vol. VIII, p. 61.
15. Ibid., Vol. VIII, p. 60.
16. Ibid., Vol. VIII, p. 62.
17. Sister Nivedita, *The Master As I Saw Him,* Udbodhan Office, Calcutta, p. 350.
18. *The Complete Works of Swami Vivekananda,* Advaita Ashrama, Calcutta, Vol. V, p. 232.
19. Sister Nivedita, *The Master As I Saw Him,* Udbodhan Office, Calcutta, p. 347.
20. Ibid., p. 346.
21. *The Complete Works of Swami Vivekananda,* Advaita Ashrama, Calcutta, Vol. IV, pp. 463-64.
22. Ibid., Vol. V, p. 231.
23. Ibid., Vol. V, p. 342.

Chapter 20

SWAMIJI'S DEVOTION TO HIS MOTHER, BHUVANESHWARI DEVI

1. Christopher Dawson, *Religion and Culture,* 1948, pp. 49-50.
2. R. K. Mission Institute of Culture, Calcutta, *The Cultural Heritage of India,* 1958, Vol. I, p. xxiii.
3. Basham, A. L., *The Wonder That was India,* 1967, p. 489.
4. *Manu Smriti,* II, p. 145.
5. *The Complete Works of Swami Vivekananda,* Advaita Ashrama, Calcutta, Vol. III, p. 291.
6. Manmatha Nath Ganguly, *Reminiscences of Vivekananda,* p. 315.
7. *Life of Swami Vivekananda,* by his Eastern and Western Disciples, Part I, pp. 8-9.
8. Ibid., p. 34.
9. Ibid., p. 516.
10. Ibid., p. 516.
11. M. L. Burke, *Swami Vivekananda in America: New Discoveries,* Prophetic Mission, Vol. II, p. 239.
12. M. L. Burke, *Swami Vivekananda in America: New Discoveries,* 1st Ed., 1958, p. 466.
13. *The Complete Works of Swami Vivekananda,* Advaita Ashrama, Calcutta, Vol. III, pp. 59-60.
14. Swami Saradananda, *Sri Ramakrishna: The Great Master,* p. 734.
15. *Life of Swami Vivekananda,* by his Eastern and Western Disciples, Part I, pp. 380-81.
16. *Letters of Swami Vivekananda,* p. 65.
17. S. N. Dhar, *A Comprehensive Biography of Swami Vivekananda,* Part II, p. 910.
18. M. L. Burke, *Swami Vivekananda in the West: New Discoveries,* A New Gospel, Vol. VI, p. 90.
19. Ibid., p. 91.
20. Manmatha Nath Ganguly, *Reminiscences of Vivekananda,* p. 345.

Chapter 21

SWAMI VIVEKANANDA ON THE FUNDAMENTALS OF EDUCATION

1. Plato, *Charmides*, p. 74.
2. *Ishavasya Upanishad,* 1.15.
3. *The Complete Works of Swami Vivekananda,* Advaita Ashrama, Calcutta, Vol. I, p. 28.
4. *Letters of Swami Vivekananda,* p. 90.
5. Lincoln-Barnett, *The Universe and Dr. Einstein,* pp. 126-27.
6. *The Complete Works of Swami Vivekananda,* Advaita Ashrama, Calcutta, Vol. IV, p. 47.
7. Ibid., Vol. IV, p. 358.
8. Ibid., Vol. VI, p. 112.
9. Ibid., Vol. I pp. 412-13.
10. Ibid., pp. 414-15.
11. Ibid., Vol. II, p. 201.
12. Ibid., Vol. III, p. 193.
13. Ibid., Vol. VIII, p. 61.

Chapter 22

EXISTENTIALISM AND SWAMI VIVEKANANDA

1. *Existentialism and Humanism,* Russel F. Moore Company, Inc., New York, 1952, pp. 65-66
2. *Aryan Path,* July 1986, Vol. 21, p. 309.
3. *History of Philosophy: Eastern and Western,* ed., Dr. S. Radhakrishnan, p. 438.
4. *The Complete Works of Swami Vivekananda,* Advaita Ashrama, Calcutta, Vol. II, p. 168.
5. Ibid., Vol. II, pp. 258-59.
6. Ibid., Vol. I, p. 181.
7. Ibid., Vol. VIII, p. 5.
8. Ibid., Vol. III, p. 189.
9. *Healthy Personality,* ed., Hung-Min Chiang and Abraham Maslow, p. 62
10. *The Complete Works of Swami Vivekananda,* Advaita Ashrama, Calcutta, Vol. VII, pp. 154-55.
11. *Chandogya Upanishad,* 6.8.7.

Chapter 23

SWAMI VIVEKANANDA AND THE MODERN INTELLECTUALS

1. *The Complete Works of Swami Vivekananda,* Advaita Ashrama, Calcutta, Vol. III, p. 159.
2. Dr. S. Radhakrishnan, *Recovery of Faith,* p. 37.
3. *The Complete Works of Swami Vivekananda,* Advaita Ashrama, Calcutta, Vol. III, p. 146.

Chapter 24

SWAMI VIVEKANANDA ON BUDDHA

1. *Life of Swami Vivekananda,* by his Eastern and Western Disciples, Advaita Ashrama, Calcutta, Fifth edition, 1981, p. 340
2. *The Complete Works of Swami Vivekananda,* Advaita Ashrama, Calcutta, Vol. II, p. 530
3. Ibid., Vol. VIII, pp. 103-4
4. Ibid., Vol. III, p. 527
5. Ibid., Vol. III, p. 528
6. Ibid., Vol. III, p. 528
7. Ibid., Vol. III, pp. 528-29
8. Ibid., Vol. I, p. 21
9. Ibid., Vol. I, p. 22
10. Ibid.
11. Ibid., Vol. I, p. 23
12. Ibid., Vol. I, pp. 116-18
13. Ibid., Vol. VIII, pp. 99-100
14. Ibid., Vol. VIII, p. 103
15. Ibid., Vol. VIII, p. 104
16. Ibid., Vol. VIII, pp. 104-5
17. Ibid., Vol. VIII, p. 100

Chapter 25

JOSIAH JOHN GOODWIN, THE FAITHFUL DISCIPLE

1. M. L. Burke, *Swami Vivekananda in the West: New Discoveries,* Advaita Ashrama, Calcutta, Vol. III, p. 339.

2. Ibid., Vol. II, p. 332.
3. Ibid., Vol. III, p. 336.
4. Ibid., Vol. III, p. 338.
5. Ibid., Vol. III, p. 338.
6. Ibid., Vol. IV, p. 334.
7. Ibid., Vol. III, pp. 338-39.
8. Ibid., Vol. III, p. 338.
9. *Life of Swami Vivekananda*, by his Eastern and Western Disciples, Advaita Ashrama, Calcutta, 1981, Vol. II, p. 272.
10. M. L. Burke, *Swami Vivekananda in the West: New Discoveries,* Advaita Ashrama, Calcutta, Vol. IV, p. 488.
11. *Life of Swami Vivekananda*, by his Eastern and Western Disciples, Advaita Ashrama, Calcutta, 1981, Vol. II, p. 235.
12. M. L. Burke, *Swami Vivekananda in the West: New Discoveries,* Advaita Ashrama, Calcutta, Vol. IV, p. 563.
13. Ibid., Vol. IV, pp. 563-64.
14. Reference is to the Mythological tradition of the god Ganesha's undertaking to write out the *Mahabharata* as the sage Vyasa would go on composing the verses and dictating them to him.
15. Swami Shraddhananda, *The Story of an Epoch*, Sri Ramakrishna Math, Madras, p. 146.

SWAMI VIVEKANANDA

A Chronology*

1863 12 January

Birth of Swami Vivekananda.

1882 c. 15 January

First meeting of Naren with Sri Ramakrishna at Dakshineshwar.

1884 30 January

B.A. examination results of Calcutta University published in *The Calcutta Gazette*, Naren passing the examination in the second division.

1884 25 February

Death of Naren's father.

1884 c. 16 September

Naren accepts Kali.

1885 11 December

Ramakrishna removed to Cossipore garden-house.

1886 March (last week)

Naren has *nirvikalpa samadhi.*

1886 April (first week)

Naren visits Bodh-Gaya.

1886 16 August

Ramakrishna's *mahasamadhi.*

1886 1 September

Cossipore establishment closed down.

1886 September-October

Baranagore Math founded.

1886 24 December

The Antpur episode.

1887 January (third week)

Viraja homa performed and monastic names assumed by Naren and *gurubhais.*

1888-89

Sets out on pilgrimage to Varanasi, etc. Initiates Sarat Gupta at Hathras. Meets Pramadadas Mitra.

1890 21 January

Naren comes to Ghazipur.

1890 4 February

Naren meets Pavhari Baba.

---

* With acknowledgements to *A Comprehensive Biography of Swami Vivekananda* by Sailendra Nath Dhar.

1890 c. 15 April
Naren leaves Ghazipur.

1890 July (middle)
Naren sets out as a wandering monk.

1890 August
Parts company with Pramadadas Mitra.

1891 January (end)
Swamiji starts wandering alone.

1891 c. 5-28 March
Swamiji at Alwar.

1891 30 April
Swamiji at Mt. Abu.

1891 4 June
Swamiji meets Maharaja Ajit Singh at Mt. Abu.

1891 7 August
Swamiji, accompanied by Ajit Singh, reaches Khetri.

1891 27 October
Swamiji leaves Khetri for wanderings in Western India.

1891 c. November (first week)
Swamiji at Limbdi, etc.

1892 26 April
Swamiji at Baroda, leaves for Bombay.

1892 June
Swamiji at Mahabaleshwar.

1892 15 June
Swamiji at Poona.

1892 July (?)
Swamiji in Central India. At Khandwa for the first time said he was prepared to go to Chicago.

1892 July (last week)
Swamiji at Bombay.

1892 22 August
Swamiji at Bombay.

1892 September (early)
Swamiji at Pune with B. G. Tilak.

1892 October (early) (?)
Swamiji at Kolhapur.

1892 8-17 October
Swamiji stays at the house of Haripada Mitra at Belgaum.

1892 18 (?) October (?)
Swamiji at Goa.
1892 October (?) end (?)
Swamiji at Bangalore.
1892 November
Swamiji at Trichur, Cochin.
1892 13-22 December
Swamiji at Trivandrum.
1892 December (end)
Swamiji at Kanyakumari.
1893 January
Swamiji at Madras.
1893 10 February
Swamiji at Hyderabad.
1893 13 February
Swamiji lectures at Mehboob College on his mission.
1893 17 February
Swamiji returns to Madras.
1893 21 April
Swamiji at Khetri on second visit.
1893 31 May
Swami Vivekananda sets sail for America.
1893 28 July
Swami Vivekananda reaches Chicago.
1893 August
Swami Vivekananda at Breezy Meadows, Metcalf, near Boston.
1893 19 August
Swami Vivekananda visits reformatory at Sherborn.
1893 21 August
Swami Vivekananda lectures to the Ramabai Circle at Boston.
1893 25-28 August
Swami Vivekananda at Annisquam with Prof. Wright.
1893 28 August
Swami Vivekananda at Salem.
1893 5, 6 September
Swami Vivekananda at Saratoga Springs.
1893 10 (?) September
Swami Vivekananda returns to Chicago.
1893 11-27 September
Swami Vivekananda at the Parliament of Religions.

1893 19 September

Swami Vivekananda reads his paper on Hinduism at the Parliament.

1893 October (first week?)

Swami Vivekananda lectures at Streator.

1893 31 October-3 November

Swami Vivekananda lectures at Evanston.

1893 20-27 November

Swami Vivekananda on a lecture tour in Wisconsin, Minnesota and Iowa.

1893 28 December

Swami Vivekananda at Chicago.

1894 13-22 January

Swami Vivekananda at Memphis.

1894 12-23 February

Swami Vivekananda at Detroit.

1894 23 February

Swami Vivekananda at Ada.

1894 (?) February

Swami Vivekananda at Chicago.

1894 9-19 March

Swami Vivekananda at Detroit.

1894 20 March

Swami Vivekananda at Bay City.

1894 22 March

Swami Vivekananda at Saginaw.

1894 23-29 (?) March

Swami Vivekananda at Detroit.

1894 14 April

Swami Vivekananda at Northampton.

1894 17, 18 April

Swami Vivekananda at Lynn.

1894 24 (?) April-6 May

Swami Vivekananda at New York.

1894 28 April

Great public meeting at Madras to felicitate Swami Vivekananda.

1894 7-16 May

Swami Vivekananda at Boston and Cambridge.

1894 June

Swami Vivekananda stays at the Hales' home at Chicago.

1894 26 July
Swami Vivekananda at Swampscott.
1894 30 July-12 August
Swami Vivekananda at the Greenacre Conference.
1894 12 August
Swami Vivekananda at Plymouth.
1894 (?) August
Swami Vivekananda at Fishkill Landing.
1894 c. 1-19 September
Swami Vivekananda at Annisquam (second visit), and Boston.
1894 5 September
Great public meeting at the Town Hall, Calcutta, to felicitate Swami Vivekananda.
1894 2-13 October
Swami Vivekananda at Melrose, Cambridge and New York.
1894 14-21 October
Swami Vivekananda at Baltimore.
1894 22 (23?) October
Swami Vivekananda at Washington.
1894 2-5 November
Swami Vivekananda at Baltimore (Second time).
1894 7 November
Swami Vivekananda at Philadelphia.
1894 (?) November
Swami Vivekananda back to New York; founded The Vedanta Society of New York.
1894 5-28 December
Swami Vivekananda at Cambridge.
1894 28 December
Swami Vivekananda at New York and Brooklyn.
1894 30 December
First lecture of Swami Vivekananda at Brooklyn.
1895 20 January-25 February
Swami Vivekananda delivers lectures at the Pouch Gallery, Brooklyn.
1895 28 (29?) January
Beginning of Vedanta classes at New York.
1895 7 June
Swami Vivekananda at Percy; has *nirvikalpa samadhi.*
1895 18 June-7 August
Swami Vivekananda at Thousand Island Park.

1895 17 August
Swami Vivekananda sets sail for Europe.
1895 22 October
Swami Vivekananda lectures at Piccadilly.
1895 (?) November (Sunday)
Miss Noble first sees Swami Vivekananda.
1895 6 December
Swami Vivekananda returns to New York.
1895 9-14 December
Swami Vivekananda holds Vedanta classes again.
1895 24 December
Swami Vivekananda goes to Ridgely Manor.
1896 15 March
Swami Vivekananda at Detroit.
1896 25 March
Swami Vivekananda delivers his so-called Harvard Lecture at Harvard University.
1896 5 April
Swami Vivekananda sets out on second visit to England.
1896 28 May
Swami Vivekananda meets Max Mueller.
1896 19 July to September (middle)
Swami Vivekananda on a tour on the Continent.
1896 September
Swami Vivekananda meets Deussen at Kiel.
1896 16 December
Swami Vivekananda leaves England for India.
1897 15 January
Swami Vivekananda reaches Colombo.
1897 27 January
Swami Vivekananda at Rameshwaram.
1897 29 January
Swami Vivekananda at Ramnad.
1897 1 February
Swami Vivekananda at Paramakkudi, Manamadurai.
1897 2 February
Swami Vivekananda at Madurai.
1897 3-5 February
Swami Vivekananda at Kumbakonam.

1897 6 February
Swami Vivekananda at Madras.

1897 14 February
Swami Vivekananda leaves Madras for Calcutta.

1897 19 February
Swami Vivekananda reaches Calcutta.

1897 8 March
Swami Vivekananda leaves for Darjeeling.

1897 21 March
Swami Vivekananda and Maharaja Ajit Singh visit Kali temple at Dakshineshwar.

1897 1 May
Foundation of the Ramakrishna Mission.

1897 6 May
Swami Vivekananda sets out on a tour in Northern India.

1897 27, 28 July
Swami Vivekananda lectures at Almora.

1897 10 September
Swami Vivekananda at Srinagar (Kashmir).

1897 21 October
Swami Vivekananda at Jammu.

1897 5-15 November
Swami Vivekananda at Lahore.

1897 c. 6 December
Swami Vivekananda at Alwar (second visit).

1897 December (middle)
Swami Vivekananda at Khetri on a second visit.

1898 c. 21 January
Swami Vivekananda returns to Calcutta.

1898 28 January
Miss Noble arrives in Calcutta.

1898 6 February
Swami Vivekananda inaugurates Ramakrishna Temple at Ramakrishnapur (Howrah).

1898 13 February
The Math transferred from Alambazar to Nilambar Mukherjee's garden-house at Belur.

1898 16 February
Miss MacLeod and Mrs. Bull arrive in Calcutta.

1898 27 February

Public celebration of Ramakrishna's birthday, for the first time held outside Dakshineshwar, Swami Vivekananda's Western disciples participating in it.

1898 25 March

Swami Vivekananda ordains Miss Noble a *brahmacharini* and gives her the name Nivedita.

1898 30 March

Swami Vivekananda at Darjeeling.

1898 3 May

Swami Vivekananda returns to Calcutta.

1898 7 May

Anagarika Dharmapala visits Swami Vivekananda at Belur Math (housed at Nilambar Mukherjee's garden-house).

1898 11 May

Sets out on a tour in Northern India.

1898 13 May

Meeting with Maharaja Ajit Singh at Nainital.

1898 16 (?) May to 11 June

Swami Vivekananda and party at Almora.

1898 2 June

Death of Goodwin at Ootacamund.

1898 22 June

Swami Vivekananda reaches Srinagar.

1898 2 August

Swami Vivekananda accompanied by Nivedita, visits the cave of Amarnath on pilgrimage.

1898 30 September

Swami Vivekananda at Kshirbhavani.

1898 18 October

Swami Vivekananda returns to Calcutta.

1898 13 November

Swami Vivekananda attends the opening ceremony of Nivedita's school.

1898 9 December

Ramakrishna's picture installed at Belur Math.

1899 2 January

Belur Math occupied by the monks.

1899 19 January

Ramakrishna's birthday celebrated for the first time at the Belur Math.

1899 19 January
Mayavati Ashrama formally established.

1899 24 March
Death of Swami Yogananda.

1899 25 March
Swami Vivekananda ordains Nivedita as a *naishthika brahmacharini.*

1899 31 March
R. K. Mission plague service initiated with Nivedita as head.

1899 c. 21 May
Swami Vivekananda visits Kalighat temple.

1899 20 June
Swami Vivekananda starts for the West on his mission for the second time.

1899 31 July
Swami Vivekananda reaches London.

1899 16 August
Swami Vivekananda leaves for New York.

1899 (?) August
Swami Vivekananda reaches Ridgely Manor.

1899 2 September
Nivedita reaches Ridgely Manor.

1899 7 November
Swami Vivekananda at New York.

1899 23 November
Swami Vivekananda at Chicago.

1899 3 December
Swami Vivekananda reaches Los Angeles.

1899 8 December
Swami Vivekananda's first lecture at Los Angeles.

1900 15 January
Swami Vivekananda's first lecture at Pasadena.

1900 22 February
Swami Vivekananda reaches San Francisco.

1900 23 February
Swami Vivekananda's first lecture at San Francisco.

1900 25 February
Swami Vivekananda's first lecture at Oakland.

1900 13 (?) April
Swami Vivekananda reaches Alameda.

1900 2 May
Swami Vivekananda reaches Camp Taylor

1900 c. 29 May
Swami Vivekananda leaves San Francisco.

1900 c. 2 June
Last meeting between Swami Vivekananda and the Hale Sisters.

1900 7 June
Swami Vivekananda at New York.

1900 26 July
Swami Vivekananda leaves for Paris.

1900 2 August
First visit of Swami Turiyananda to Shanti Ashrama.

1900 3 August
Swami Vivekananda reaches Paris.

1900 7 September
Swami Vivekananda attends a sectional meeting of the Paris Congress.

1900 17 September
First visit of Swami Vivekananda to Perros Guirec.

1900 c. 28 September
Swami Vivekananda visits Mt. St. Michael.

1900 15 October
Second visit of Swami Vivekananda to Perros Guirec.

1900 24 October
Swami Vivekananda leaves Paris for tour in Eastern Europe, accompanied by Madame Calvé and others.

1900 25 October
Swami Vivekananda and party reach Vienna.

1900 28 October
Death of Capt. Sevier at Mayavati Ashrama.

1900 30 October
Swami Vivekananda and party reach Constantinople.

1900 2 November
Swami Vivekananda delivers a lecture at Seutari.

1900 c. 10 November
Swami Vivekananda and party leave for Athens.

1900 (?) November
Swami Vivekananda and party reach Cairo — Swami Vivekananda suddenly announces his intention to leave for India.

1900 26 November
Swami Vivekananda at Port Tewfick on way back to India

1900 9 Deccmber
Swami Vivekananda reaches Belur Math.

1900 27 December
Swami Vivekananda leaves for Mayavati.

1901 3 January
Swami Vivekananda reaches Mayavati Ashrama.

1901 18 January
Swami Vivekananda leaves Mayavati.

1901 18 January
Death of Maharaja Ajit Singh.

1901 24 January
Swami Vivekananda reaches Calcutta.

1901 18 March
Swami Vivekananda leaves Calcutta for pilgrimage in Eastern India.

1901 19 March
Swami Vivekananda reaches Dacca.

1901 27 March
Swami Vivekananda at Langalbandha along with his mother.

1901 30, 31 March
Swami Vivekananda lectures at Dacca.

1901 7 April
Swami Vivekananda and party visit Chandranath for pilgrimage.

1901 c. 12 April
Swami Vivekananda and party leave for Assam.

1901 12 May
Swami Vivekananda returns from Shillong to Belur.

1901 18-21 October
Swami Vivekananda performs Durga Puja at Belur Math.

1901 28-31 October
The Indian National Congress holds its seventeenth annual session in Calcutta — B. G. Tilak and others meet Swami Vivekananda.

1901 (?) November
Rev. Oda and Kakuzo Okakura meet Swami Vivekananda

1902 6 (?) January
Swami Vivekananda at Bodh-Gaya.

1902 12 (?) January
Swami Vivekananda at Varanasi.

1902 February (end)-March (beginning)
Swami Vivekananda returns to Belur.

1902 4 July
Mahasamadhi.

GLOSSARY

ABHAYA. Fearlessness; an epithet of Supreme Being.

ABHIH. Fearless.

ABHYASA. Practice

ADVAITA. Non-duality; a school of Vedanta philosophy teaching the oneness of God, soul, and universe, whose chief exponent was Shankaracharya (A.D. 788-820)

ADVAITIN. Advaitist.

ADVAITIST. A follower of Advaita, the philosophy of non-dualism.

AKASHA. The first of the five material elements that constitute the universe; often translated as "space" and "ether." The four other elements are *vayu* (air), *agni* (fire), *ap* (water), and *prithivi* (earth).

AMRITA. Immortality.

ANANDA. Bliss.

ANANTAM. Infinite.

ANIRVACHANIYA. Inexplicable and indefinable.

ANTARATMAN. Supreme Spirit or soul residing in the interior of man.

ANTARYAMIN. The Inner Controller.

APAURUSHEYA. Superhuman; of Divine origin.

ARJUNA. A hero of the epic *Mahabharata* and a friend and disciple of Sri Krishna.

ARYAN. An anglicized derivation from Arya, literally, noble; in ancient times, an inhabitant of Aryavarta or Vedic India; in later times, a member of any of the first three castes of Hinduism.

ATMAN. The Self or Soul; denotes both the Supreme Soul and the individual soul, which, according to Non-dualistic Vedanta are ultimately identical.

ATMANAM VIDDHI. 'Know the Atman'.

ATMAPRITI. Love for the Self; self-satisfaction.

AVATARA. Incarnation of God.

AYAMATMA BRAHMA. 'This Atman is Brahman'.

BHAGAVAD GITA. An important Hindu scripture, comprising eighteen chapters of the epic *Mahabharata* and containing the teachings of Sri Krishna.

BHAGAVAN. The Lord; also used as a title of celebrated saints.

BHAGAVATAM. A well-known scripture dealing mainly with the life of Sri Krishna.

BHAKTA. Devotee of God.

BHAKTI. Love of God.

BHAKTI YOGA. The path of devotion followed by dualistic worshippers.

BHARATA. India, so named in honour of Bharata, the celebrated hero and monarch of ancient India from whom a long line of kings descended.

BHARATA DHARMA. Indian ethos; Indian way of life.

BHAVA. Feeling; emotion; ecstasy; samadhi; also denotes any one of the five attitudes that a dualistic worshipper assumes towards God. The first of these attitudes is that of peace; assuming the other four, the devotee regards God as the Master, Child, Friend, or Beloved.

BHAVA SAMADHI. Ecstasy in which the devotee retains his ego and enjoys communion with the Personal God.

BHISHMA. A hero of the *Mahabharata*, celebrated for his devotion to truth.

BHUMAN. The incomparably great.

BRAHMACHARYA. The first of the four stages of life; the life of an unmarried student..

BRAHMAN. The Absolute; the Supreme Reality of the Vedanta philosophy.

BRAHMANUBHUTI. Knowledge of Brahman through realizing one's identity with It; the highest spiritual realization.

BRAHMA SUTRAS. An authoritative treatise on Vedanta philosophy, ascribed to Vyasa.

BRAHMATEJA. The glory that surrounds a Holy man.

BUDDHA. The Enlightened One; title of Gautama Siddhartha (563-483 B.C.), the founder of Buddhism, who was born in northern India and is considered by the Hindus to be an Incarnation of God.

BUDDHI. The determinative faculty of the mind, which makes decisions; sometimes translated as "intellect."

BUDDHISM. Religion and philosophy of Gautama Buddha, teaching that *nirvana* is the ultimate goal of life.

CHARAIVETI. 'Move on'.

CHIT. Consciousness.

DAYA. Compassion.

DEVATMASHAKTI. God's self-conscious power.

DHARMA. Righteousness, duty; the inner constitution of a thing, which governs its growth.

DHYANA. Concentration; meditation.

DHYANA-SIDDHA. Adept in meditation.

DVAITA. The philosophy of dualism.

EKAM SAT. Truth is one.

GARGI. A woman seer mentioned in the Vedas.

GAUNI-BHAKTI. Preparatcry devotion.

GITA. Same as *Bhagavad Gita.*

GURU. Spiritual preceptor.

GURUBHAIS. Brother disciples; disciples of the same *guru*, or spiritual teacher.

HATHA-YOGA. A school of *yoga* that aims chiefly at physical health and well-being.

HOMA. A ritual consisting of offering oblation into the sacred fire.

HRIDAYAKASHA. Space in the heart.

ISHTA-NISHTA. Single-minded devotion to the Chosen Ideal.

ISHWARA. The Personal God.

JAGAT. Universe.

JANAKA. A king in Hindu mythology who was endowed with the knowledge of Brahman.

JAPA. Repetition of the Lord's name or of a sacred formula taught to the disciple by the spiritual teacher.

JIVA. (Lit., living being) The individual soul, which in essence is one with the Universal Soul.

JIVATMAN. The embodied soul.

JNANA. Knowledge of Reality arrived at through reasoning and discrimination; also the process of reasoning by means of which Ultimate Truth is attained.

JNANA YOGA. A form of spiritual discipline mainly based upon philosophical discrimination between the real and the unreal, and renunciation of the unreal.

KALI. (Lit., the Black One) An epithet of the Divine Mother; the Primal Energy.

KAMANA. Desire.

KAMANDALU. A *sannyasin's* wooden water-bowl.

KARMA. Action in general; duty. The *Vedas* use the word chiefly to denote ritualistic worship and humanitarian action.

KARMA YOGA. A spiritual discipline, mainly discussed in the *Bhagavad Gita*, based upon the unselfish performance of duty.

KHEER. A sweet pudding made from milk.

KRISHNA, SRI. An Incarnation of the God described in the *Mahabharata* and the *Bhagavata.*

KSHATRAVIRYA. Manliness of a warrior.

KUBERA. God of wealth.

LILA. The divine play.

MAHABHARATA. A celebrated Hindu epic.

MAHARSHI. A great *rishi* or seer of truth.

MAHASAMADHI. The highest state of God-consciousness; the word also signifies the death of an illumined person.

MAHA-SHAKTI. Great Power.

MAHATMA. Great soul.

MAHAVAKYA. Great utterance or declaration; name given to certain sacred dicta in the *Upanishads*, such as *Tat tvam asi*, "That thou art."

MANAS. The faculty of doubt and volition; sometimes translated as "mind."

MANAVA ADVAITAVADA. Humanistic monism.

MANAVA MAHATMYA. The glory of man.

MANTRA. Sacred word by which a spiritual teacher initiates his disciple; Vedic hymn; sacred word in general.

MANU. The celebrated ancient lawgiver of India.

MAYA. A term of Vedanta philosophy denoting ignorance obscuring the vision of Reality; the cosmic illusion on account of which the One appears as many, the Absolute as the relative.

MOKSHA. Liberation or emancipation, which is the final goal of life.

MUKTI. Liberation from the bondage of the world, which is the goal of spiritual practice.

NAISHTHIKA BRAHMACHARINI. A woman who takes the vow of life-long chastity and student life even after the prescribed period.

NARAYANA. An epithet of Vishnu, or the Godhead.

NAVAVIDHA BHAKTI. Ninefold devotional discipline — listening to the stories of the Lord, singing His glories, constant remembrance of the all-pervading Lord, serving Him in His devotees, ritualistic worship, constantly saluting the Lord, doing all work for His sake, friendship with the Lord, and complete self-surrender.

"NETI NETI". (Lit., "Not this, not this.") The negative process of discrimination, advocated by the followers of Non-dualistic Vedanta.

NIRGUNA. Without attributes.

NIRGUNA BRAHMAN. (Lit., *Brahman* without attributes). A term used to describe the Absolute.

NIRVANA. Final absorption in *Brahman,* or the All-pervading Reality, by the annihilation of the individual ego.

NIRVIKALPA SAMADHI. The highest state of *samadhi,* in which the aspirant realizes his total oneness with *Brahman.*

NIVRITTI MARGA. The Path of Renunciation (of desires).

OM. The most sacred word of the Vedas; also written "Aum." It is a symbol both of the Personal God and of the Absolute.

OTA-PROTA. Through and through.

PARA-BHAKTI. Supreme love of the Lord, characterized by the complete selflessness.

PARAMAHAMSA. One belonging to the highest order of sannyasins.

PARAMATMAN. The Supreme Soul.

PATANAJALI. The author of the *Yoga* system, one of the six systems of orthodox Hindu philosophy, dealing with concentration and its methods, control of the mind, and similar matters.

PAVHARI BABA. An ascetic and *yogi* of great distinction who was a contemporary of Sri Ramakrishna.

PRAHLADA. The young son of the wicked demon king Hiranyakashipu, who nevertheless developed supreme devotion to God.

PRAKRITI. Primordial nature; the material substratum of the creation, consisting of *sattva, rajas,* and *tamas.*

PRANA. The vital breath, which sustains life in a physical body; the primal energy or force, of which other physical forces are manifestations.

PRATIKA. Substitute.

PRATIMA. Image.

PRATYAGATMAN. The individual *atman.*

PRAVRITTI MARGA. The Path of Desire, — (a preliminary course of spiritual discipline).

PREMA-BHAKTI. Ecstatic love of God.

PREMASWARUPAH. Of the nature of Ecstatic love.

PRITHA. Mother of Arjuna. Also known as Kunti.

PUNYA. Merit, virtue.

PURANAS. Books of Hindu mythology.

PURUSHA. (Lit., person) A term of Samkhya philosophy denoting the individual conscious principle. In Vedanta the term *Purusha* denotes the Self.

RAJAS. The principal of activity or restlessness in nature.

RAJA YOGA. A system of *yoga* ascribed to Patanjali, dealing with concentration and its methods, control of the mind, *samadhi,* and similar matters.

RAKSHASA RAJ. Demoniac rule.

RAMAYANA. A famous Hindu epic.

RIG-VEDA. One of the four *Vedas.* See *Vedas.*

RISHI. A seer of truth to whom the wisdom of the *Vedas* was revealed; a general name for saint or ascetic.

RITA. The fixed way or course.

SADHAKA. An aspirant devoted to the practice of spiritual discipline.

SADHANA. Spiritual discipline.

SADHU. Holy man; a term generally used with reference to a monk.

SAGUNA. Endowed with attributes.

SAGUNA BRAHMAN. *Brahman* with attributes; the Absolute conceived as the Creator, Preserver, and Destroyer of the universe; also the Personal God according to the *Vedanta.*

SAMADHI. Ecstasy, trance, communion with God.

SAMSKARA. Mental impression; a tendency inherent in the mind.

SANATANA DHARMA. (Lit., the Eternal Religion.) Refers to Hinduism, formulated by the *rishis* of the *Vedas.*

SANNYASIN. A Hindu monk who has renounced the world in order to realize God.

SARVA-BHUTA-ANTAR-ATMA. The inner Self of all beings.

SARVA-SEVA-VADA. Advocacy of the Vaishnava doctrine of service to all, recognizing their inherent divinity.

SARVATMA-VADA. Advocacy of the Advaita doctrine of the oneness of the soul — oneness of all existence.

SAT. Reality; being.

SATCHIDANANDA/SAT-CHIT-ANANDA. (Lit., Existence-Knowledge-Bliss Absolute.) A term for *Brahman*, or Ultimate Reality.

SATTVA. The quality of tranquility, purity, virtue, and illumination; one of the three *gunas,* or constitutive elements of phenomena.

SATTVIC. Pertaining to *sattva.*

SATYA. Truth.

SAUNDARYA. Beauty.

SEVA. Service.

SHAIVA. Auspiciousness; also the worshipper of Shiva.

SHAKTI. Power, generally the Creative Power of Brahman; a name of the Divine Mother.

SHANTI. Peace.

SHASTRA. Scripture.

SHIVA. The Destroyer God; the Third Person of the Hindu Trinity, the other two being Brahma and Vishnu.

SHLOKA. A Sanskrit verse; also a hymn or verse in praise of a deity.

SHRADDHA. Faith and reverence.

SHRI/SRI. The word is often used as honorific prefix to the names of deities and eminent persons, or of celebrated books generally of a sacred character; sometimes used as an auspicious sign at the commencement of letters, manuscripts, etc., also as an equivalent of the English term, Mr.

SHUDDHA. Pure.

SHUKA (DEVA). The narrator of the *Bhagavata* and son of Vyasa, regarded as one of India's ideal monks.

SITA. The wife of Rama.

SOMVAR VRATA. Fasting and praying on Mondays.

TAMAS. The principle of dullness or inertia in nature.

TAMASIC. Pertaining to, or possessed of, *tamas*.

TANTRA. A system of religious philosophy in which the Divine Mother or Power, is regarded as Ultimate Reality; also the scriptures dealing with this philosophy.

TAPASYA. Austerity.

TATHAGATA. (Lit., 'One who has come from there.') It is one of the names by which Gautama Buddha is known. It is a word which conveys the sense of "Messiah."

TAT TVAM ASI. (Lit., "That thou art.") A sacred formula of the Vedas denoting the identity of the individual self and the Supreme Self.

TYAGA. Renunciation.

UPADHI. A term of Vedanta philosophy denoting a limitation imposed upon the Self or upon Brahman through ignorance.

UPANISHADS. The well-known Hindu scriptures containing the philosophy of the Vedas. They are one hundred and eight in number, of which eleven are called major Upanishads.

VAIDHI-BHAKTI. Devotion to God characterized by formal rules regarding food, worship, etc.

VAISHNAVAS. The followers of Vishnu; a dualistic sect which emphasizes the path of devotion as a spiritual discipline.

VEDANTA. (Lit., the essence or concluding part of the Vedas.) A system of philosophy mainly based upon the teachings of the *Upanishads*, the *Bhagavad Gita*, and the *Brahma Sutras*.

VEDANTA SUTRAS. Same as *Brahma Sutras*.

VEDANTIC. Pertaining to the Vedanta system of philosophy.

VEDANTIST. A follower of Vedanta.

VEDAS. The revealed scriptures of the Hindus, consisting of the *Rig-Veda*, *Yajur-Veda*, *Sama-Veda*, and *Atharva-Veda*.

VIJNANA. Special knowledge of the Absolute, by which one affirms the universe and sees it as the manifestation of *Brahman.*

VIJNANI. One endowed with vijnana.

VIRA. Hero.

VIRAJA HOMA. A Vedic rite preparatory to one's entering the life of a monk, consisting of offering oblations into the sacred fire with the chanting of certain Vedic texts indicative of renunciation.

VISHISHTADVAITA. Qualified Non-dualistic Vedanta, as expounded by Ramanujacharya.

VYASA. The compiler of the Vedas, reputed author of the *Mahabharata* and the *Brahma Sutras,* and father of Shukadeva.

YOGA. Union of the individual soul and the Supreme Soul. The discipline by which such union is effected. The *Yoga* system of philosophy, ascribed to Patanjali, is one of the six systems of orthodox Hindu philosophy, and deals with the realization of Truth through the control of the mind.

YOGI. One who practises *yoga.*

YUDHISHTHIRA. The eldest of the five sons of Pandu; one of the heroes of the *Mahabharata.*

SUGGESTIONS FOR FURTHER READING

The best introduction to Vivekananda is not to read about him but to read him. The Swamiji's personality, with all its charm and force, its courageousness, its spiritual authority, its fury and its fun, comes through to you very strongly in his writings and recorded words . . . .

Reading his printed words, we can catch something of the tone of his voice and even feel some sense of contact with his power . . . Vivekananda-English recreates his personality for us even now, three-quarters of a century later.

— CHRISTOPHER ISHERWOOD

If you want to know India, study Vivekananda. In him everything is positive and nothing negative.

Vivekananda's message lights up for man's consciousness the path to limitless liberation from the trammels and limitations of the self. His message is a call of awakening to the totality of our manhood through work, renunciation and service.

— RABINDRANATH TAGORE

Swami Vivekananda was a multifaceted personality whose entire life and actions were permeated by divine consciousness. An unusual phenomenon of all times, he was not only an illumined Soul of the highest order but also a philosopher, an orator by divine right, a brilliant conversationalist and dynamic worker. But he was always rooted in divine consciousness and in his inmost heart he was a lover of God. A humanist with unparalleled sympathy and understanding, he was also an introspective *yogi.* In spite of his multifarious roles in different contexts, he was a wonderfully integrated character who could easily move in the world of action without ever losing his strong grip on divinity. A lover of mankind, he drained out every ounce of his energy in disseminating the lofty message of Vedanta. His speeches welling forth from his direct and intuitive experience of Divinity made a deep impact on the human mind, removing doubts and ignorance immediately. Romain Rolland, his biographer, wrote in 1928, "His words are great music, phrases in the style of Beethoven, stirring rhythms like the march of Handel choruses. I cannot touch these sayings of his, scattered as they are through the pages of books at thirty years' distance, without receiving a thrill through my body like an electric shock. And what shocks, what transports must have been produced when in burning words they issued from the lips of the hero!"

In his message, the goal or purpose of life is to realize the divinity which is within every individual. He was therefore a voice of vision and wisdom. Let everyone remember his or her true nature — divinity. Self-culture and self-transformation, culminating in a spiritually oriented character development will bring spiritual revolution in us. A transformation of inner life, the purification of our emotions, was one dominant theme of his message. Peace and prosperity are absolutely dependent on this inner transformation of the individual life. Modern symptoms of destructive forces authenticate the teachings of Swamiji that a "man with excess of knowledge and power without holiness is a devil." "Man-making is my mission of life," said Swamiji; "You try to translate this mission of mine into action and reality."

Swami Vivekananda has inspired millions of people with the noble ideals of "Be and Make." Studying his eventful, noble life and invigorating teachings will certainly open a new vista of wisdom sadly lacking in the present age.

"The more the life and teachings of the great Swamiji are made known, the more will the spiritual perspective of humanity be widened, thereby paving the way for enduring world peace everyone is hankering after."

BOOKS BY AND ON VIVEKANANDA — A SELECTION

Swami Vivekananda's writings and speeches are collected in *The Complete Works of Swami Vivekananda* (in 8 volumes), and published by the Advaita Ashrama, 5, Dehi Entally Road, Calcutta-700 014 (India). They have also brought out many other books by and on Swami Vivekananda among which the reader may consult the following with profit:

Life of Swami Vivekananda (in 2 volumes), by his Eastern and Western Disciples.

The Life of Vivekananda and the Universal Gospel by Romain Rolland.

Vivekananda — A Biography in Pictures.

Reminiscences of Swami Vivekananda by his Eastern and Western Admirers.

Swami Vivekananda in the West — New Discoveries (in 6 volumes), by Marie Louise Burke.

What Religion Is (in the words of Swami Vivekananda) by Swami Vidyatmananda.

Swami Vivekananda's Four Yogas — Condensed and Retold by Swami Tapasyananda.

The Philosophical and Religious Lectures of Swami Vivekananda — Condensed and Retold by Swami Tapasyananda.

The Nationalistic and Religious Lectures of Swami Vivekananda— Condensed and Retold by Swami Tapasyananda.

Lectures From Colombo to Almora.
Letters of Swami Vivekananda.
Teachings of Swami Vivekananda.
Selections from Swami Vivekananda.
Talks with Swami Vivekananda.

Other Select Publications:

Basu, Sankari Prasad and Sunil Behari Ghosh, *eds.* — *Vivekananda in Indian Newspapers, 1893-1902,* Basu-Bhattacharya & Co., Calcutta, India.

Chetanananda, Swami, *ed.* — *Vedanta Voice of Freedom,* Vedanta Society of St. Louis, St. Louis, MO.

Dasgupta, R. K., *general ed.* — *Swami Vivekananda: A Hundred Years Since Chicago,* Ramakrishna Math & Ramakrishna Mission, Belur, West Bengal, India.

Dhar, Sailendra Nath — *A Comprehensive Biography of Swami Vivekananda,* Vivekananda Kendra, Madras, India.

Dutta, Tapash Sankar — *A Study of the Philosophy of Vivekananda,* Sribhumi Publishing Co., Calcutta, India.

Gupta, Harish C., *tr.* — *Swami Vivekananda Studies in Soviet Union,* R. K. Mission Institute of Culture, Calcutta, India.

Jackson, Carl T. — *Vedanta for the West,* Indiana University Press.

Jyotirmayananda, Swami — *Vivekananda: A Comprehensive Study,* 137, Mount Road, Madras-2, India.

Lokeswarananda, Swami, *ed.* — *Books on Vivekananda: A Bibliography,* R. K. Mission Institute of Culture, Calcutta, India.

Majumdar, Amiya Kumar — *Understanding Vivekananda,* Sanskrit Pustak Bhandar, Calcutta, India.

Majumdar, Dr. R. C. — *Swami Vivekananda: A Historical Review,* General Printers and Publishers Pvt. Ltd., Calcutta, India.

Myren, Ann and Dorothy Madison, *ed.* — *Living at the Source: Yoga Teachings of Vivekananda,* Shambhala Publications, Boston, Massachusetts.

Nikhilananda, Swami — *Vivekananda: A Biography,* Ramakrishna-Vivekananda Center, New York.

Nikhilananda, Swami, *ed.* — *Vivekananda: The Yogas and Other Works,* Ramakrishna-Vivekananda Center, New York.

Rao, M. Shivaramakrishna and Sumita Roy, *Reflections on Swami Vivekananda,* Sterling Publishers Pvt. Ltd., New Delhi, India.

Someswarananda, Swami — *Vivekananda's Concept of History,* Samata Prakashani, Calcutta, India.

Stark, Eleanor — *The Gift Unopened: A New American Revolution,* Peter E. Randall, Portsmouth, NH.

Tapasyananda, Swami — *Swami Vivekananda: His Life and Legacy,* Sri Ramakrishna Math, Madras, India.